CONCEPTUAL FOUNDATIONS OF ORGANIZATION THEORY

EDWIN HARTMAN

BALLINGER PUBLISHING COMPANY
Cambridge, Massachusetts
A Subsidiary of Harper & Row, Publishers, Inc.

International Standard Book Number: 0–88730–251–3

Library of Congress Catalog Card Number: 88–19312

Printed in the United States of America

Library of Congress Cataloging-in-Publication Data

Hartman, Edwin, 1941–
Conceptual foundations of organization theory.

   Bibliography: p.
   Includes index.
   1. Organizational behavior. 2. Organization.
I. Title.
HD58.7.H36985
1988
302.3'5
88–19312
ISBN 0–88730–251–3

CONTENTS

About the Author

ACKNOWLEDGMENTS

It was Ed Freeman who first suggested to me that someone ought to write a book about conceptual issues touched upon by organization theory. Freeman gave me a few ideas of his own and pointed out others that seemed to him wrong but insufficiently challenged. Since then he has sufficiently challenged some of my ideas.

Rutgers University gave me a semester's leave and, earlier, a fellowship in its new Center for the Critical Analysis of Contemporary Culture. I thank the university for its generosity and the other fellows of the center for criticizing my half-formed thoughts and introducing me to others whose pertinence to the present enterprise I had not understood.

Some Rutgers colleagues, particularly Nancy DiTomaso, George Faris, Frank Fischer, and Joel Harmon, provided useful reactions to early drafts of parts of the manuscript. Jeff Slovak read a late draft through to save me from blunders in discussing issues that relate to sociology. Martin Bunzl gave me good bibliographical advice.

The New Jersey Department of Higher Education supported my research and planning for a conceptually oriented course in business policy, and so indirectly contributed to this effort. The department also put me on its Task Force on Thinking, whose members listened politely to a version of one of these chapters and gave me some helpful reactions.

Ballinger Publishing Company recruited anonymous referees whose critical remarks have immeasurably improved the manuscript. I doubt I have solved all the problems they raised, but that is not their fault.

Ballinger's Marjorie Richman and Barbara Roth have shown their mastery of the agreeable art of being critical without being discouraging.

Jay Howland did an extraordinary job of copyediting. I am indebted to her, and so are all who read any part of this book.

Finally I thank Mary S. Hartman and Sam Hartman for their unconditional forbearance and support.

For M.S.H.

INTRODUCTION
What This Book Is About

This is a book not about organization theory but about its conceptual foundations. I shall not review the literature of organization theory, nor shall I undertake a thorough investigation of all its fundamental concepts: a few crucial concepts will give us enough work to do. My purpose is to give organization theorists a clearer idea of what they are doing, particularly as opposed to what others are doing, and to help them avoid certain mistakes and see certain opportunities.

Although my primary targets are assumptions and methods, this account often takes sides on actual theories. I shall argue in favor of structural-functionalism and the systems approach to understanding organizations, in favor of the viability and importance of psychological explanation. I shall argue for rational individualism, and for interpretation as a way of explaining individual behavior that organization theorists cannot ignore. I shall argue too for a collective approach, irreducibly different from one based on psychology and focused on individuals, to explain what organizations do. In fact, a collective approach, including reference to corporate culture, is required for explaining not only organizational but individual behavior. I shall argue for limits on both the scope and the objectivity of the scientific method, but against a tendency to use paradigm talk as a substitute for coherent theorizing and argument.

The two primary adversaries are empiricism and subjectivism. Both have done some damage to organization theory and call for more criticism than they have received from within the field. Both are easily mistaken for correct positions. I have not, however, identified a gang of empiricists and a gang of subjectivists. The field does not break down along these lines, with the result that it is hard to see who is propagating false doctrine. It can turn up anywhere, even on both sides of a bitter dispute.

There is little consensus among organization theorists on most conceptual issues, still less where the issues are discussed explicitly. One of the remarkable features of this field is the extent to which organization theorists discuss these issues without being aware of what others in the field have said about them. The point is illustrated by the books on organization theory that have had the greatest influence on this one.

Roberts, Hulin, and Rousseau's *Developing an Interdisciplinary Science of Organizations* (1978) shows a frequently subtle understanding of the interplay of the languages and theories from which organization theorists borrow.

Lawrence B. Mohr's *Explaining Organizational Behavior* (1982) concentrates primarily on how motives explain behavior. Mohr's interests intersect those of Roberts et al., but he does not cite their work.

Jeffrey Pfeffer's *Organizations and Organization Theory* (1982), an extraordinarily thorough critical survey of the field, refers to Roberts et al., but far less frequently than it might profitably have done.

Gareth Morgan's provocative *Images of Organization* (1986) mentions only Pfeffer's book, not Roberts et al. or Mohr, though they ought to have been of interest.

Lex Donaldson's *In Defence of Organization Theory* (1985) cites only Morgan (1980 and 1981), though the others all contain material relevant to Donaldson's well-wrought argument.

Of the five, only Roberts et al. even mention Cronbach and Meehl's brilliant and important "Construct Validity in Psychological Tests" (1955), which should be required reading for all organization theorists and many other social scientists as well. Its argument affects them all.

Each of the five has an extensive bibliography; each selects certain others' views for particular scrutiny (and I have profited from their doing so, as will be evident). But the bibliographies overlap surprisingly little, and the five argue with each other almost not at all.

The sheer mass and disarray in the field will be evident to those who read this book and see what I have left out: I am aware that there are vast areas of organization theory on which I have said nothing. You may or may not share my opinion that this is preferable to making claims about all these areas but not arguing for them. If the published work in our field were more fully organized into groups of clear positions, then it would be easier to cover it.

Another sign of disarray is the apparently low level of communication among those writing in the field. In few fields, not even in philosophy, do we find such frequent accusations of bad argument, missing the point, ignoring this or that. If we cannot agree on what the questions are, we are certainly going to have some disputes about the answers.

This relative lack of communication is partly a consequence of the field's interdisciplinary nature. Organization theory raises questions that are or appear to be amenable to treatment from a great variety of vantage points, and its practitioners are often committed to one approach rather than another. No consensus is in sight. We shall not soon have reason to rule psychology or sociology or economics off the field, or any way to rid ourselves of the clash among the views characteristic of those disciplines about what is basic and what must be explained.

This conflict is not necessarily a bad thing. It does remind us that disciplines characteristically take for granted some propositions that are not self-evidently true, and it forces us to think critically about them. Nor is the disunity in the field fatal: the various schools go about their work and find useful results in spite of each other. So the field seems not to require a high level of coherence and consistency.

Yet organization theorists do communicate, and do have some problems and some methodologies in common. As I shall emphasize frequently, the different approaches to issues in organization theory are not all separated by unbridgeable paradigmatic gulfs. Sometimes, in fact, apparent disagreements are only apparent.

Methodological and epistemological self-consciousness has led to brave talk about reality, epistemology, the function of language, paradigms, and other juicy philosophical topics. I have tried to resist the temptation to add to it unduly. So do not expect me to spend a great deal of time talking about—for example—whether reality exists apart from our cognitive faculties.

One hazard of any interdisciplinary work, and in particular of bringing one discipline to bear on another, is that one constantly makes statements that some of one's readers consider humdrum and perhaps oversimplified, and others consider radical and wildly improbable or obscure. A case in point is my discussion of free will in chapter 4. I regard freedom of the will as having nothing much to do with one's decisions being caused, but much to do with one's decisions being caused by the right sort of thing in the right way. To some this will sound familiar, to others bizarre. If you are among the latter, try to reexamine your position rather than assuming—what may be true but ought not to be assumed—that scholars familiar with twenty-four hundred years of work on the problem have failed to consider something that seems immediately obvious to you.

On some issues, such as the viability of explanation by intentions, there is lively debate among organization theorists. Occasionally in this debate there will be a reference to a philosopher who has written about the issue. (Donaldson often notes what something called "the philosophy of science" has to say on this or that topic.) Sometimes there is recognition that a number of philosophers have thought more intensively, if not necessarily better, about an issue than have most organization theorists.

Sometimes, on the other hand, organization theorists who would never argue a point of mathematics without support from a mathematician argue a philosophical point without paying any attention to the views of people who have a professional concern with the issue in question. One way to explain this state of affairs is to point to the apparently small amount of progress in philosophy and consensus among philosophers. Why should anybody be convinced by people who cannot convince each other? That question, doubtless familiar to some economists as well, is by no means unreasonable. The trouble with it is that there are so many points at which the alternative to thinking philosophically—that is, being open to conceptual considerations—is carelessly choosing a position that sounds good and sticking to it even if you cannot defend it. Responsible theorists want to avoid that if they can. The best way to deal with conceptual arguments, here and elsewhere, is neither to defer to them nor to reject them because they sound as though they come from a philosopher, but to consider them and find satisfactory reasons for accepting them or not.

Philosophers who know something about organization theory do not in any case have an automatic advantage over organization theorists who know something about philosophy. The best people in any field are usually capable of considering the questions that others do not think to ask. That should be particularly true in an interdisciplinary field. There is nothing magic about the ability of the organization theorist March, the economist Friedman, and the psychologist Meehl to contribute to conceptual discussions. In addition to being very clever, they wrestle seriously with the pertinent arguments.

Organization theorists do philosophize freely, often explicitly. Some invoke language games, paradigms, meanings, and other subjects of recent analytical philosophy. This is all to the good, but sometimes enthusiasm outruns due care.

William James said that philosophy characteristically makes the familiar look strange and the strange familiar. Insofar as this book involves philosophy, it aims at the second of these tasks more than the first. Some recent attempts at the first have created needless strangeness. Consider the following claim, made by Morgan (1980) and others: Reality is not just "out there." It is in some sense socially constructed. Few people would simply disagree with that claim, but even fewer could tell you exactly what is being claimed and on what basis. Under some interpretations the claim is false; under others it is true but uninteresting. I believe there is at least one interpretation that is important, that is not universally agreed to, and that makes the statement true. Similarly, social action theorists invite us to consider meanings and to see certain events in their own particular terms, rather than as instances of covering laws. That invitation sounds mysterious and radical, and it is not always either explicated or defended very well. I shall offer a plausible explication of it and then argue that what is called the interpretability of some behavior does not in fact rule out its being law-governed.

My strategy is minimalist: keep the conceptual conversation as clear as possible by arguing carefully for some points that are no more extravagant than necessary. Inevitably some of what I say will seem elementary. That is good insofar as it indicates that the reader understands what I am saying and why. My aim is not to surprise anyone with the news that (say) reality is socially constructed, but to give plausible content to such provocative but somewhat vague statements.

Arguable and specific claims tend to be minimal and undramatic relative to grand-sounding ones. On the other hand, I trust my claims will be relatively comprehensible, and they may also be true; and after you have considered them, you may have a better idea of why organization theorists or even managers should care about them.

I put a premium on clarity; but valuing it is not the same thing as achieving it, and the latter can be a problem in an interdisciplinary undertaking. If you are an organization theorist or a philosopher and not both, some terms I use will cause skepticism, if not puzzlement. But the cry, "Define your terms!" is no mere call for clarity. In an interdisciplinary context, particularly, it is also a challenge to show that a theory of a certain kind is tenable. Many definitions in organization theory and else-where in the human sciences have substantive implications; so their defi-nition is not arbitrary, or even always possible without some defense. Much of what I say here is in effect argument for definitions of terms like *organization* and *mind*.

Here is a fact from which an extraordinary flood of other facts follows: in certain important cases it is not possible to distinguish between truth by definition and truth by virtue of how the world is. I shall argue, first in chapter 2, that it follows that experience provides no firm basis on which to build or to test one's theories. It follows too that one cannot always tell whether certain theories conflict or are instead compatible but are talking about different things. For this and related reasons it is often difficult, though seldom impossible, to adjudicate among competing theories. It also follows that our best explanations of behavior must presuppose an in-determinate level of rationality and therefore are invariably uncertain. All that is implicit in the impossibility of distinguishing truth by definition from truth as a matter of fact.

Sometimes defining or defending a vocabulary takes an argument—as, for example, when in chapter 4 I give an account of what free will is and is not. But the term *free will* and its surrogates appear prominently in our literature, and in an unexplained state have done considerable damage. So I shall try to defend my definitions of them.

ESCAPING PHILOSOPHY

When human knowledge was less systematic and extensive than it is now, philosophy covered most of it. Gradually some sciences managed to pull away and establish themselves as respectable and autonomous: physics, astronomy, and others over a long period of time; psychology only in the past hundred years or so, and perhaps less than some psychologists think.

A science frees itself from philosophy by first getting clear on what it is about—that is, developing a useful and fairly precise vocabulary and some agreement about what counts as evidence for or against the kind of proposition it generates. Where measurement is possible, the freedom of the science from philosophy is all the greater. The limiting case is the one in which consensus on fundamental theories and concepts permits clarity on what counts as evidence for all possible claims; but no science ever escapes philosophy to this extent.

Sciences characteristically achieve a local and useful but not neces- sarily perfect consensus on what counts as evidence. Their view of the world does not rest on the solid rock of unassailable observation, but still provides a basis for our agreement, and disagreement as well. A science creates a community that shares rules about how to communicate; that in- volves adjudicating acceptably and usefully between right and wrong.

Communication is certainly more difficult between communities that do not share the enabling rules. Arguments between them cannot be settled according to the canons of one community or the other. Some- times it is not obvious that settlement is possible at all. It is a purpose of philosophy to effect whatever reconciliation, or at least communication, may be possible. In an interdisciplinary field like organization theory we should therefore expect philosophy to play a significant role.

In many areas of organization theory it is difficult to tell whether an issue is conceptual or empirical or both. Sometimes we can approach an issue most effectively by doing what the natural sciences have often done with success: recast what sounds like a profound philosophical issue so that it is amenable to evidence. For example, I shall argue in chapters 4 and 5 that the problem of free will is largely a problem about the extent to which behavior can be explained by reference to reasons, and not a prob- lem about the absence of causality. For individuals and for organizations the solution to the problem is largely an empirical one: we can often iden- tify and sometimes classify the situations in which there is some point in explaining an organization's success by adverting to the availability of re- sources, say, as opposed to or in addition to the skill and imagination of the strategists. On the other hand, talk about what there is some point in doing suggests that there may be arguments about the appropriateness of one sort of explanation rather than another; and arguments about appro- priateness are not always empirical arguments.

The slightest self-consciousness about one's craft—and many organi- zation theorists have more than a little—raises conceptual questions. Some of these questions I present from a new point of view and couch in a slightly different vocabulary; but if you are an organization theorist you will probably find that, rather like Molière's bourgeois gentleman, you have been doing philosophy all your life.

One must be careful, however, about inflating manageable questions to philosophical size. Serious talk about whether the population ecology model or the strategic choice one is right sometimes begins to sound like discussion of the Nature of Man. Questions like Is reality socially constructed? and Do people (or organizations) really reason? are sometimes obscurantist renderings of specific and manageable questions, or conflatings of several different questions.

Not all deep-sounding philosophical questions can be analyzed into bite-size questions that some science understands as empirical. Not all conceptual questions are immediately available to evidence or measurement. We have moved in that direction in many cases, but there is no evidence that it is always possible to move farther. There is danger in too readily operationalizing, or talking too facilely about what one can learn from observation, about how clear one can be about criteria, and so on.

In short, we have two extremes to avoid. One is the view that we can judge theories about organizations on an empiricist basis, and that it is accordingly appropriate to ask, "How can you operationalize (or quantify) that concept or falsify that proposition?" On this view, anything more is an unwarranted ideological position. The other extreme is the view that the big issues in organization theory are all philosophical issues, and that consequently they are characteristically subjective, or at least impervious to criticism based on anything like what the natural sciences do. The proponents of this view include people who talk about the myth of objectivity and say all classification is ideological, which is much like saying that no boats are entirely dry inside and therefore all boats are as good as sunk. A common corollary of this last view is that the political meaning of a theory is a good guide to whether it is true or not, since the political benefit of a theory clearly indicates the intention with which it was formed. Roughly (and not entirely fairly), the first view can be associated with Pfeffer (1982), the second with Silverman (1971) and with Burrell and Morgan (1979). Even more roughly, the first view conjures up natural science, causality, and statistics fully liberated from philosophy; the second invokes teleology, intention, meaning, and interpretation.

The latter approach is right insofar as it suggests that there are points at which one cannot choose between theories on any standard empirical basis. In fact, as I shall argue in chapter 6, it is sometimes justifiable to use a theory that is wrong, or two theories that are incompatible. But I shall warn against inferring from the difficulty of finding pure empirical truth to the view that we have no rational basis for choice among alternative conceptual frameworks. There can be good and bad reasons for choosing a kind of theory; it is just not always textbook scientific method that gives us the good reasons. At a certain point in choosing among theories we must bring to bear the kind of experienced intuition no less characteristic of a good manager than of a good scientist.

Not only do I want to effect a compromise between the methods of science and the methods that use categories of reason, meaning, and so on: I want to argue that these methods are compatible and in some cases mutually reinforcing. There is no incompatibility between explanation by reference to an agent's reasons and ordinary causal explanation, or therefore between voluntary action and caused action. On the contrary, no sound account of action as voluntary can avoid seeing it as caused as well. Similarly, behavior that can be successfully explained by interpretation is not necessarily unavailable to hypotheses based on statistics.

I oppose the notion that one must choose a certain orientation and then stick with it, forsaking all others. I oppose equally the notion that no orientation can be criticized from outside. I shall undertake to show that certain orientations are unsound; and in doing so, I shall be giving reasons for adopting certain other orientations. At other points my argument will be that certain apparently different frameworks are compatible or even complementary.

Simon (1957 and elsewhere) propounded the justly noted argument that acquiring the appropriate kind and amount of information is an economic problem for managers, and that the solution requires taking into account the cost of the information. Beyond a certain point accuracy is not worth the price: the manager "satisfices"—that is, decides that what is available suffices for the purposes at hand—rather than maximizes. Winter (1964, 1975) added an important argument: that in some cases identifying that certain point is itself not worth what it costs; so the decision about how much information to gather cannot be an altogether rational one. I shall argue that the same is true in the case of theories: beyond a certain point, which we cannot identify by the application of scientific method, there are no scientific or even economic bases for theory choice. The experienced theorist simply decides to make do with what is available. We can call this the doctrine of theoretical satisficing.

This doctrine is not an invitation to heavy-handed positivist-bashing and paradigm-invoking. Still less does it advocate theoretical license, or any form of believing whatever you like; that makes no more sense than to drive on the left side of the street because space is only relative anyway. If natural scientists had proceeded that way, they would have made little progress.

The truth, as Lady Bracknell observed, is rarely pure and never simple. In this case it is less dramatic than either of these two of its competitors, whose proponents argue or declare with infectious enthusiasm. Be prepared for words like "on the other hand," "matter of degree," and so on. Accuracy demands such caution where life is complex.

THE TEA BREAK: AN ILLUSTRATIVE CASE

The owner of a small manufacturing company in England learned from an industrial engineering study that his workers' tea break at eleven o'clock each morning was seriously interfering with production.[1] The break itself lasted only twenty minutes, but the time required to stop work and restart it doubled the down-time and made the interval between "elevenses" and lunch short and unproductive.

As the shop was not unionized, the managing director unilaterally eliminated the morning tea break, lengthened the lunch hour by twenty minutes, and undertook to share the productivity gained with the workers through a small wage increase.

The result was disastrous. To the managing director's surprise, the workers clung fiercely to the notion that the tea break was an essential right that should not be tampered with. Grumbling did not subside for weeks, morale suffered, absenteeism rose, and productivity fell—most sharply between eleven and lunch, but measurably throughout the afternoon as well. In due course the managing director relented, and operations quickly returned to something close to normal.

Why was the reaction so calamitous? What can we learn from the incident? These two questions may have the same answer if the covering law theory of causality, long considered basic to scientific method (see, for example, the classic Hempel and Oppenheim paper [1948], discussed further in chapter 1) is correct: the causal explanation of the event invokes a general principle, or more than one, that a manager may learn and then use to avoid such trouble on another occasion.

The answer, whether or not it is a simple one, is not found within the case as thus far described. It would be helpful to know, what the case does not state, that people who eat a starchy breakfast typically experience a depressed blood sugar level towards the end of the morning, and in many cases consequent faintness and irritability. It would be useful to know that among employees of this company a starchy breakfast was common, and more useful in the long run to know that in working-class England a high-carbohydrate breakfast has traditionally been the rule.

Whether a tea break at eleven was a longtime custom in this company is relevant; so is whether it is customary in English factories; so is whether there was significant socializing at the tea break. In any of these cases, the owner's cancelling it was likely to cause repercussions.

Whether relations between the owner and the workers had been good to this point is significant: a poor relationship creates negative attitudes towards changes that would not disturb a good relationship. (Clearly, it will be useful to describe the relationship in terms more reliable and informative than *good* or *poor*. The better description may make reference to corporate culture, about which more in due course.)

Workers' attitudes are in part a function of their individual personalities: some personality types are more amenable than others. (That too could be stated in more precise language.) But if we do not know much about workers' personalities, we may infer something about their preferences from their age, nationality, economic situation, class membership, length of service, and so on.

Two second-order questions emerge from this case. The first is, What kind of explanation is appropriate here? Physiological? Psychological? Sociological? Political? There is no reason to rule out any sort as inappropriate by nature. The information available for the explanation will affect the appropriateness of one kind or another; so will the nature of the question asked, which is at the moment somewhat vague; so will the purpose to which the answer is to be put, though some answers are much likelier to be useful than others; so will the measuring instruments available, and the cost of using them. Blood sugar level may be a factor, as may the employees' attitude; and both may be more accurately predictable if we have some knowledge of the workers' social class.

The last remark may suggest that physiological and psychological explanations are somehow more basic than sociological ones. One can no doubt construct a sense in which they are. But social arrangements themselves are not functions of physiological and psychological states alone, and they substantially affect those states.

What one may safely take for granted affects the appropriateness of a proffered explanation as well. We do not usually explain a fire by saying that the house in question was made largely of wood or by pointing out that oxygen was present, but we could. Managers of complex organizations ought to be at least as open to interdisciplinary explanations and as practical in using them as firemen.

The other second-order question is not very different: Is there anything in the tea break situation that makes it unamenable to the scientific method?

The physiological explanation is surely scientific enough: a high-starch breakfast affects blood sugar levels in many cases, and indirectly affects mood and performance. Dietetics is a less exact science than physics, but it is a science. We have a causal explanation here even if we lack some information about the individuals' physical makeup and therefore cannot predict who will be affected and how much, even if we cannot find a set of principles that would ever make such a prediction possible given the sort of information we could possibly get.

In some respects an organization theorist is like an academic dietitian. Neither of them is a scientist in quite the way a theoretical physicist is, but neither is unscientific in method or general outlook. Dietitians describe certain events and states on so gross a level that only approximately accurate diagnoses, predictions, and recommendations are possible. The regularities they postulate and use lack the precision and definitiveness of scientific laws, but allow the dietitians to achieve their objectives far more effectively than if they could use only standard scientific laws, whose application would be hopelessly cumbersome.

Much the same can be said of organization theorists, though their theories are even more remote than the dietitians' from anything like physics. Organization theorists form testable hypotheses, try to define terms clearly, use public, replicable procedures that they have some reason to consider sound, build on others' work, and aim to explain, predict, and control. As in dietetics, the phenomena they have chosen to study are dauntingly complex at the level at which they study them: to find deterministic relations among the phenomena, one must look to deeper levels. But something of the sort may be said of almost any science, even arguably of physics as it now stands. As dietetics and meteorology are sciences and use the scientific method, we need not be embarrassed about applying the scientific method to the systematic study of organizations.

There is, however, an objection to applying standard scientific criteria to organizations or to anything for which the social sciences are designed. Theories in the social sciences are about people. In determining the effects of some events and states on people and vice versa we must take into account how people perceive and intend. If the workers do not notice that the tea break has been eliminated, the change may affect them less. If they do but decide it is all for the best, the change will have little effect. A theory that covered workers' perceptions and intentions would be extraordinarily complex. It would be a psychological theory but something more as well.

An explanation of the workers' behavior would have to answer questions like, What does the elimination of the tea break mean to them? How do they perceive it? How do they think it will affect them? How important do they take it to be? There is nothing unscientific about postulating internal states—perceptions, beliefs, intentions, and so on—that account for how the workers behave. But we must also attend to possible effects of past experience and training, social and economic class, corporate culture and custom, expectations about the owner and about owners in general, and many other factors that do not fall within the usual purview of the ordinary organization theorist. All this is part of the *interpretation* of the workers' behavior: that is, a form of explanation that seeks to understand and take into account the workers' view of the situation, motivation, and therefore beliefs and rationality. In fact, some of it involves attributing interpretation to the workers themselves, who will probably try to understand the owner's behavior.

In chapter 3, then more extensively in chapters 4 and 5, I shall take the position that interpretation is indeed a valuable form of explanation, but that it neither eliminates nor is eliminated by standard forms of scientific explanation. In fact natural scientists too must sometimes resort to a form of interpretation in arguing for and choosing theories.

This case raises many of the issues to be discussed hereafter. From time to time I shall refer back to it, and in due course I shall argue for the following answers to the two second-order questions posed earlier. First, there is no one kind of explanation that explains the workers' behavior well enough to justify excluding all other kinds. Second, the discussion of interpretation does not show that the workers' behavior is beyond the reach of scientific explanation.

A SUMMARY OF THE REST OF THE BOOK

Chapter 1 argues that organization theory does provide us with theories that support causal explanations, and in aid of that argument indicates the criteria—not all of them perfectly compatible—for good theory. We do have reasons for doubting that organization theory can be scientific, but some excessive pessimism on that issue may be related to problems inherent in the standard account of causal explanation. Science is justified by its success, not by its conformity to any simple textbook notion of how scientists ought to proceed.

Like psychology, organization theory rests on functional explanation, which is neither incompatible with ordinary causal explanation nor inferior to it. In showing why this is true, I lay the basis for subsequently arguing that psychology is a viable form of explanation and that the organization theorist should be hospitable to a variety of kinds of explanation.

Chapter 2 takes up the time-honored notion, long associated with scientific method, that knowledge is based on well-measured observation and that the meaningfulness of a theory depends on its being connected to observation. But it is a major mistake to suppose that a theory is translatable into the evidence for it. Excessive zeal in operationalizing is a form of just that reductionist mistake. In chapter 2 I deny that we should reduce postulates to pure observables, affirm that we should attend more closely to the nature of constructs and construct validity, and argue that there are no pure observables. Every observation comes wrapped in concepts, or it is not observation at all. The distinction between observable entities and theoretical ones is so thoroughly blurred that one can neither keep them wholly separate nor reduce the latter to the former.

Stated in the abstract, these points are familiar; but where they are applied to practical matters, such as organizational climate, they prove incompatible with some of what organization theorists believe and do.

Chapter 3 applies the discussion of observations and postulates to psychological states and events, and answers criticisms of psychology that attack it for countenancing unobservable entities. But it is true that psychological theory does not conform very well to the standard criteria for good theory mentioned above. Its central propositions do not appear to be falsifiable, and its concepts are poorly defined relative to what is observable and to each other. Beyond that, insofar as psychology focuses on the individual abstracted out of organizational and social context, it falsifies what it sets out to explain. All of an individual's knowledge of his or her mental states and events is mediated by and presupposes a system of social intercourse. These issues, serious though not fatal, teach some general lessons about the nature of theory. For example, in order to assess the central concepts of psychology we must bring to bear the issue of construct validity, and with it a better understanding of the sound concepts of both natural scientists and behavioral theorists, including not only psychologists but organization theorists.

Chapter 4 defends the rational model of individual and organizational behavior as essential to the explanation of behavior of either sort. Intentions, rational or not, are causes of behavior; and no account of intention can omit reference to rationality. To suppose otherwise is to misunderstand the relationship between covering law and causation. Equally important, it is to misunderstand how the attribution of rationality is a crucial part of a very respectable form of explanation, and how the attribution of causation is a crucial part of the attribution of rationality, hence free will. A coherent and defensible account of the nature of persons and of organizations presupposes just what some opponents of rational individualism deny.

Chapter 5 asks whether the organization itself can be considered a rational entity, with something analogous to the intentions and objectives of a person. It can; and there are corporate values distinct from those of its managers. That answer entails consideration of corporate culture and, in turn, of interpretation, which is widely supposed to be what distinguishes the natural from the social sciences. The explanation of a wide range of individual or collective human behavior entails reference to the shared rules under which people think and talk about the world and agree about what is rational and what is not, even if they do not always act just that way. Anthropologists explain reason-based behavior in part by reference to the collective view of what is reasonable that is imposed by the local culture and carried in its language. To understand individual behavior, then, it is necessary to understand the rules of the culture—it may be an organization's culture—under which it makes sense.

Having established all this, we are well prepared to deal in chapter 6 with the question whether organization theory can be reduced to psychology. Certainly it cannot. The question, not so difficult in itself, prompts a discussion of what is involved in reducing something to something else and of how different and even incompatible theories may give different kinds of viable explanation of the same events and states. A theorist or a user of theories sometimes "satisfices" in the same way as a decision-maker does—that is, chooses an imperfect theory because the cost of a "better" one is prohibitive. Understanding organizations and theories about them requires an appreciation of the ways in which distinct and even incompatible theories contribute to both knowledge and practice.

Chapter 7 takes a pragmatic position on how theories in the natural and behavioral sciences are justified. Both involve making some rational and defensible choices with no rock-bottom justifying foundation of self-evident truth to use as a basis for choosing. These choices are more difficult when the theories in question are not only incompatible but incommensurable, so that they cannot be translated into a neutral language and compared. In such cases the proponents of one theoretical framework may have to assess another, incommensurable one by interpreting its proponents' reasons for embracing it in much the same way an anthropologist interprets exotic language and behavior. In this way one paradigm can indeed critically assess another and find fault with it; for you can identify a conceptual framework as a conceptual framework only if it has enough in common with your own that you can also criticize it, though not as straightforwardly as empiricists believe two theories can be compared. This sort of criticism as much as anything else is what philosophers do; and organization theorists do it too.

Neither Kuhn nor Burrell and Morgan (1979) nor anyone else has found reason to doubt that some theories are good and others bad, but what is required in choosing between theories may be more like the successful manager's experienced intuition than any empiricist would acknowledge.

If the central arguments of this book are sound, organization theory is not in a comfortable position. Neither facts nor concepts can always be pinned down with the kind of certainty we have traditionally associated with science. On the other hand, there is a difference between good theories and bad ones, and an enormous premium on knowing the difference. Theorists cannot be expected to like that position. But philosophers and managers, each in their own way, have to live with it every day.

The rational model, free will, interpretation, the indeterminacy of translation, the difficulty of distinguishing necessary from contingent truth, incommensurability, the viability of psychology, the special status of mental entities, reducibility, construct validity, personal identity, functionalism, materialism, paradigms, the social construction of reality, rule-following behavior, and the covering law model of causal explanation—at least some of these will be separately familiar to most readers. Please join me in considering how they are related.

NOTE

1. This case, altered for the usual reasons, is based on some findings discussed in a lecture by Russell L. Ackoff, who offers a shorter version of it in Ackoff (1978, 106ff.). I have no doubt the story is firmly based on fact, but I cannot vouch for this version of it, and its truth does not matter for present purposes.

1 SCIENCE
Laws and Theories

To write usefully about organization theory requires some understanding of what a good theory is. That, in turn, requires us to address the foremost means by which good theories are produced—that is, the scientific method.

I shall argue that the scientific method and the sort of theory it generates are well, but not perfectly, suited to the explanation of organizational behavior. The human sciences raise two kinds of problem for the scientific method. First, the phenomena that the social sciences undertake to explain are uncontrollably complex and indeterminate. Second, explanations that take intentional action seriously have an evaluative aspect or something much like it, with the result that the standard methods of science do not provide all the kinds of explanation organization theorists need. To prove all this, I shall attack incautious views of what purports to be the nature of science as well as mistaken criticisms of legitimate views.

It should be obvious that organization theory is not much like physics. In spite of some similarities explored here and later, organization theory has no prospect of achieving the physicist's precision and justified confidence in prediction. But this is not because organization theorists have perversely or indolently failed to use some readily identifiable procedure called the scientific method. In fact, as I shall argue more than once, even scientists do not always adhere to any such procedure. Much damage has been done through the careless application of some plausible notion of the scientific method. No less damage has been done when skepticism about the scientific method has led to the view that the behavioral and the natural sciences are both essentially subjective enterprises.

1. WHAT SCIENCE DOES

Why should organization theorists take scientific method seriously? The best reason is its successful track record in explanation, prediction, and control. It may not be everywhere applicable, but it is clear that organization theorists, at any rate, have learned some useful techniques from it. What is not so clear is whether organization theory has taken sufficient advantage of what science has to offer; for organization theorists have not always been sufficiently careful in applying the methods of science so far away from their original home.

To speak of scientific method obscures an obvious fact: there are a good many sciences, each with its characteristic methods as well as subject matter. Science is not methodologically uniform, and it is not clear that it ought to be. Geology and meteorology, for example, seem to lack the precision of physics. Biology has some techniques of its own, and has succeeded with them. Anthropologists do not follow all the physicists' criteria for theoretical soundness. We need to be cautious in describing *the* scientific method or the nature of all good theories.

Scientists' successes in many fields raise doubt that philosophers or other critics have any business trying to set down rules a priori that scientists are supposed to follow. It is wiser to look at what scientists have actually done and to distill from their successes some lessons from which future scientists, philosophers, and others in pursuit of knowledge can learn. When a scientist comes along and breaks the textbook rules and seems to succeed—Darwin's theory is a good example—it is not at all clear that one should simply rule that enterprise out as being bad science. The least this shows is that identifying the methodological principles that make science successful is difficult; and for all we know it may be impossible to find unexceptionable principles. History does not in any case permit us to be confident that at any given moment most scientific theories are right, or even methodologically sound.

Organization theory has a problem that some other behavioral sciences do not: as actually practiced, it is interdisciplinary. For better or worse, it seems now to be developing its characteristic methods and canons that

distinguish it clearly from, say, sociology; but that development is a matter of controversy among organization theorists every step of the way. So the question whether its methods are like those of some natural science is complicated by its having no set of clearly recognizable methods.

Central to the scientific method as traditionally understood is the idea that it is the scientist's function to identify laws of nature, which support causal claims. Whether organization theorists can or should do the same in support of their kind of explanation is another matter.

1a. Law and Causality

The standard device for explicating scientific explanation is the hypothetico-deductive model. It takes the form of a syllogism of which the first premise is a purported law of nature, the second a statement of particular fact that is an instance of the purported law, and the conclusion, which follows deductively from the two premises, an event to be explained. The second premise states the cause—that is, a sufficient condition—of the conclusion.

Hence:

Purported natural law: anyone who has been eaten by a bear is dead.
Statement of particular fact: Smokey has eaten Jones.
Conclusion: Jones is dead.

If one asks why Jones is dead, it is normally an adequate reply to say that Jones was eaten by a bear. Pressed, one might refer to the lawlike generalization, or "covering law," as it is sometimes called, to the effect that when a bear eats you, you die. Pressed further, one might refer to generalizations that explain why being eaten by a bear is fatal.

This plausible model has evoked an endless stream of criticisms and suggestions for improvement or abandonment.[1] One of the great difficulties is distinguishing between first premises that are genuine natural laws and those that are not. So-called accidental generalizations—for example, that every woman in this room is divorced—do not permit us to explain Smith's being divorced by stating that she is in this room. Not all cases are so easy to identify, however.

Another difficulty is that the model does not always distinguish cause and effect in an intuitively satisfying way. If the second premise is a necessary as well as a sufficient condition of the conclusion, then the conclu-

sion logically must also be necessary and sufficient for the second prem-ise. So, for example, we intuitively believe that the length of a pendulum is the cause of its period, and not the other way around. But the model gives us no way to distinguish the cases.

In some apparently clear instances of causation the model is of limited help. We might say that lightning had caused a forest fire, but there is no natural law that says a forest fire starts when lightning strikes a forest. Conditions must be right: the wood must be adequately dry; there must be no one there to extinguish the fire before it spreads, and so on; and oxy-gen must be present. But given all that, there seems no definitive basis for saying that the stroke of lightning caused the forest fire and the presence of oxygen did not. We must use a criterion of this sort: the stroke of lightning was the unusual or unexpected factor.

In another, similar way the model fails to engage the difficulties of real causal explanation. Suppose a pitcher is hit on the leg by a line drive and suffers a tibial fracture. To the question, "Why does Bob Gibson have a broken leg?" a respectable answer would be, "Because a line drive off Roberto Clemente's bat hit him on the leg." But being hit on the leg by a line drive—even one of Clemente's—was never in itself a sufficient con-dition of a broken leg. We have good reason to attribute a cause in some cases of this sort even when we do not know the applicable law in ques-tion, even when we cannot describe the situation accurately enough to identify a truly sufficient condition. We can identify causes with confi-dence even when, given the way they are identified, they are not suffi-cient conditions. Importing statistics helps, but it does not always solve all the problems. If we could establish that a line drive to the leg was fol-lowed by a broken tibia only thirteen percent of the time, it would nevertheless remain true that on those occasions the line drive caused the tibia to break.

Sometimes organization theorists find causes without strong correla-tions. Sometimes they find correlations where the issue of causality is very much in doubt. Linking cigarette smoking and cancer illustrates the point, but it is easy to think of additional evidence that would strongly support the causal hypothesis. In some other cases there are excellent cor-relations without any trace of causation; thus, apparently, the case of pen-dulum length and period. There is a law according to which thermal and electrical conductivity are perfectly isomorphic, but it does not support even as much explanation as the pendulum law does. It might help in making a prediction, but you could not control electrical conductivity by manipulating thermal conductivity. (Cummins [1983, especially chapter

1] discusses most of these examples in his helpful treatment, though he is one of many to have made the general point.)

Consider the case of the tea break, described in the Introduction. The physiological explanation is scientific enough: a high-starch breakfast (to describe it crudely) affects blood sugar levels in many cases, and so indirectly mood and performance as well. We may have a causal explanation here even if we lack some information about the individuals' physical makeup and therefore cannot predict who will be affected and how much, even if we cannot find a set of principles that would ever make such a prediction possible given the sort of information we could possibly get.

Neither an organization theorist nor an academic dietitian is a scientist in quite the way a theoretical physicist is, but in neither case would we deny that the method of the discipline is scientific in general because its "laws" are imprecise and its subject matter out of control and subject to exogenous forces.

Organization theorists form testable hypotheses, use replicable procedures, and so on. (The next section goes into more detail on what is scientific.) So do dietetic theorists. That the phenomena they study are dauntingly complex at the level at which they study them is no argument against applying scientific methods to the study of organizations, or of the weather.

In arguing that theories support causal explanations we have raised an issue of obvious importance: what makes a theory a good theory? What is it about a physicist's theory that makes it better than an alchemist's or an astrologer's? Why do we suspect that theories about organizations may not be quite respectable?

1b. Good Theories

One of the primary goals of science is to find first premises of the hypothetico-deductive "syllogisms" that are true and explain events. A good theory gathers together a network of such premises that explain well in part because the relations among the premises themselves deepen the explanations of individual events, in part because the premises are true. But as theories are not the simple inductive sum of orderly experience, it is often difficult to determine whether a theory generated to explain certain phenomena is true, and which of competing theories consistent with the phenomena is true. Scientists have made these choices and defended them

successfully. The heart of the scientific method is the means by which scientists generate hypotheses that account for observed phenomena and predict those yet to be observed.

In part because issues about the nature and methods of science are neither deducible from what successful scientists do (even assuming we all agree on what counts as success) nor discoverable a priori without regard to what scientists do, this set of criteria for good theories will inevitably be controversial—in fact, there will be some disagreement about what I have already said in this subsection—and it is not clear how the controversy can be solved. But I think the criteria will sound persuasive to most readers.[2]

1. A theory must fit the publicly observable facts of the case, and its predictions must be true as well. Where the facts in question have been generated by experimentation, this criterion is supplemented by standards of measurement, publicity, and replicability of procedure intended to ensure objectivity. A theory that makes essential use of probability is harder to undermine, but there the inferior theory can be made to look pretty silly, particularly if there is a superior alternative available.

2. A theory must say something that could be shown to be incompatible with the observed facts, present or future. A theory that is compatible with anything that happens—hence unfalsifiable in principle—tells us nothing about the world. So it should be testable in a way that makes falsification conceivable.

3. A theory should contain no internal contradictions. This condition, roughly the converse of the previous one, forbids that a theory should be wrong no matter what happens.

4. No theory stated in language that only its propounder can understand is very valuable. There is surely little reason to accept a theory whose terms have no connection to any we use to describe our actual or possible experience.

5. There is reason to be skeptical of a theory that is incompatible with a great many of our other beliefs. One of the promising features of a new hypothesis is that it explains or is explained by other hypotheses we entertain. It fits consistently into the network of these hypotheses. Of course the entire network could be wrong, but that is less likely where other propositions in it have survived rigorous examination.

6. Other things being equal, simpler hypotheses are better. We choose the hypothesis that postulates fewer entities for the same reason we

reject a hypothesis that postulates one entity when the available evidence can be accounted for by postulating none.

7. The more general, the better. Newton's theories gained great credibility by explaining the movements of both heavenly and earthly bodies by the same laws. If a hypothesis is too narrow-gauged, it begins to look like a mere random fact or ad hoc collection of facts not able to explain anything (recall "All women in this room are divorced"). Note how this criterion relates to the sixth: any theory can achieve generality if it is stated with enough conditions and complications.
8. As elsewhere in life, modesty is a virtue. Hypotheses that run too elaborately beyond the evidence lose plausibility.

You have probably noticed that the last two criteria tend in opposite directions. You may also have noticed that simplicity and modesty do not always coincide, the simplest hypothesis sometimes being a very bold one. In fact, many successful scientific theories have not been modest, or refutable by any readily describable possibility, or simple, or compatible with most of the rest of what the theorist or anyone else believed, or compatible with everything sincere observers claimed to have seen. These criteria are guidelines rather than strict rules. Each, with the arguable exception of the third, has been violated by some good theory. But they are all important, and not only to natural science.

The scientific method is a way to get theoretical knowledge from experience, which is at the very least an important source of it. But the success of science is not evidence in favor of empiricism.

1c. Empiricism

If science produces knowledge par excellence, then it is at least worth considering that all real knowledge is scientific knowledge. The purest empiricists, the logical positivists, chief sponsors of that position, argued that knowledge was built up from fundamental observation, that explanation was backed by discovered laws of nature, that any proposition that no observation could either confirm or disconfirm was meaningless. Some positivists and sympathizers argued for operationalism, which claims an even closer relationship between meaning and experience : a theory is no more, means no more, than the observable evidence for it. Nothing more—in particular, no unobservable entities—may be countenanced. Temperature, for example, is not what causes the mercury to rise:

temperature is to be defined by direct reference to the mercury rising. This leads to embarrassment when we consider platinum-wire thermometers, whose use is based on the assumption that electrical resistance varies with temperature. How, in this case, do we define temperature?

The positivist position can be attacked in several ways. One way is to say that not all knowledge is scientific knowledge, and not all understanding is knowledge of subsumption under a law of nature. Another is to find incoherence in the positivist position. A third is to hold that scientists do not and cannot work the way positivists claim they do. Advocates of this third way have had the greatest effect on organization theorists. One name stands out.

It was Thomas Kuhn (1970) whose celebrated scrutiny of the way successful scientists have worked throughout history led him to argue that the soundest of possible scientific practice differs radically from the ideals of old textbooks, according to which scientists gather available knowledge into theories in cumulative and austerely objective fashion. Kuhn claimed that the relations among evidence, concept, and theory in successful and accepted scientific practice are not as straightforward or as unproblematical as most admirers of scientific method believe. His strictures, couched in provocative and not always readily comprehensible language,[3] have not merely made people more realistic about what science does. Some readers have interpreted Kuhn as a radical subjectivist and have themselves adopted a permissive attitude toward "different paradigms"; this now fashionable expression usually suggests that there is no reasonable way to show that one kind of theory is better than another.

To many behavioral scientists Kuhn seems a godsend. Feelings of inferiority give way to the satisfaction of discovering that even natural scientists are uncertainly anchored and subject to the tides of politics as well as fact. All organization theorists know something about Kuhn and can use the word *paradigm* on demand; few dismiss or even seriously dispute what they take to be his claims. If asked, most would agree in the abstract that there is no one paradigm that is self-evidently correct. An unwarranted tolerance of subjectivism is an extreme response to Kuhn—and to Quine (1960 and 1961) and Wittgenstein (1953) and Rorty (1979) and others—and on the whole a misreading of his intent. A somewhat more measured and justifiable reaction is to bash positivism, as though everyone who took theories seriously were a positivist. If there is anything on which most organization theorists can agree, it is that *positivism is bad*— or at the very least not the final answer.

Yet while Kuhn and the others have been widely influential, not all the implications of his work or that of his best successors have been fully absorbed, or even accepted.

On important methodological and substantive issues, many organization theorists are empiricists, and their empiricism creates theoretical and practical problems. Positions taken and arguments made in the field often presuppose that knowledge arises from experience and that experience serves as an ultimate check on claims about the world. Kuhn is one of many who have argued that the relationship between experience and knowledge is not as straightforward as it may appear; and overconfidence in empiricism—not truly characteristic of natural scientists— can lead not only to bad theory but to bad practice as well. This overconfidence has generated some unsound criticism of psychological explanation and of other techniques characteristic of the human sciences, and has had other negative effects on the study of organizations.

Attacking empiricism in organization theory is not a new idea. On the contrary, the wonder about empiricism is its weedlike tenacity in this most unpromising soil. One reason for its remarkable vigor is that there seems to be no good alternative to it. With nothing else to cling to, many of its critics among organization theorists—for example, Morgan (1980 and elsewhere)—seem unconfident that there is any reality outside our individual and collective minds. (We discuss some of the subjectivists' positions in chapters 2 and 7.)

One of the attractions of empiricism is that it seems to offer objectivity, which seems to be required if we are to distinguish sound theories from those that we would simply like to be true. So Pfeffer calls for objectivity in organizational theory and denounces "lay preaching" that comes forward in scientific guise (1982, 293f.). It is just possible, however, that at some points lay preaching is unavoidable and that in those cases our only realistic hope is to find ways of distinguishing good sermons from bad ones.

My aim is to argue for the scientific method as one way of generating knowledge about organizations, but at the same time to criticize empiricism. I claim the important issue in justifying theory is to determine what we can infer about what is the case from what works.

Two kinds of theory seem to differ considerably not only from the canons of empiricism but also from the scientific method as I have described it. They are important for two reasons: first, both are frequently used in organization theory; second, both are legitimate ways of explaining, not in violation of any rules of natural science, though they differ from what natural scientists usually produce. Each occupies one of the two following sections.

2. PROCESS THEORIES

Some organization theories are similar to what Mohr (1982, especially chapter 2) calls process theories. These differ from variance theories, the staples of our journals, which seek necessary and sufficient conditions for the states and events they explain on the basis of statistical evidence. A typical process explanation of an accidental fire would tell a story of successive causally related events that in this case form a chain leading to (say) a fire, but which cannot be expected always to work in the same way. Mohr claims process theories are about necessary rather than sufficient conditions and probabilistic processes rather than efficient causes. So we might have a theory about accidental fires to the effect that .03 percent of all wooden houses with wood-burning stoves will burn down in any given winter. In such a case as this, however, we have not only a statistical regularity but also the basis of an explanation, because there is clearly some causal relation between how a wood-burning stove operates and the ignition of the flammable material near the stove.

It is clear that we can identify Jones's wood-burning stove as the cause of the fire that destroyed the Jones house even though there is no scientific law stating that having a wood-burning stove is followed by a house-destroying fire. Mohr seems correct, too, in identifying probability as central to the theory. We can have a statistical theory to explain a non-inevitable event, and on the other hand we could hardly be said to have a theory without at least some statement of the probability of B given A. A statistical theory may be the best we can do, and it may be good enough to be extraordinarily useful to homeowners and managers as they make decisions.

But we do not need statistics to know what caused this fire. Without statistics one can tell the story of how the fire ignited and then, unchecked, flared out of control. The insurance investigator could prove a case in court without the support of statistics. What we need statistics for is a theory that helps prevent fires, or at least helps set insurance rates. So it is in the case of organizations. We can reasonably conclude that the work force was unproductive last quarter because Smith decided on ideological grounds to foment discontent among the hourly employees, and can explain in detail how it happened; but that is far from a theory. Managers as well as theorists have good reason to be interested in theories as well as causes. The identification of causal relationships after the fact may tell you whom or what to blame, but what is required is some way of designing the organization that reduces the probability of the unwelcome outcome for the future.

Mohr resists the notion that statistical explanations of the kind in prospect here are based on our ignorance of the true laws of nature. For some areas of the world he postulates a "probabilistic metaphysic." "Not all recurring events are causal, especially because what is considered an event depends on how reality is construed" (1982, 52). We know the first clause is true, but it is equally true that all caused events would recur under the same circumstances. It is also true that scientific laws relate events under certain descriptions and that events so related may have other descriptions under which they are not related by laws of nature, but it does not follow and it is not true that the way anyone describes or construes reality determines which events are in fact causally related.

Mohr is willing to use the intuitive notion of cause to distinguish process theories from mere sequences that happen to recur, while at the same time resisting defining causes by reference to natural laws.[4] The notion of lawlike generalization smacks too much of variance theories, and suggests that anopheles mosquitos cause malaria in everybody and every wood-burning stove causes a fire. Here Mohr's probabilistic metaphysic seems to lead him to overstate his case. He need not deny that there are lawlike generalizations covering malaria and fires; it is enough to say that, as in the case of line drives and broken legs, we need not be able to find them in order to attribute a cause. (In the discussion in chapter 4 of how intentions cause actions this becomes a crucial point.) His more important point is that probability is enough—perhaps more than enough—to support a perfectly respectable process theory.

The weakness of process theories is their strength. To postulate a causal chain beginning with a wood-burning stove or an anopheles mosquito is to make a significant statement of great practical value. At the same time, however, it does not permit a prediction that any individual will get malaria or that a certain house will burn down. On the other hand, the kind of detail that might seem required to "improve" a simple but approximate model of the spread of disease or the diffusion of technology (it could be the same model for both) might well render it so complex and circumscribed as to be useless. For example, to try to improve a certain economic or sociological model by the addition of reference to different individuals' traits and motives might give a hopelessly unwieldy result.

Process explanation is one of the two apparently deviant but legitimate forms of explanation we have to discuss. The other, no less important and apparently more confusing, is functional explanation.

3. FUNCTIONAL EXPLANATION

The topic of functional explanation is one whose connections radiate out in an extraordinary number of directions. It touches on several issues, particularly psychological explanation, to be discussed primarily in chapter 3. It also provides an opportunity to take a position on the issue of what Donaldson (1985), for one, has called traditional organization theory, or contingency theory,[5] or the structural-functional approach, or the design tradition in organization theory. According to that view, organizations are systems whose parts have functions that, arranged in the appropriate structure, lead to achieving organizational goals. And organization theory is concerned primarily with finding the appropriate structures for organizations, given their contexts.

The methods of the design tradition therefore conceive of an organization as an entity that is subject to functional analysis; that is, analyzing systems into their functions is one way of explaining what they do. To turn the point on its head: arranging functions into a structure is one way of getting the system to do what you want it to do. I shall use the notions of functional analysis and instantiation (the terms will be explained below) in discussing organization theory.

Functional analysis has an honorable history in both the natural and social sciences. It focuses on what something is made of and on what its components do and therefore cause to happen.[6]

Not all the theories that explain something by reference to how it is constituted are causal theories. To state that the temperature of a gas is the mean kinetic energy of its molecules is not to give an arbitrary and conventional definiticn of heat: there is an actual scientific theory to that effect. But the theory does not claim that the mean kinetic energy of molecules *causes* heat. Whatever causes heat also causes the mean kinetic energy of molecules, because these phenomena are, as a matter of discovered scientific fact, identical. The theory in question explains something's possession of a property by analyzing the property (heat, in this case) into certain properties of that something or its components (in this case, the kinetic energy of the molecules constituting the gas), then theorizing that this something has the property (twenty degrees Celsius) if and only if its components have certain properties (the mean kinetic energy of the molecules is such and such). In some cases the components must also be arranged in a certain relation. This is a standard explanatory move in chemistry. Where the properties of the components explain the properties of the whole, there may or may not be any similar explanation of the component's properties.

In such cases the laws to which such explanations appeal are not causal laws but "instantiation" laws, of this form: anything that has such and such components arranged so and so has a certain property. Often the property to be explained is a dispositional one. We explain the water-solubility of something or its brittleness by invoking the law that anything that has components of a certain sort arranged in a certain way is water-soluble or brittle.

A similar but not identical way of explaining a disposition is to analyze it into its component dispositions, or *functions*. The purported explanation truly succeeds in explaining if the functions are simpler than the whole disposition and their arrangement in a certain structure creates the disposition of the system as a whole. Now there is a crucial difference between explaining the temperature of a gas by finding that it is the mean kinetic energy of its molecules and explaining a disposition of a system by analysis of it into subsystems with subfunctions. In the latter case it does make sense to say that the activities of the subsystems *cause* the disposition of the system as a whole.

So we can consider a factory a system that has this dispositional property: it is capable of manufacturing something. It has this disposition or capacity because it contains and can be broken down into comparatively simple functions, such as tasks on an assembly line. The concept is familiar in electronics. A schematic diagram of a complex device analyzes its capacities into those of its components, suitably organized. In biology, too—the body has certain systems, defined by their capacities, that contribute to the life of the body. Insofar as the capacities of the whole system are different from and more sophisticated than those of the subsystems and (for that reason, presumably) depend on a complex organization of the subsystems into the system, the functional analysis has

explanatory power. A computer program analyzed into a complex serial
set of simple operations is an example attractive to those who think the
cognition of computers is similar to that of the human brain from the
point of view of functional analysis.

The functional analysis may be just the first part of a more thorough
explanation of a system's capacity. The capacity of the subsystem to perform a certain function may be explained by reference to its physical
parts and their structure and appeal to the appropriate instantiation law.
Where components that are physically different can perform the same
function in a system, the explanation of how the physical structures of the
two different subsystems generate the functions may be different. In that
case we say that a particular function is *instantiated* in two different
structures. A flowchart or its analogue expresses the functional analysis
of a system's capacity; the capacity itself can be expressed by a statement
of the relationship between the system's input and its output. Many
different configurations of hardware may accommodate the program in
question.

A system may be described at various levels of abstraction.[7] In the case
of a computer, at least, it can be described as a series of physical movements causing other physical movements, perhaps in machine language; it
can be described as a series of states in a program, presumably in the appropriate programming language; or it can be described in input-output
terms, in some user-friendly language. This way of talking suggests that
there is just one system, one set of events, and they are being described in
different ways, at various levels. But although we are talking about identical rather than different events, the functional analysis *explains* the system, and the specification of how the subsystems are instantiated *explains*
the subsystems. The identity does not undermine explanation: neither descriptions nor explanations of an entity need be reducible.

If a computer (or a person) can add, it can produce output that is the
sum of certain inputs—that is, output that is symbolic in the sense that it
can be interpreted as the sum of what the inputs can be interpreted as. The
relations among such states are not only causal, not only functional: they
may conform to certain rules of logic or language or evidence as well.
Where this conformity is in question, one can describe a symbolic output
from the point of view of correctness: it may fail to conform to the applicable rule and therefore be wrong. The law that supports the causal claim
is a law of electronics couched in machine language terms; it does not
state that the appearance of the premises is always followed by the appearance of the conclusions, nor is that true. But in this case, by virtue of

a law of electronics the premises cause the conclusion; and by a rule of logic they justify them.

Any system is subject to functional explanation, and to say that some piece of behavior can be analyzed into subsystems in some way is to say at least that that behavior is the effect of the states or activities into which it is analyzed. In this clear sense, functional explanation is a form of causal explanation. Similarly, the work of a group of subsystems in an organization is a cause of the achievement of an organization's goals.

But there is another feature of genuine systems that makes them functional in a stronger sense. Not only does the system generate goals—results that are in some way beneficial for the system—but the goals themselves exert a causal influence on the work of the subsystems: they help maintain the subsystems and thus the system by means of a feedback mechanism in the system. The feedback mechanism involves a conscious process where management decides, on the basis of the organization's goals, to develop or alter the subsystems. In some cases, however, the process is not conscious. For example, the Chicago School argues that firms that maximize profits survive, but that managers do not choose objectives because they know they will maximize profits; they choose them rather out of habit or imitation. The firms whose managers have the right habits survive. One may be tempted to believe that a system's goals explain the system just because the goals are in fact achieved; but where there is no feedback mechanism, that is not so.[8]

Consider the computer case again. It is possible to demand an explanation of the computer's operation that does not describe some component computation in a larger program, but instead details the operation of the hardware in machine language or some other terms. That such an explanation is possible at that juncture—or at any, for that matter—does not make an explanation in software terms or in more user-friendly terms useless. A flowchart of the computer's program does provide an explanation of the relationship between input and output. It describes subroutines that, organized properly, add up to an entire task-accomplishing program.

This is a good way to explain the wide range of phenomena that can be viewed as input followed by output. But part of the strength of that sort of explanation is that it is perfectly compatible with further explanation of a different kind. At a certain point one may say, in effect, Don't tell me what role this component plays. Tell me how the component came to be here. At this point a computer programmer can say something about the physical states of the machine that instantiate the states described in the program, and how the machine was constructed. A biologist may abandon functional analysis and turn to a microanalysis (perhaps characteristic of chemistry more than of biology) of some of the components of the organism and a story of how they got that way. Any functional explanation that focuses on the roles of the subsystems and does not go into detail about the operative causal relations, including those of the feedback mechanism, can be expanded on demand if one knows enough.

We can also describe an organization this way. Something like a flow-chart can map its input and output as well as its subsystems and sub-functions and indicate how the latter contribute to the economy of the whole. But in answer to persistent questions about just how the subsystems operate, one might go into detail about who does what and about how the control system works. As each of the subsystems of tasks may be instantiated in a variety of ways—for example, by different people or different machines—consistently with one functional analysis of the whole, a story about exactly how the essential tasks are done and even how the organization was put together in the first place could add significant new information.

4. ORGANIZATION THEORY AS FUNCTIONAL EXPLANATION

One of the primary purposes of the standard kind of organization theory that Donaldson (1985) and others have called the design tradition and the structural-functional approach is to assist managers in managing. It does this by trying to discover the necessary conditions for an organization to achieve success. The question can be put this way: given the organization's context, what is required, as well as sufficient, for success? Organization theories state which combinations of context and structural conditions will lead to success and which will not. The manager determines what the context is, then adjusts organizational conditions so as to bring them into optimal combination.

This standard approach to organization theory regards organizations as systems, with goals and components. The achievement of the goals of an organization—indeed, its very existence—depends upon the nature of its components and the way they are organized. Typically the organization is divided into subsystems that are supposed to perform their functions in aid of achieving the organization's goals. Among the many interactions in an organization, the recurring ones that have to do with the arrangement of subsystems, like centralization and specialization, are the elements of structure. It is one of management's primary tasks to adjust the organization's structure—that is, to coordinate the subsystems of components of the organization—so as to achieve its goals. If the manager is adequately knowledgeable about organization theory, he or she knows which way of coordinating the subsystems will generate the desired results and adjusts the coordinating mechanisms on the basis of feedback.

This conception of the organization and of the point of organization theory has been subjected to heterodox attack at almost every point, as Donaldson has shown. Some of the objections are within the scope of this book, and for the most part I agree with Donaldson's position on them, if not with every detail of his defense.

Silverman (especially 1968 and 1971; cited by Donaldson) and many others object that in talking about organizational goals and needs the traditional approach *reifies* organizations and endows them illegitimately with properties that only persons have. Reification comes up in chapter 2; it is discussed in the context of the attribution of psychological properties in chapter 5. In the same chapter we shall also discuss the claim, from Mintzberg particularly (1978 and, with Waters, 1985), that some highly successful organizations do not deliberate about strategy.

There are problems about the explanatory value of the notion of goal, but there are solutions to these problems. We shall discuss how goals explain in chapters 3, 4, and 7.

The traditional approach sets little store by individual intentions and values. Similarly, strategy is about choice, and the structural-functional approach raises hard questions about choice. Chapters 3, 4, and 5 deal with these questions.

The traditional approach is criticized as being ideologically tainted: it serves the interests of the managing classes. Chapters 4, 5, and 7 touch on the issue of ideological taint. There are opposite temptations to be avoided: being unrealistic about the possibility of escaping ideology, and being unduly permissive about accepting some ideological position.

A related point has to do with paradigms and frameworks. The traditional structural-functional approach to organization theory is one among a number of possible paradigms, and there is some question about the basis for choosing it as opposed to a different approach. There are some extraordinary difficulties in defending the choice of one framework over another when one cannot even translate statements within one framework into another. Chapter 7 undertakes to put the problem of translation into perspective. A problem it is, but it just does not have the awful consequences of which we are sometimes warned. Rational theory choice is possible.

One complaint about the structural-functional approach is that it fails to deal with the causes of structure but attends only to its effects. According to this criticism, Marxists and others perform the more important work of considering issues like the causes of the distribution of power in organizations.[9]

To some extent this criticism is accurate. Theorists in the design tradition do not concentrate on the causal bases of structures in organizations. They ask what structures are appropriate in certain situations, rather than what structures are generated by certain situations. There is a difference between the questions, but there is some overlap. The traditional view sees the consequences of the structure at a particular time as having a causal influence on the subsequent structure: managers develop structures that contribute to organizational goals, and they change what does not work. That is the feedback loop. But the design theory does not say how an organization gets a particular structure in the first place, whereas theorists who attend more closely to social influences have something to say on that matter.

The criticism does not damage the design tradition, however. That traditional approach aims to get at appropriateness—that is, to see what mix of context and structure causes success. The kind of explanation the theory gives is similar to the kind given by the functional analysis discussed in the previous section. A functional analysis of a body, an ecosystem, or a computer program explains by showing how the subsystems contribute to the whole. The question of how the subsystems were generated raises different issues, but useful ones for some purposes—for example, preventive medicine or building a computer. These questions sit perfectly compatibly with those that demand functional analysis; they are just different questions. The primary focus is on finding the structures that will generate success, but there would be no point in doing this if management could not then do whatever was necessary to put those structures in place and maintain them.

Functional analysis is a significant part of a legitimate way to explain a system that has subsystems. It is not identical with causal explanation on the Hempel-Oppenheim model, but it is not usually incompatible with it either. Here is one of those false oppositions posed between ways of explanation that are compatible, or nearly enough so for practical purposes. Deterministic and choice-based models constitute another example. The need to be hospitable to a variety of explanations but not promiscuous is a recurring theme in this book. An accompanying and supporting theme is skepticism about the possibility of a firm foundation on which all knowledge can be built, and even about the possibility of a coherent language in which all knowledge can be expressed.

NOTES

1. The model is often named after Hempel and Oppenheim, whose discussion of it (1948) is a classic, though there were previous similar formulations and there have been subsequent ones. But for thirty years and more it was Hempel above all others who defended the model and its accompanying "hypothetico-deductive" method against criticisms. See, for example, Hempel (1965).

2. The list is a standard one, not much different from what you would find in a good text. Quine and Ullian (1970) offer a fairly orthodox but more than usually sophisticated set of criteria, with a provocative commentary presented deadpan, and mine borrows from theirs as much as from anyone's.

3. That was not necessarily careless writing on Kuhn's part. Kuhn can be interpreted as holding that people who accept a certain overall view of the world will necessarily have trouble communicating with those who accept a radically different view, in part because some key definitions will be different. If so, the reader whose view of the world differs from that of Kuhn may have trouble understanding Kuhn. We return to this point in chapters 2 and 7.

4. He regards the notion of causality as "metaphysical," rather than observable, and thus somehow mysterious. As will become clear in chapter 2, I do not think unobservability is fatal, or even necessarily metaphysical. It must be clear that I share some of his exasperation over the notion of cause, but he is on dangerous ground when he is tempted to abandon it. It is bad policy to abandon what has been a useful term just because it cannot be operationalized. We have some difficulty in saying why the period of a pendulum does not cause its length, but the certainty of our intuition on the matter will be accommodated rather than eliminated by a successful analysis of the concept of cause. If the Hempel-Oppenheim analysis does not account for our notion of cause, then perhaps the problem is with the analysis rather than the notion. So where Mohr is using an incompletely analyzed concept of cause to explain process theories, he is not necessarily wrong.

5. As the term "contingency theory" is often associated with the view that organization theories must be of strictly limited scope, I shall speak instead of the design tradition or the structural-functional approach in this context.

6. This section is heavily dependent on Cummins (1983, chapters 1 and 2). I have deviated from his account at certain points, and I have profited from

the work of others who take a functional approach in giving an account of psychological states. (See, for example, the Block anthology [1980].) As Cummins's account is aimed primarily at explicating psychological explanation, however, the application to organization theory is largely mine. But Cummins himself does use the notion of a production system to help make a point about functional analysis.

7. Cummins would apparently disagree with this view, which in effect takes one side of a long-lived and complex argument.

8. See Elster (1984, especially chapter 1). He notes that sociologists and organization theorists occasionally conclude that if X causes Y and Y is beneficial for Z then there is a feedback mechanism involved and something is explained, but he argues correctly that that does not follow. This false move is a temptation for Marxists particularly, since they often seek to explain certain events and institutions by showing them to be beneficial to (say) the ruling class. But showing who benefits is not by itself an explanation.

9. If Elster is right in criticizing Marxists for ignoring the importance of identifying feedback mechanisms in functional explanations (see note 8), then it is not surprising that Marxists should think that in identifying the causal bases and the beneficiaries of organizational and institutional arrangements one has given essentially all the explanation anybody could reasonably want.

2 SOME PROBLEMS ABOUT EMPIRICISM

Empirical work is essential to any successful science, and to organization theory. Empiricism, which is to empirical work as arson is to central heating, does more harm than good. The fundamental problem about empiricism is overconfidence in observation and a consequent impatience with the difficulties and uncertainties that theorists encounter when they go beyond observing and operationalizing to theorizing. That last activity usually involves postulating states and events that are not themselves observable but are causes of states and events that are.

This much discussion brings us back to the question: what makes a good theory good? The right answer is not simple, but a popular wrong one is easily found: a good theory is one based firmly on what we know by observation to be true. Though not entirely wrongheaded, that wrong answer has some bad consequences for organization theorists. Among them is an abiding fondness for operationalism, which undertakes to base theory firmly on observation by assimilating statements about theoretical entities to statements about the observable evidence for them.

Observation, a basis for knowledge only insofar as it comes equipped with concepts, not only supports theory but presupposes it too. It does not reliably serve as a definitive way of verifying or falsifying theory: we cannot always evaluate competing ways of explaining organizational behavior simply by reference to predictive ability. We may not even assume there can be a common language in which one could say everything worth saying about organizations or anything else, nor that there is always a way of reconciling or even comparing the competing kinds of theory put forward to explain and deal with organizations. Yet some theories are better than others, and good local theories are better than no theories at all.

We can make sound choices among theories without the assumption that observation provides a firm basis for all knowledge. Let us see why that assumption is false.

1. OBSERVATION AND KNOWLEDGE

1a. Observables and Theoretical Entities

The time-honored empiricist way to establish that something is the case is to observe it. In the absence of direct observation of the thing or the fact itself, we make do with the observation of evidence for it. According to the extreme version of empiricism we call positivism, a proposition can be shown to be true only by being verified directly or indirectly (i.e., through evidence) by way of observation. Necessary truths aside, a proposition is meaningful only if we know what sort of observation would count as verifying or falsifying it, directly or indirectly; a term is meaningful only if it can play an essential role in such a proposition. Under the influential sponsorship of Popper (1959 and elsewhere), the criterion of falsifiability became a favorite of theorists: if a proposition is not falsifiable under any conceivable circumstances, then it is compatible with anything that could go on in the world, and consequently gives no information about what does or will go on in the world.

One of Popper's favorite examples is Freudian theory, which he regards as unfalsifiable, hence bankrupt. The theory of psychosexual development, for example, predicts rigidity of personality as a result of early toilet training; but if the opposite comes to pass, the theory is again vindicated, because the person's easygoing personality constitutes a "reaction formation." Heads, the theory wins; tails, it wins. But that, the empiricist argues, is exactly what is wrong with this and certain other psychological theories.

The organizational literature has its share of propositions and theories that do not readily admit of falsification. One of the most noted and plausible of motivation theories, for example, is Vroom's (1964) expectancy theory, the nerve of which is that an individual chooses to behave in a way that appears to lead to a reward that he or she values. Stated just that way, the theory is not very informative, for it is not clear what would falsify it. What would count as evidence that an individual is pursuing behavior motivated by something other than a valued reward? If on the whole the best guide to what people genuinely value is not what they publicly espouse but what they actually work towards, then a significant component of expectancy theory is impervious to any possible undermining evidence, and therefore trivial.

There are problems with this view, however. To begin with, the notion that theoretical statements must be individually verifiable or falsifiable to be fit for meaningful discourse seems just unrealistic. In practice we verify and falsify statements on the assumption that other statements are true or false; so it is always a complex of statements that we judge in the court of experience. (Quine [1961] was not the first to make this point, but his defense of it has been most influential.)

It is therefore impossible to overturn an entire theory on the basis of one counterexample. The defender of the theory can point out that where a theory predicts some specific event it is also assuming a number of facts; and when the prediction goes wrong, there is always the possibility that one of the assumptions is false, with the result that the failed prediction says nothing damaging about the theory. One familiar way to challenge a counterexample is to claim that conditions were not standard, as required by the theory. As behavioral scientists are not always precise or thorough in stating the conditions under which their laws hold, it is altogether too easy to make that claim, as any economist will tell you; but the same sort of escape hatch, albeit harder to find and get through, is available to the natural scientist. Another way out is to decide that we did not observe what we thought we observed, or (in a pinch) that the theory needs some minor qualification to cover special cases of this sort.

Without doubt some statements or complexes of statements are more resistant to falsification than others. The laws of logic most of all; theoretical statements less so. Metatheoretical statements of the kind philosophers like to make fall somewhere in between. Even certain individual statements close to experience may be less straightforwardly falsifiable than we might suppose. Could we not finally say that the apparent falsifying evidence is the result of a bad piece of observation? It happens.

Now if it were true that every empirically meaningful statement could be reduced to some set of observation statements, then we would have a way of clearly seeing the meaning of each, and could more easily adjudicate among their competing claims to be true. On two counts this will not do: the reduction is not possible; neither is the observation. The two counts are related, and we turn to the first now and the second immediately afterward.

The extreme of empiricist skepticism about all but observation is the reductionist view that the whole content of a theory is exhausted by statements of the form, "If this happens, then that happens." There is no need to postulate a set of unobservable theoretical entities behaving in lawlike ways. We need only concepts defined by direct reference to what can be observed, and variables defined by direct reference to the operations required to measure them. What a theory postulates is not real: a theory simply represents a device for speaking efficiently about observables, which are real. What we can observe and measure is not evidence for the concept: it just is the concept. That is operationalism in its crudest form.

It is not a very practical position. If it were followed in medicine, for example, then it would be a matter of defining the disease by reference to its symptoms, and treating it that way too, for better or for worse. In fact, of course, medical scientists cannot take seriously the view of an operationalist who argues in effect that there is no reason to believe in unobservable theoretical entities. Among other things, what is not observable now may be available for viewing later.

A strong form of operationalism[1] would hold that intelligence is not a mental capacity that causes people to perform well on IQ tests and in certain other enterprises, but is instead by definition whatever IQ tests measure. An IQ test is then by definition a direct and adequate measure of intelligence. On this telling, intelligence is not some capacity that Binet and Wechsler and others glimpsed but imperfectly understood, as in the case of Newton and light. It is not something that James D. Watson, the Nobel laureate, has in abundance though his score on a standard IQ test (it is about 110) does not show it; rather, Watson is not very intelligent. An IQ test does not provide evidence about one's intelligence: rather, intelligence is reducible to one's score on a certain kind of test.

But consider why anyone has bothered to develop tests of intelligence in the first place. We have reasons for wanting to determine how much individuals have of what distinguished Aristotle and Newton and Mozart, and Watson as well, from the general run of people. There are efficiencies to be gained from assigning certain tasks and opportunities on the basis of intelligence, and education will be more effective if we can find a way of measuring innate intelligence as opposed to the mental skill that instruction and experience impart.

All this is to say that there is no point in trying to operationalize intelligence. To explain what intelligence is is to indicate its logical and causal relations not only to results of IQ tests but also to other observable states and performances, and to other unobservable states and events as well. That last step, the connection of unobservables by logical and causal relations, is of the essence of theorizing. In psychology, as in organization theory, there is a great deal of theorizing and constructing of postulates still to be done.

There is nothing wrong with postulating unobservable entities. Scientists of all kinds must do it. In this case, as in some others, what is readily measurable is not precisely what most interests us. A science looks for lawful relationships in aid of predicting the future or creating it, and creates theories precisely because these relationships do not always obtain among observables. If we assume that the operationalized concept—the disposition to score high on IQ tests—is the cause of the behavior we take to be evidence of intelligence, we shall likely use IQ tests as instruments for dispensing tasks and opportunities. This social practice, theoretically austere though it is, has ideologically significant consequences. It is the policy equivalent of trying to cure the symptoms rather than the disease.

To define every concept just by reference to the observable evidence for it is to assimilate "A is evidence for B" to "anything one can say about B is translatable into talk about A." This has the apparent advantage of bringing B out of the shadow of possible doubt and into the range of observation if A itself is observable. The disadvantage is that the explanatory power of theory is reduced virtually to nothing; for the regularities that explain relations among observed events are usually postulated regularities among theoretical entities, and theoretical entities are seldom observable. Reduction to the observable therefore makes science hopelessly inefficient. The appropriate response to the question, "How would you operationalize that?" is usually, "Why should I want to?"

None of this ought to come as a surprise to anyone who takes the notions of construct and construct validity seriously, as many organization theorists do.[2] Behavioral scientists call tests valid that test the thing of interest and not some other thing. Construct validity in particular is a property of a test that successfully indicates (for example) intelligence, since intelligence is a construct—an entity defined by reference to a (fairly sophisticated) theory, and generally conceded not to be observable.[3] A purported intelligence test is not construct valid if it is really testing socioeconomic background. And, to use an example to which we shall frequently return, a test that tested corporate climate (that is, people's avowed views on certain topics) rather than culture would be invalid if it advertised itself as a test for culture.

Cronbach and Meehl (especially 1955)[4] have given what is now widely considered a standard account of the construct validity of a test. The salient point of that account is that there is a theory, implicit or otherwise, behind the test; and this theory may be good or not so good. If a person's intelligence is not reducible to a score on an intelligence test but is instead a construct, then intelligence is defined by its role in a theory that explains how it is that some people score higher than others on IQ tests—and on some other tasks as well, since otherwise there would be no point in trying to determine people's IQs. The test of the construct is the test of the theory: you derive hypotheses from the theory and test the hypotheses against experience, presumably at least for their ability to predict.

If the only thing your theory says is that intelligence (the construct) causes good performance on IQ tests, then you have a not very useful construct in a not very useful theory. But if you can fit the concept into a theory that relates intelligence to genes or environment or something else in at least a fairly specific and consistent way, then you have a valid construct[5] because you have a theory that explains rather than merely restates.

Think of a theory as a network of propositions that form a coherent whole. The meanings of even the most basic propositions are a function of their relations (logical, evidential, and a combination of both) to other propositions. Defining the sophisticated construct (and few are simple, or it would not be necessary to construct them) and defending the theory turn out to be inseparable parts of the same enterprise. If so, then what is true of the construct by definition is not wholly separable from what the theory claims is true of it. To put it a bit more dramatically, there is a problem about determining whether two very different theories about a concept are really disagreeing, because in some sense they are not talking about the same thing.

Recall how this discussion of operationalism began: stated in a certain way, expectancy theory is allegedly bankrupt because what it puts forward as fact looks to be true by definition. Now we find ourselves in a similar position: in the case of intelligence we cannot quite distinguish what is true in fact from what is true by definition. But if this is a difficulty, it is one that damages the most respectable of sciences. Consider the basic Newtonian laws. It is impossible to divide the propositions into those that define mass and the other constructs on the one hand and those that make claims about how as a matter of fact mass is related to other things on the other. Few would dare argue that Newton's theories are trivial on this account. The lesson is rather that it is a mistake to demand that a theory be a set of purely empirical statements, or to hold that any given statement is either true by definition or true in fact, or even to hold that any given statement has an empirical component and, separately, a definitional component.[6]

How, if there is finally no way to distinguish between differences in substantive claim and differences in meaning,[7] is communication possible between two theorists who seriously disagree? If my theory differs significantly from yours, then my constructs differ accordingly, with the result that the meanings of the terms I use differ. The empiricist's answer is that observation is the arbiter: experience distinguishes between theories as it vindicates some and not others; so whatever the difficulties of understanding between theorists, at least one of them will be embarrassed by falsification into giving up the theory and its language. But we have noted that experience does not always adjudicate satisfactorily between competing theories, or easily explode any single one.

To reject operationalism and embrace theoretical entities does invite us to ask how words get their meaning if not from the evidence for the entity defined. A partial answer is that one knows the meaning of a word if one can consistently use it in generating statements that other members of the linguistic community take to be true, and therefore also that these members think they understand, in the sense that they are prepared to judge whether they are true or false. In a theoretical context we say roughly the same thing: knowing the meaning of a word is a matter of knowing how to use it in a theory, and therefore knowing what role it plays in the theory.

If this is right, then it will sometimes be difficult to tell whether a speaker is saying something factually false or just using words in a deviant way in trying to express a true proposition. In the latter case, the hearer may have no way of knowing whether to interpret a statement as meaning "p" and being false or meaning "q" and being true. The general rule is to give a statement whatever interpretation makes it true; but that rule cannot be airtight as long as people ever make false statements. (This point will recur, especially in chapter 5.)

This view of meaning reinforces the point that some words have different meanings for people who hold significantly different theories. That is plausible: Aristotle, Newton, and Einstein did not all have the same concept of space. It does raise the question, not raised by the operationalist view of meaning, how people who have different theories can communicate. The answer is, Sometimes not very well. But when two intelligence theorists differ about the definition of intelligence, the difference cannot readily be dismissed as "just a matter of semantics." So when Miner (1980 and 1982; the books have essentially the same forthright methodological introduction) and other organization theorists call for clarity in definition of concepts—not unreasonably, as it is a standard criterion of theoretical soundness, as I indicated in chapter 1—they may be demanding more than they realize. You and I cannot reach clarity and agreement over significant theoretical concepts without generally agreeing on the theory itself. If Putnam (1962) is right (see note 6), a theoretical term has many statements true of it, of which proponents of different theories must agree on many if they can be said to be talking about the same thing. Hence communication deteriorates the greater the difference between theories—not least theories about organizations.

1b. Operationalizing and Theorizing: An Example

Consider organizational climate. There is a standard use of the concept according to which climate is operationalized by (and in that sense reducible to) the responses of employees to a certain kind of questionnaire. Climate just is what the employees think it is. Their perceptions are taken as logically authoritative, on the principle that perceptions matter as much as that of which they are accurate or inaccurate perceptions.[8] Climate can therefore be directly measured with considerable accuracy. Culture, on the other hand, is typically postulated as a cause of employees' behavior and perceptions. (See Sathe [1985] and Schein [1985], for example.) It is at least logically possible, though not very likely, for the employees of a company to be mistaken about what the culture is like. For example, the culture might be a highly competitive one, but competition might be encouraged so subtly that employees did not realize they were being pitted against each other. The climate might in that case be an uncompetitive one. In such a case there is a climate and there is a culture; but the congruence between them is less than usual.

There is nothing wrong with either concept; each has its place. If a manager is trying to build an environment that will ensure productivity and satisfaction for the long run, then culture will probably be the issue of primary concern. If the manager wants a quick and economical reading of certain effectiveness-related features of the organization, then a test for climate will do. No doubt it will serve other purposes as well, since there is some evidential relationship, albeit not a very reliable one, between climate and effectiveness; and it may be that no more reliable relationship than that is required for the projects at hand.

We may dispense with the concept of culture where its superiority over climate for diagnostic and developmental purposes appears not to justify the additional trouble involved in working out what the culture is like. To ascertain the nature of a culture is always difficult in part because there is both vagueness and disagreement about what culture is. To say we do not know quite what culture is is the same as saying that we do not have a theory that links culture to other concepts and to other facts we can readily know. We therefore have no valid way of measuring culture or describing it with precision.

Does it follow that in explaining individuals' behavior in organizations we should stick with climate and not chance our hand with culture? The kind of explanation available would then be thin, as is usually the case when we restrict ourselves to the readily observable. We go beyond climate because we believe there is some further explanation of the relationships between climate data and organizational behavior and among the pieces of climate data. We believe these further, explanatory facts go beyond psychological facts about individuals in organizations and bring in some effects of aggregation, interaction, and structure over a period of time. Our ignorance of the details here does not imply that we should abandon the search, or that we should stop talking about culture in particular cases. Even if there is every reason to believe that we shall never find a tight theory that uses anything like the vocabulary of corporate culture, we are justified in talking about culture and using it to explain and predict until someone propounds a better theory. That better theory may do all the explanatory work we expect of the concept of culture without postulating anything like what we now call culture, in which case the concept of culture would go the way of the concept of phlogiston. But now, despite its problems, the concept of culture cannot be replaced by anything better.

None of this shows that operationalizing is always wrong, or that the concept of climate in particular is a bad one. The point is rather that in some cases and for some purposes we are better off adverting to culture, which is in effect a construct or theoretical entity, in developing explanations, even though the theory in question has great holes in it, even if there is no prospect of filling in the holes in a theory of that structure. The literature on culture and practice in the area of corporate culture make a good case that the concept is a viable one.[9]

Sometimes the disparity between perceptions and reality, hence between climate and culture, is crucial. Most experienced consultants have seen senior managers manipulate climate in hopes of generating a culture. Some years ago I became familiar with a large and geographically dispersed firm whose culture proved on close inspection to be stodgy and risk-averse to a degree that was probably inappropriate to its competitive environment. Top management had persuaded most of the professionals who were actually producing the firm's services to think of themselves as aggressive, daring, unconventional, and even highly paid gunslingers. As one device for creating a climate and, it was hoped, eventually a culture, management had fabricated and circulated stories whose heroes had shown several of the desired qualities of intellect and personality and had consequently been rewarded.

This device, along with a few others, had succeeded in leading most professionals to state with evident sincerity that aggressive behavior was a key to success in this organization. That is, it had created an aggressive climate. But the culture was not so aggressive. For in spite of what they said, in spite of the widespread (though by no means unanimous) belief in the official stories, most of the professionals were still cautious. They had reason to be so: they were modestly rewarded for successful risks and severely punished for unsuccessful ones. So they only talked a macho game.

It would have been impossible to understand this organization very well on the basis of a climate survey. On the other hand, a thorough understanding of its culture would have been difficult to come by, and would not have been a good basis for presenting useful diagnoses to top managers, who seemed to set great store by the notion that the culture was an aggressive one.

But even climate is not as observable as it looks. In that respect it is like most observables.

1c. Some Problems about Observation

To this point I have taken for granted that there are things and states that are unproblematically observable—that is, something can be known about them by way of direct experience without any theoretical overlay. We see and hear behavior; we can record and quantify questionnaire responses. These data seem to serve as the firm basis on which we erect a theoretical structure. That view of the theoretical house built on the rock of observation is a staple of empiricism. But it is not tenable.

What sort of thing or event is naturally observable? There are some experienced doctors who can observe that a patient has typhoid fever. That is, they can be in the presence of the disease and say immediately and credibly that the patient has typhoid.[10] They say things like, "I just smelled typhoid." Others cannot; they observe that the patient is running a certain temperature and has some other symptoms, and then they infer. What a doctor can observe is in part a matter of training and experience in the application of theory. Much the same can be said of a consultant who spends a few hours walking around an office and then delivers an accurate and trenchant report on the organization's culture. This kind of ability calls into question the clarity of the distinction between observable and theoretical.

The argument can be complicated endlessly. Do I observe that Jones has an angry expression on his face? Or do I infer anger from the arrangement of his features? Even if I am not conscious of the arrangement of his features when I am noting his anger? One can construct a theory of unconscious inference, but it risks triviality: any observation has causal conditions, and the theory may have difficulty distinguishing causal conditions from what is directly observed. Consider whether we observe something when we look at it through a microscope or a sophisticated kind of telescope. Consider what particle physicists say is observable. There are no agreed boundaries here, and it is not clear that we need any.

It is a commonplace among experimenters that subjects give honest conflicting reports about things and events that are observable if anything is. The very act of gathering data through questionnaires and other noticeable devices affects the data not only in the Hawthorne way but more subtly too: it imposes a structure on responses and regiments them according to the experimenter's chosen categories, which may be associated with a substantive and even ideologically potent theory. This imposition is as likely to happen where the questionnaire is intended to diagnose climate as it is where culture is in view.

Imagine a climate survey designed by a devout and credulous Puritan researcher and administered in Salem Village in 1692. For purposes of the present argument, the interesting aspect is not that the responses will provide evidence of belief in witches, but that the survey itself will. The questions themselves, and the vocabulary in which they are framed, organize the respondents' experience according to a theory in which witches play a causal role. In the actual Salem trials, testimony was elicited not by questionnaire but by deposition. There were at least two things wrong with the testimony. First, some witnesses gave false reports of what they had observed, because they made mistakes both in observing and in remembering. Second, and more to the present point, they spoke a language that embodied the regimentation of their observations according to the supernatural theory. The language presupposed that certain supernatural events were observable.

This cannot come as shocking news to survey researchers. I want to go further, though, and argue that the whole notion of observability is too frail to bear the weight that has routinely been piled onto it. The practical difficulty is that observation can be influenced and distorted; the conceptual difficulty—the real point of the present discussion—is that all observations are to some degree concept-loaded if not theory-loaded. (The latter term, invented by Hanson [1958], has come into common and sometimes reckless use.)

Already in talking about climate we find ourselves detached from the secure certainty of observation, as concept-free observations are impossible. Although some kinds of thing are easier than others to observe, and some people are better than others at observing certain kinds of thing, there is no kind of entity that is by its nature readily observable to all who would observe it. Different theories, bringing with them different categories for organizing experience, might disagree on the description of a particular thing or state, or they might agree on the description but disagree on whether it is observable, or on whether it is observable under that description—that is, whether its being of that description is observable. A functional description, as of the state of a computer, would obviously involve commitments beyond those of an alternative description that did not involve its function.

The grounds for belief in an unobservable entity—that is, for reifying it—will depend on the soundness of the theory that postulates it; but much the same can be said of certain allegedly observable entities. When we deny that someone has observed a witch, we are not being skeptical about whether the light was good enough or the person's eyesight sufficiently keen. The same is true of a great many concepts, for the meaning of a term that stands for a concept is determined by the concept's role in a theory, or at least in a cluster of beliefs. We can say that any concept presupposes a theory, if we allow for thin or obvious theories; and some concepts make no sense at all without considerable theoretical background.

To know anything at all, however simple, requires the use of concepts, and concepts make sense only within a network that is built up over a period of time and that presupposes a great many causal connections. So observation cannot afford you any knowledge if you do not have any concepts. On the other hand, if you know enough, you can sometimes directly observe typhoid fever. Or if you believe enough, you can report observing a witch.

Depending on the concepts you bring with you to the point of observation, you will use certain criteria to classify certain observations and thereby to consider them similar or dissimilar. Observables do not organize themselves into natural groups of bite-size components. In this respect observers impose order on the world, rather than discover it there.

Consider how a scientist doing research on stimulus and response in monkeys reports observations. Unquestionably the scientist can observe the monkey pull the lever and eat the banana, but that description of what the scientist observes is not the only possible accurate one. The scientist might have reported the movement of the monkey's paw through certain spatial coordinates, the motion of the lever, the opening and closing of the monkey's jaw, the disappearance of the banana, and so on. Equally accurately the scientist might have reported events in terms of muscles or even of molecules. The scientist's vocabulary, built into the observation reports, mandates that certain events be classified together, though they could have been classified separately. In effect, the vocabulary reifies events of a certain sort. On two occasions the monkey's body moves, and on both occasions the motion is described in the same way—pulling the lever—even if in one case two fingers are used and in the other case three, and even if the motions differ in other ways as well. The concepts used to organize the observed events into like and unlike effectively presuppose that the monkey is capable of action that is purposive. (And if the monkey could talk, our hearing it do so would presuppose more than purpose.) The concepts are remarkably hospitable to a stimulus-response theory of behavior; and to the extent that that theory is viable, the concepts and the classification they mandate are viable as well. But neither they nor any other concepts that might be used in the accurate description and classification of the observable events are immediately apparent to the conceptually naked eye. In fact, nothing at all can be apparent to the conceptually naked eye.

This is not to say that all observations are theory-loaded in every possible sense. If I know by observation that something is a table, then I have a concept that presupposes, what is perhaps not self-evident, that the world is populated by middle-sized material objects and that this particular object is of a kind that has a certain standard use. The "theory" here is at best a rudimentary one arguably not worthy of the name. And one can observe something and accurately call it a planet by the absence of twinkling even if one does not know how planets and stars differ otherwise.

If one can observe only what one knows some particular scientific theory postulates, then observation is of essentially no help in deciding among theories. But I am not prepared to go so far. I am rather talking about matters of degree, and warning that in some cases what we gather from observation is heavily determined by what we believed in advance. Those cases include many in which we need some way of adjudicating among theories, and observation is not always as decisive as we might wish. (See Hacking [1983, 167-185], who is indebted to Shapere [1982].)

On the continuum of statements running from highly theoretical to crudely observation-based there is no point at which one can say, Here the observable ends and the theoretical begins. Neither is there any statement justifiable by observation untainted by any concepts. Empiricists and partisans of common sense are therefore mistaken in taking the observable to be the unproblematically knowable basis on which sound theory rests.

It is often useful for organization and policy theorists to take the trouble to notice how much and what sort of commitment is already being made just by the vocabulary in which observations are stated. For example, consider what is presupposed when a consultant points out that a manager is being defensive. One might object that defensiveness is not observable; but it is, to some degree, if there are people who can give reasons for claiming to be able to observe it.

One more point deserves attention. The doubts I have raised about observation tend to undermine operationalism and all related views that hold that only observables exist and that postulated entities are nothing more than convenient fictions to help us manage our dealings with observables efficiently. Operationalists and others sometimes warn against reifying one's postulates. But if there are no pure observables, then everything we believe in is a postulate from some point of view. Arguably, in fact (see Quine [1960 and elsewhere]), the best reason for reifying some sort of thing is that it is postulated by a sound theory. What better reason could there be?

This is emphatically not a purely conceptual point. It is the sort of thing strategists, for example, ought to consider.

1d. Observation and the Explanation of What Organizations Do

Hayes and Abernathy (1980) complain that American firms have been hurt by their overconfidence in portfolio theory and in other theories, models, and languages that ignore or obscure causal factors essential to corporate success and failure. Part of the problem is that the language of portfolio theory sounds stronger than any version of the theory actually is. PIMS and various consulting firms offer what amount to theories predicting the success of a business unit based on its competitive strength and the attractiveness of its market; and those two indices are typically defined by reference to competitive and market properties that are supposed to bear the requisite causal relationships to return on investment and cash flow. Slavish adherence to the definitions and therefore to the theory in designing business unit strategies is an extreme case of overconfidence. On a less extreme plane, the very use of the language associated with the model predisposes one to a theory that does not work in all situations and therefore may encourage some bad decisions. What is needed no less than a sound theory with correspondingly sound indices of the operative causal factors is an understanding of the shortcomings of what we have now.[11]

The trouble is not all in portfolio theory. The languages of accounting and finance themselves are designed to assist managers in making decisions and assessing their effects within a rather narrow range. Insofar as the concepts embedded in this language permit the measurement of some things and not others, they enforce a certain discipline on what managers may consider pertinent information when making decisions. Profit is a thin construct in much the same way IQ is, and it has some of the same potential problems. Each is operationalizable, quantifiable; as a result, neither relates unproblematically to the sort of success it was designed to predict.

There are stupid people with high IQs, and profitable companies with dangerously deteriorating cash flows. The accounting profession has struggled to find a coherent and perspicuous language that describes the world in ways useful to the managers who make decisions about it; and that struggle continues.

All theorists use constructs, but in the business-related academic disciplines there is less recognition of the conceptual issues related to constructs and theoretic soundness in general than there ought to be. Roberts,

Hulin, and Rousseau (1978), however, are notable for the seriousness with which they consider the problems associated with the constructs available for the organization theorist's use. Their aim is clarity if not reconciliation among multidisciplinary theories. They give a quite sophisticated statement of a subtle empiricism that is implicit in the work of many organization theorists. Precisely because they are not crude empiricists, the extent to which they accept parts of the empiricist program indicates its pervasiveness. Whether they are right or not—and they are by no means always wrong—their work raises important questions and proposes significant answers more thoughtful than those of most organization theorists.

They consider Fiske's (1978) classic statement of a strong form of empiricism—his claim that social scientists must work towards redefining their variables by reference to behavior observable by independent judges with a high degree of agreement. What I have argued thus far implies that Fiske is envisaging an impossible goal. There is no reason to believe we can ever be in a position to be sure that independent judges will report a class of events, however observable, in the same language—unless, of course, it is certain that they will all bring to bear the same set of concepts in giving their descriptions. But in that case there will be grounds for doubting that the concepts will have been defined by reference to observable behavior.[12] Roberts et al. seem to regard Fiske's quest as utopian, but do not object to it in principle. They raise no problems about getting judges who can agree on what they observe without having committed themselves to certain common concepts in the first place.

They note that theorists filter their observations in accordance with their theories, but they do not suggest that that practice is unavoidable. They decry certain kinds of filtering—for example, collecting observations by using a level of abstraction that fails to collect individual response differences. They state misgivings about the influence of characteristic "paradigmatic filters" on the various theorists' inferences (Roberts et al. [1978, 28]), even on their observations (47). The result, they claim, is that some essential variable may be omitted and different kinds of event may be classified together; so theorists are assuming what they set out to prove. For example, those who regard roles within groups as important determinants of behavior are likely to exclude the possible differential influence of the characteristics of individuals playing the social roles; those characteristics leak through the holes in their insufficiently fine sieve.

"Thus," Roberts et al. write, "the exclusion of individual responses in the study of social collectives appears to reflect a convenient paradigm with unvalidated assumptions rather than the absence of individual variability in conformity to social roles." (41) The suggestion is that the partisans of social collectives are by methodological fiat ruling out what their theories then—not surprisingly—can find no reason to postulate as causes. Roberts et al. seem to find this sort of practice unscientific—verdict first, trial afterward.

The appropriate reply to this criticism, which is correct at least in noting the methodological fiat, will take some time and argument to construct. But the crux of it is this: if the "convenient paradigm" is sufficiently and appropriately convenient, then its convenience is precisely what validates its assumptions.

Roberts et al. prefer that organization theorists try to construct theoretical networks with well-established relations among well-defined constructs and solid grounding in observation. A construct like job turnover, which they subject to extended discussion, is especially problematical. Whether it is operationalized or a construct, there is no reason to assume it does or can have the same definition from one theory to the next. When a psychologist and a labor economist are both studying turnover, the first may be studying an individual's decision to leave a job, while the second may be trying to determine causes of increase in the number of departures per thousand. Are the two even studying the same thing? The use of the single word *turnover* to describe both objects of study could hardly answer the question, as Roberts et al. are surely aware.[13]

With matters in this state, it is easy to see why knowledge in organization theory has not been cumulative. Roberts et al. suggest a program for making the best use of the various applicable disciplines by forging connections among them at and around the level of observation. Organization theorists, they propose, should try to develop theoretical networks that link sound constructs to each other and, in a variety of ways, to observation. They are aware of the difficulty of what they advocate, for it involves integrating the work of disciplines whose units of analysis are defined at a variety of levels. On the other hand, they do not see how the field can progress so long as theorists make no attempt to find common ground.

Roberts et al. are fundamentally too optimistic about the unification project, for there is a crucial difficulty they do not squarely address. It is not that organization theory is incapable of developing constructs that relate to each other as tightly as do those of physics. Nobody should expect organization theory to be like physics, nor is there any need for it to be. The more lethal problem is that the differences among the units of analysis from the various disciplines may be irreducible. There is no a priori reason to believe that among distinct theories there can be any common language that truly carves the world at its joints.

Roberts et al. cite Cronbach and Meehl on constructs; the latter give the clue, as I have suggested, to why different disciplines cannot agree on a common language. The validity of a construct is in part a function of the truth of the theory that gives it its meaning; so constructs from different theories may easily have different meanings. But there is more. The doctrine of construct validity has implications that have not been universally understood, nor extended into every area in which they are relevant.

To observe that something is the case, even to identify something by observation, is to bring to bear a classificatory scheme that is no better than the theory (or theories) behind it. Normally no controversy is involved, but on occasion the observation can be challenged on the grounds that it reifies some dubious entity like a witch (or a mental event, or an organization). So while we can settle some arguments by reference to observation, profound disagreements about what the world is like will often appear in the different ways in which observables are classified and reified. My view of construct validity is that the construct is no better than the theory in which it plays a role.

We are inclined to say that theories are built on observation; but in fact, observations are built on theories, in the sense that a theory determines the kind of thing one can observe. This is not just the psychological fact that our theories predispose us to notice what conforms to them and ignore what does not. Even if that psychological theory were false, it would remain true that identification requires classification and classification governs reification and presupposes a theory.

The most significant example of this—the centerpiece of chapter 3—is psychology. We think we can be directly aware of certain mental events, but in fact, even though we can reliably report them, our identification of them is no better than the psychological theory that postulates them in the first place.

Roberts et al. are saying, in effect, that we have to be aware of the different ways in which different theoretical schools view and explain turnover, which they take as an example of the kind of thing theorists of various orientations discuss. That is right as far as it goes. But if reification follows theorizing, then there is no reason to be confident that those who hold different theories can agree about just what turnover is—and the same goes for any other observable.

Roberts et al. follow the long but now questionable tradition in the philosophy of science of considering a theory a hierarchy, with observations at the base of the structure, operationalized constructs on the level above them, and theoretically defined constructs on the next higher level (19; cf. Kerlinger [1986, 30f.]). But in putting matters that way they obscure a crucial fact: the choice of constructs significantly influences what one observes and the kind of entity that is counted as an observable. Roberts et al. are aware of this for the case of theories that operate at different levels—they are conscious of the problems of aggregation—but it goes for entities on the same level as well.

In the case of turnover, a psychologist with certain theoretical predispositions other than behaviorist ones is likely to regard voluntary actions as observable and distinguishable by observation from involuntary ones in part because such a distinction is compatible with the view of persons as potentially motivated by reasons for action.[14] A labor economist would not necessarily take the behaviorist view that one cannot observe a voluntary action, but would consider mere departures from jobs the units of analysis, because that is what his or her theory postulates as the units of analysis and undertakes to explain. As a result, the psychologist and the labor economist may not be talking about the same concept when they use the word *turnover*. It may not save the situation to get the psychologist and the labor economist to agree to talk about voluntary departures, for it is quite possible they will have very different notions of what counts as voluntary. And the point can be generalized further: even if two theories are at the same level, their observables may be defined differently. This is not a matter of carelessness or stubborn independence. It is the inevitable result of significant theoretical differences, as for example between behaviorists and psychologists of other kinds.

Each theorist says this, in effect: in aid of explaining, predicting, and controlling the world, I postulate these entities that have these lawlike relationships to each other. I say (this is the psychologist talking) there are these voluntary actions, as opposed to those involuntary actions, that have these features. Other theorists postulate not only other features, but other entities, possibly with no distinction between voluntary and involuntary. As the next section indicates, some economists will not recognize what psychologists take to be basic units of behavior.

Roberts et al. call themselves Lockean in data collection and Kantian in data interpretation. They do appear to be too much under the spell of

Locke's empiricism, which envisages the imprint of the experience on the mind without prior benefit of concepts, to be sufficiently alert to the inevitability of theory-based interpretation in characterizing data. So, for example, when setting out their theory-neutral framework for analyzing theories, they seem to use the same functional taxonomy that sneaks into behaviorists' description of behavior: "responses," as they call units of behavior, are classified in part according to their intended ends (59-62).

Let us be clear. It is not only that different theories may have different units of analysis and different constructs—a point that Roberts et al. not only recognize but emphasize. It is that different theories may have different observables just because they have different constructs. It might be confusing to say that all observables are really constructs or postulates; but the similarities are very much worth keeping in mind.[15]

2. COMPETING THEORIES

Different theories commend different states and events as observable. What then can we really observe? We can observe at most what is postulated by the best possible theory. Once again, how can we tell which theory that is?

This notoriously difficult question has been addressed by a great and methodologically scrupulous social scientist. Milton Friedman (1953; in this paper he somewhat misleadingly calls himself a positivist) argued that theories have merit if they enable one to predict something that needs predicting, and not if they do not. An assumption is epistemologically justified if and only if it passes the test of predictive power. Further questions about truth are not worth worrying about. It is not that economists' assumptions are a false basis for theory, Friedman argues, but that economists' theories are to be thought of as applying to that range of situations—including those that appear in models only and not in the real world—in which they are true, or close enough to the truth that the difference does not matter.

One thing Friedman does not do is suggest that economists expand their theories to take account of more of the complexities of human motivation than the homo economicus model does. This omission is no accident. For one thing, we cannot assume the labor economist has a theory that is merely simpler than the psychologist's and can readily be expanded to encompass it. But even if that were so, Friedman would find the new hybrid theory so complex as to defeat the purpose of any explanatory model, which is to explain the world by simplifying it. No doubt he would advise a labor economist on the issue of turnover: maybe you can find a way of distinguishing voluntary turnover from involuntary, but why bother? The expense would overwhelm the benefit to anybody who uses labor statistics. (It will become increasingly clear that I think Friedman's position on this question has something to be said for it.)

If Friedman's position is right, the issue between those whose theory refers to (say) organizational roles and those who bring in individual characteristics is only this: whose theory predicts better? If the organizational-role approach enables us to predict adequately, then that fact in itself is the strongest possible evidence that individual characteristics have no causal influence. And if accurate prediction of events on which individual characteristics are alleged to exert a causal influence is possible without reference to them, the assumption that there are no individual characteristics seems to be vindicated. If what we observe is in part a function of the theories we apply to the world, to state that individual characteristics absolutely must be there because we observe them is no more convincing than to point to an apparently abnormal woman and claim to be observing a witch.[16]

Even if we can agree on this, however, our problems are not over. We have considered several criteria for assessing theories and found predictive power prominent among them, but it was not the only one. One trouble with the predictive criterion for judging theories is closely akin to the trouble with reliance on verifiability and falsifiability in determining the meaning, if any, of propositions; we have seen some of the problems that causes. Another is that a theory might predict economic phenomena well but other phenomena, aggregate as well as individual, badly. Of competing theories it seldom happens that one unfailingly makes superior predictions on all matters on which they both have something to say. If a theory generates a false prediction, then the theorist may plead that some unexpected extraneous condition interfered. Where one theory seems superior to the other, therefore, the question arises whether its apparent predictive superiority is only temporary or local.

It is common to evaluate models and theories according to usefulness; so simplicity and wieldiness count enough to override exact but irrelevant or costly or questionably repeatable accuracy, even assuming such accuracy were possible. Applicability to a particular problem counts for something as well. Hence a human-factors engineer uses a classifying filter too fine-meshed for a sociologist but too gross for an industrial psychologist. Traffic engineers, psychotherapists, and human-factors engineers will view similar situations differently, and the theories of each will have their limited areas of superior usefulness.

We seem at this point to be without any prospect of a unified and consistent vocabulary—never mind a theory—for describing and explaining organizational phenomena, given how theories determine the meanings of the words used in stating them, and given the limitations of predictive power and other criteria in helping us distinguish good theories from bad ones.

We have so many disciplines in part because widely varied problems require widely varied and sometimes incompatible groups of theories. Roberts et al. are right to try to narrow down these incompatibilities. Whether it is possible to remove them entirely from the interdisciplinary field of organization theory is another matter. One message of this book is that it is neither necessary nor possible.

There are serious problems in the way of reconciling the various disciplines' methods of explaining collective behavior. A commitment to a certain kind of theory—rational individualism, Marxism, holism—carries with it a commitment to methodological rules, including rules about what counts as observable, what counts as evidence, and what counts as perspicuous language. There are no handy rules of translation from one theory to another, and no ultimate laws for settling disputes.

Lest this sound like radical subjectivism, there is no justification for saying that we can never understand each other and never settle disputes, or that no "paradigm" can be shown to be better than another. But for settling disputes across disciplinary lines—and, significantly, for communicating clearly about such disagreements—what is required is less a knowledge of the rules that apply to a rule-bound situation than an experienced intuition about what rules, including rules of thumb, apply to the situation at hand.

We have undermined the notion of raw observation as the foundation of all knowledge and the precursor of concepts and theories. We have raised doubts about the criteria of verifiability and falsifiability and the related criterion of predictive power. We have suggested that it is hard to find a language common to all theorists for some of the same reasons it is hard to find a theory on which all people agree. We have found reason to believe that the choice among competing theoretical frameworks will sometimes be extraordinarily difficult. But it bears saying now that we do and should use competing theoretical frameworks, even if they are irreconcilable. In some cases, I shall argue, explanations with profoundly different conceptual roots need each other in order to make sense.

NOTES

1. In this discussion I criticize a position that, so far as I know, no organization theorist explicitly holds, except perhaps in the form of a casual behaviorism. (Strong and crude operationalism was first propounded by the physicist Bridgman [1927], who soon moderated his views.) The purpose of the discussion, however, is to lay a foundation for two arguments that come later: first, in chapter 3, the critique of certain critics of psychology, who I think do tacitly adopt strong operationalism; then, at various points in that chapter and thereafter, the "reification" of certain things that others would prefer to consign to the realm of fiction.

2. See for example Schwab (1980), Hughes, Price, and Marrs (1986), Venkatraman and Grant (1986), and Peter (1979, 1981). For most of these the primary concern is sound measurement, but they are all far beyond operationalism.

3. I do not distinguish between constructs and postulates. In this chapter I shall begin to build a case that the distinction between constructs and more familiar entities is not so solid as some (e.g., Kerlinger [1986, 27]) have supposed.

4. For a somewhat updated summary, see Cronbach (1984). Peter (1981) claims that in the first paper Cronbach and Meehl are instrumentalists, and so regard theoretical entities as fictions, but necessary ones. I do not interpret them that way, but nothing I have to say on the subject depends on their intent.

5. This is a rare locution but a justifiable one, since it puts some emphasis on the soundness of the theory behind the construct, and that is where the emphasis ought to be.

6. Putnam (1962) argues that we know the meaning of a theoretical term if we know most of what the theory says about it. The point is that there is no set of statements about the theoretical term that constitutes its definition as opposed to factual claims that the theory makes about it.

7. By no means do I claim to have proved this point, which has been the subject of great controversy among philosophers. The most notable contribution has been that of Quine (1961). His challenge to the distinction did not destroy it, but never since then have most knowledgeable philosophers been confident of it or believed it could be used to prove anything controversial.

8. See Gordon and Cummins (1979), for example. Schwab (1980) cites Hellriegel and Slocum (1974) and Schneider and Hall (1972), and notes that Payne and Pugh (1976) distinguish two forms of climate, structural and perceptual. Schwab, whose concern is construct validity, suggests that there is

44   CONCEPTUAL FOUNDATIONS OF ORGANIZATION THEORY

some lazy theorizing here; but at least some of these authors know what they are doing and why.

Chapters 5 and 7 refer to an argument over psychological and organizational climate. That dispute, typified by the exchange between James, Joyce, and Slocum (1988) and Glick (1988), is over whether there are organizational states that are more than the sum or the average of the psychological states of employees. James, Joyce, and Slocum say no; Glick says yes, as I do, and for similar reasons. But the former seem to commit themselves to genuine individual psychological states, not necessarily operationalizable in questionnaires. If so, their conception of climate is slightly heavier theoretically than that of Gordon and Cummins and the others, and is therefore a less good example of operationalizing. Glick's organizational climate is similar to what I am now calling culture in all respects relevant to the points I want to make.

9. In suggesting an analogy between disease/symptoms and culture/climate I am not trying to deny that diseases are much easier to define and deal with than is culture. They are now, at any rate.

10. Bringing in credibility suggests that observability is in part a question of whether there is good reason to take the observer's report as being in some way authoritative. That good reason, in turn, would have to involve reference to something like the observer's record for accuracy. I think this is a correct approach, and I shall return to it in chapter 3, when we discuss mental states and events.

11. There have been some promising attempts at both. See, for example, Venkatraman and Grant (1986) and Hambrick (1980, 1981a and b, 1982, 1983). For an attack on the "vulgar and destructive vocabulary" of portfolio theory, see Andrews (1981).

12. Fiske's work as a whole shows him to be no unreflective empiricist. In this case he might more charitably be read as urging that social scientists try to improve their variables, but not as expecting that they will ever find judges to be unanimous in observing them. When we abandon empiricism we run some risk of coming to believe—what is clearly false—that observation just does not matter.

13. The Steers and Mowday (1981) model, for example, refers to states of affect and intention as causes of job-leaving.

14. Steers and Mowday (1981) characterize certain behavior by such terms as "effort" and "search." Their conceptual apparatus, and that of similar models, makes possible some fine distinctions among such events as leaving a satisfactory position for a better opportunity, leaving out of dissatisfaction, leaving under pressure, and so on. These are not distinctions that normally concern the Bureau of Labor Statistics. More to the point, Steers and Mowday explicitly define certain states (for example, job expectations; see 241-

244) in idiosyncratic ways characteristic of their theory. A claim to observe or otherwise detect that some individual or group entertains certain job expectations will not be credible to someone who considers the Steers-Mowday theory profoundly wrong.

15. This attention to their work indicates my view of its subtlety and importance. Our area of agreement is sufficiently large that some of my views represent something like an adjustment of theirs.

16. This point will be put to extensive use in chapter 3. It is tempting to charge economists like Stigler and Becker (1977) with stubborn refusal to acknowledge the manifest fact of individual states of mind as causes of economic behavior. They are saying, in effect, that they will observe such entities only if they have theoretical warrant for doing so. If there is a problem, it lies in their suggestion that economic warrant is the only kind of theoretical warrant there could ever be. There is more on this point and related matters in chapter 4.

3 PSYCHOLOGICAL EXPLANATION

Critics have attacked psychological theory for being detached from observation, for being vacuous, for relying on hypothetical entities inside our heads, and for being bound to individualist ideology rather than to solid fact. (Pfeffer [1982] collects these criticisms in his first two chapters, essays no replies, and recapitulates them in his concluding chapter.) There is something to these criticisms; yet there is nothing wrong with psychological explanations so long as they are kept in their place, which is a respectable one. Like standard organizational theory, psychology makes extensive use of functional explanation.

One point of clarification: not all psychological theories resemble each other very much. In some areas, for example those having to do with perception, there is precision and conceptual clarity any geologist and many biologists would envy. In others, such as psychoanalysis, looseness abounds. (Meehl [1986] makes this point in the process of arguing against easy subjectivism in discussing the social sciences.) I shall be thinking of psychology as that cluster of theories that use concepts of perception, personality, and motivation to explain, predict, and control an individual's behavior. Industrial psychology would be included. Most of what I shall say about psychology would apply as well to the kind of explanation an intelligent person would provide for an individual's behavior, opinions, or demeanor.

This is not to say that psychology is what organization theory should be all about. The argument is only that psychology can explain behavior in ways of interest to organization theorists and managers.

1. THE UNOBSERVABILITY OF PSYCHOLOGICAL ENTITIES

Some empiricists consider mental states or events unrespectable in part because they are unobservable, in the sense that each is manifest to at most one person, and then sometimes unclearly. The would-be science of psychology is not based on a public, checkable objective foundation. (See especially Mayhew [1980 and 1981]; cf. Pfeffer, 20ff.)

An extreme form of empiricism would hold that science is primarily in the business of finding regularities among observable entities; consequently it raises doubts about atoms as well as pains and preferences. But it is possible to be an empiricist to a greater or lesser degree. You may agree that not every state or event worth believing in is observable, and that there is often some choice as to which of several possible candidate propositions to abandon in the face of recalcitrant experience; but you may nevertheless insist that a proposition have some connection, direct or otherwise, to observation. Some psychological theories are compatible with quite a range of outcomes and falsifiable by only a few. In such cases, as we shall see, the crucial question is whether we can find a more useful theory than one so hard to put to the test. The more of an empiricist one is, the less permissive about theories with tenuous connections to experience—hence, the less tolerant of psychological explanations.

Psychological entities are indeed not so readily observable, even to their owners, as they may seem. The problems about observability do not wholly vindicate psychology's critics, however. They are problems for other respectable and widely used forms of explanation of other states and events as well. And since no form of explanation rests firmly on observation, the argument against psychology cannot succeed just by charging that the entities in question are unobservable. But as I have already indicated, it does go beyond that charge.

What may strike us as downright perverse about objecting to psychological entities on the grounds of unobservability is that certain of them, such as pains and perceptions, seem the most securely observable entities of all. In fact, our hesitation in calling them observable rests in part on the notion that observing suggests that a mistaken observation is conceivable. But how? I may be mistaken in believing that I have sinusitis, but not in thinking that I have a headache. I may be wrong about the color of the cows in the sunset, but not about their immediate appearance to me.

Whatever causes my impression, I cannot be mistaken about the impression itself. Skepticism is appropriate only when we consider whether the cause of the impression is what the so-called evidence of our senses leads us to think it is. That is the old standard story, anyway.

There are some problems with it, however. You can perhaps "observe" your own toothache; I cannot. How do I know you are telling the truth when you say you have one? Something of which only one person can be certain does not appear to be evidence of the kind empiricists say we should build knowledge on.

To this point the argument has been one that an empiricist can accept. Not only Pfeffer but such hard-nosed theorists as Watson and Skinner would agree so far. But the next step of the argument depends on the application of the anti-empiricist lessons of the previous chapter. It tells against mental entities as being straightforwardly reportable, but it defends psychology by pointing to similar problems for any sort of entity sponsored as observable. Mental states and events, like others, are observable and reportable only as mediated by concepts that may or may not be the best we can get. There is no rock-bottom certainty here, but there is none anywhere else, either.

I have questioned the easy distinction between what is observable and what is not, with its suggestion that there are items that are naturally observable just as they are. It is worth noting that not all cultures at all times have had the concept of the mental or given evidence of noticing what we consider most apparent. If there is good reason to be generally skeptical about states that psychologists postulate, then there is good reason to be skeptical about common-sense mental states as well. Like witches, pains and thoughts are no better than the theories behind them. But how good are the psychological theories behind them? Given their looseness and certain other differences from those typical of natural science, are they respectable?

Thus warned, we can go on and discuss how we are acquainted with certain of our mental entities (I shall use *entities* to cover things, states, and events) and how we can support our claims to knowledge of them.

2. REPORTABILITY AND TRUTH

When I am having a headache I need not infer the fact. It is at least as immediately evident as any event I can observe. On the other hand, it is logically possible for me to be mistaken in my belief that I have a headache. I might, for example, have a mistaken notion of what it is like to have a headache. I cannot reliably report my headache until I have to some degree mastered the concept of a headache. Having once mastered it, however, I can report my headache so reliably that under ordinary circumstances it would be irrational for anybody to believe me mistaken in reporting it. The convention of accepting the owner's evidently sincere reports of a range of mental events is well supported by our experience: in the absence of any better way of determining mental events, the practice generally permits smooth communication with a minimum of surprise. The success of the practice not only testifies for the convention of accepting these reports but also provides some evidence in favor of their accuracy. Much the same is true of most simple statements of belief, of many statements of immediate desire, and of some statements of personal principle.

This may be an opportune time to make a point about terminology. Insofar as we make a distinction between mental events and psychological ones, we usually reserve the term *mental* for the ones that common sense provides to the owner's attention and *psychological* for those that it does not. We are therefore more likely to consider psychological events theoretical entities. But I argue that mental events are as secure as the explicit or implicit theories that postulate them, and no more so. In fact, given that spatio-temporal objects are usually publicly observable and mental events are not, we have strong reason for saying that mental as well as psychological events are postulates.

The success of the convention of believing speakers about their mental events does not show that what one says about one's mental states and events is a particularly good or thorough description of them. To say I have a headache is at best rather vague. It tells the listener little more than that my current state is (1) one normally associated with a disorder in the head, (2) one I normally wish not to have, and (3) one that characteristically causes certain behavior aimed at avoidance or palliation. The descriptions we can give of such states turn out to be closely related to behavior and the environment: they are usually tied to causes and effects of publicly observable events.

This is no coincidence. Consider a red patch in one's visual field, an immediate and private object of sense. One is inclined to say that its color is not only immediately but infallibly evident to its owner, but that is not so. If a little girl who has been totally blind from birth is fully cured by eye surgery, so that she can see clearly the moment the bandages come off, will she then be able to identify the color of some red object held directly before her face? Will she be able to identify the color of the sense impression it causes? Surely not: she does not know what red looks like. She will be able to describe the color and her sense impression only after someone has taught her how to talk about them. And if for some reason a red object causes her to have a blue impression—assuming it even makes sense to talk about the colors of impressions—she will never know. Like anybody else, she can have knowledge of only those properties of impressions that are parasitic upon properties of publicly observable objects. In knowing the color of your sense impression you know, approximately, that it is of the kind normally caused by red things in good light.

But you might have been taught very differently about your mental states. Some warped person might have taught you to report the color red or a headache, and quite sincerely and confidently, under circumstances different from standard ones. Or you might have been taught a language tied to a radically different underlying theory of what goes on under your skin, so that you might say, not "I have a headache," but "Satan is punishing my brain." The existence and nature of such mental entities are not immediately given to untutored sensation. I can know about myself only the kind of thing I can learn in a public forum to attribute, and my attributions are no better than the theory behind them.[1]

Since I can identify in myself only the sort of event I have learned in the public forum to identify in others as well as myself, my knowledge of myself is shaped and limited by what goes on in that forum. It is a psychological fact that people's views of themselves may be influenced by their interaction with others: our social experiences and the roles we have thrust upon us have a deep influence. But a further and quite distinct point is that all concepts that one can apply to oneself—or withhold from oneself, for that matter—one must be able to apply to or withhold from others as well. So applying the vocabulary of the mental to oneself entails thinking of oneself as interacting with other people who are like oneself in having mental events and states of certain kinds. Solipsism—the view that one's mind is the only entity that exists—is not only implausible but incoherent, for it presupposes what it then denies.

Our knowledge of our mental events is inevitably and irreducibly social. What I am able to know and say about my sense impressions—including that there are any sense impressions—is organized and limited by the ways in which people talk about things in the public forum. I can communicate with others about them—in fact, I can learn about them in the first place—because they bear certain causal relations to public things and events. Many observation-based claims, even simple ones, rely on some theoretical background, and all rely on some concepts that embody a view of what the world is like. So even though one may reasonably claim to be able to observe mental states and events, one can be as wrong as the theory is. The burghers of Salem Village observed witches; we are aware of mental events. The latter kind of cognition is superior if and only if psychological theory is superior to any theory that postulates witches.

Particularly as the discussion turns to corporate culture, we shall consider the claim that an individual's reality is socially constructed. That is not an empty claim, although it is hard to see precisely what it amounts to. It suggests at the very least that one's environment affects how one thinks and perceives; and the argument just given specifies some ways in which that happens. I shall argue that corporate culture and values are not reducible to those of individuals, in part because the former help determine the latter through socialization. In that and other ways organization theory does not follow from psychology. (See Berger and Luckmann [1967].)

It is not unusual for psychologists to regard psychological states as constructs, rather than as operationally definable in a straightforward way, as in the case of behaviorism. So, for example, Cronbach and Meehl's (1955) account of construct validity in effect argues for psychological traits as theoretical entities related to observation in the way postulates of natural science normally are, except that the latter usually have a place in a tighter and more fully articulated theory. Cronbach and Meehl do not, however, explicitly consider mental entities like pains, thoughts, and desires postulates.[2]

It follows that attributing a mind to something is not a matter of speculating about whether some realm impervious to others' eyes and ears contains the same sort of state and event of which we are immediately aware in our own case. It is instead a matter of deciding what has to be postulated in order to have a theory substantial and accurate enough to account for the behavior of the bodies in question, including our own.[3]

If the argument is correct so far, then our normal ability to report certain of our mental states betokens a highly useful convention of believing such reports when they are made by evidently sincere people. That the convention is useful does suggest something about the truth of the reports: it is not mere chance that when a child complains of a headache her father can improve the situation by giving her a painkiller.

To this point we are making an argument for the mental and for psychological events as postulates of a handy theory. But how handy is it, really? When I explain an action by reference to a desire to perform an action of that sort, what information is being added other than that the action has in fact taken place? The objection is not that psychological theory is inaccurate, but that it is vacuous. One can make the same objection in a slightly different way by denying that any psychological theory is superior to behaviorism.

3. WHY BOTHER? THE POSSIBILITY OF BEHAVIORISM

The behaviorist starts with the necessity that mental entities be identified in the public forum and goes on to infer that what can be said about them is definable by statements about actions and dispositions to act. (In philosophy we associate behaviorism primarily with Ryle [1947], and in psychology with Skinner [1938 and elsewhere]. But Skinner has lasted far better in his field than Ryle in his.) So, for example, a headache is a disposition to clutch one's head and complain of having a headache. A belief that something or other is the case is a disposition to state that something or other is the case, or to act accordingly. An intention to do something is a disposition to do it in certain circumstances. There is no need to postulate inner states: all there is is just actual and potential observable behavior.

Behaviorism will appeal to operationalists, who characteristically fail to see the point of postulating anything unobservable. Earlier I argued that operationalism has no clear advantages over postulating unobservable entities—particularly if one is not confident about the distinction between observables and postulates—and some serious disadvantages. So behaviorism itself reduces headaches to dispositions to head-clutching and taking aspirin and complaining; for clutching, taking aspirin, and complaining are relatively observable. But a disposition to perform these acts is surely as unobservable as what it is supposed to replace; so it is hard to see what is gained. For the notion of disposition has to be sufficiently robust to account for the difference between intended and unintended actions (or inaction), unless the behaviorist cares to deny that there could possibly be any such thing as intention without action or action without intention. Why put one's faith in dispositions so robust (and so unobservable) while shrinking from postulating internal states of the person?

Consider the concept of brittleness. (And keep your eye on it: it came up in the discussion of functional explanation in chapter 1, and it will be used repeatedly hereafter.) A behaviorist would consider brittleness just a disposition. Thus Ryle, for example. It is in fact a state defined by reference to the behavior of the brittle object under certain vaguely specified circumstances. When something is in a state of brittleness, it has certain components in a certain structure and as a result breaks easily when you drop it. I might (reassuringly) explain that the glass broke when you held it not very tightly in your hand because it was extraordinarily brittle and not because you were holding it too tightly. If pressed, I could go on to say something about the structural cause of its being brittle.

Here we see one of the advantages of taking mental states to be actual (that is, not just dispositional) states definable by reference to causes and/or effects, including some unobservable ones. If pressed, and if one has the right information, one can expand one's explanation by specifying the causal basis of the state of brittleness. For example: Jones flared up because he is brittle, not because you were particularly insensitive. And further: Jones is brittle because he is having problems at home, or because he is not taking his medication, etc.

This is an important point, because there is a great temptation to criticize psychological explanation for being trivial. If a desire is defined largely by reference to what follows it, then it is not very enlightening to explain an action by reference to a desire to do it. But an explanation like that can be filled out by reference to other states of mind. We postulate mental states and events that have an effect not only on behavior but also on each other. So a desire to do A may not lead to one's doing A, because a scruple against it might be stronger.

In fact, a desire for X leads you to perform a particular action A only if you believe that A will lead to X; a belief that proposition p is the case will lead you to state that p only if you want to. Hence any translation of a statement of desire into a statement about actual or possible action must make essential reference to belief, and a translation of a statement of belief into a statement about action must assume a desire; so neither can be reduced to action without the other being left as a remainder. So it is quite impossible to translate statements about mental events into statements about behavior.[4]

Most important, behaviorism just does not reduce mental entities to the purely observable because behavior itself is not purely observable. As I claimed in chapter 2, when behaviorist psychologists report what happens with animals, food, lights, and levers, they do not normally report observable bodily movements like the movement of an arm .34 centimeters. Instead they describe the phenomena by organizing them into pieces of behavior like pushing the bar. Careful as they generally are, Roberts et al. (1978) seem to agree that behavior is sufficiently observable, described in behaviorist terms, to be a basic item in theories from a variety of disciplines.

The behaviorist vocabulary for describing the observable phenomena is laden with taxonomic commitments redolent of precisely the sort of theoretical entity that empiricists say has no place in the bare description of what is observed. It is at least a teleological vocabulary where actions are grouped together on the basis of intended sameness of results. Now whether a state is teleological is not readily observable. Behaviorists and their sympathizers have tried to state observable necessary and sufficient conditions for teleological events and states (see Rosenblueth, Wiener, and Bigelow [1968]), but without success (see Taylor [1968] and Woodfield [1976]). A behaviorist could simply rule teleological states out of the theory and allow only bodily movements to be mentioned in the lawlike regularities discovered by psychology, but then very few such regularities would ever be discovered.

Many behaviorists' descriptions presuppose belief, and thereby also presuppose that the behavior allegedly under observation follows certain social rules. On an individual occasion, far from being observable, it may be downright hard to prove that a certain piece of behavior is not only consistent with a rule—for example, a linguistic rule—but actually follows it. When we attribute to some person a complex belief— say, that federal deficits do not cause inflation—we are presupposing, what is not immediately and naturally observable even if the person is making noises, that he or she is capable of reasoning and of language, a socially-based phenomenon. It is not always clear whether certain noises constitute meaningful language.

The unobservable that the behaviorist's description of behavior presupposes is not a mysterious realm of private events, but rather the social base on which even the behaviorist's vocabulary rests. I cannot know I have a headache unless I learn in the public forum how to identify my headache. Nor can I have beliefs and other language-related states and capacities unless I am a participant in a language. In those respects, one's mental life is based on and defined by one's social experience, and is not immediately observable.[5]

The behaviorist cannot even handle the possibility that the monkey is not aware of the light going on, for that would raise questions about the monkey's mental state. So the explanation of what the monkey does has to assume—what is not always the case—that the monkey acts appropriately if the light goes on. Perception is cancelled out; so misperception is impossible. Stimulus has to lead to response.

A common theme in these objections to behaviorism is that pains, intentions, and other mental events are *causes* of behavior, as well as of each other: to revert to my earlier example, they are related to behavior as a disease is related to its symptoms. It makes even less sense to define a mental event by reference to its observable manifestations than to define a disease by its symptoms, for a symptom is usually a more reliable criterion of a disease than a piece of behavior is of a mental event or state. The only respect in which disease is more deserving of status than a mental state is that it can sometimes be identified as a physiological state observable separately from its symptoms. But diseases are not always identifiable that way. When they are not, we do not legislate them out of existence. Neither should we legislate mental states out of existence on that basis.

One of the difficulties we noticed in defining diseases by reference to symptoms is that physiology would have a hard time making a science of itself if it were confined to discovering laws linking only observables and not postulated states. Much the same is true of whatever science might undertake to explain human behavior by finding causal relationships only among instances of observable behavior, while resolutely ignoring possible relations among unobservable ones. Why should explanation be hamstrung in this way?

Pfeffer (1982, chapters 1 and 2) and others are skeptical about psychological explanation because they are inclined to identify clarity with the operationalization of psychological concepts. That standard of clarity would do neither psychology nor any other kind of science any good.

We can avoid some unnecessary difficulties by explicitly dropping operationalist scruples and considering behavior evidence for mental states and events rather than holding that sentences about behavior are translatable into sentences about mental states and events. In that case individual statements about mental entities, like statements about theoretical entities, need not meet the absurd standard of being individually verifiable or falsifiable by reference to observable facts on every occurrence. They can affect each other. We can (but not necessarily must) distinguish between intentional and unintentional action by holding that in the former case an intention is present and active. We need only depart from hard empiricism to the extent of permitting entities that are unobservable in the way theoretical entities are unobservable. Particularly for one skeptical about the very notion of observability, that is a reasonable departure.

But the defense of mental entities and of psychology in general cannot rest there, for it does little to show that either the inchoate psychological theory behind ordinary mental entities or any more sophisticated psychological theory is a good theory. The fact is that much of psychological theory does not approach the sort of precision we find in the hardest of the natural sciences. Even where we can rule out environmental effects, even where we can know for certain what the subject's state of mind is, we cannot confidently make such a simple inference as this: given that Jones wants to eat a banana and that this object is a banana and that Jones believes that this object is a banana, Jones will eat this object; for it is altogether possible that Jones will not eat this object. More sophisticated psychological theories do not substantially improve upon this situation. They generate predictions that rarely permit quantification and come equipped with unspecified "ceteris paribus" clauses. Insofar as explanation takes the hypothetico-deductive form described in chapter 1, approximation is the best psychology has to offer. (Mohr [1982] makes this and similar points, some of which we shall discuss further in chapter 4.)

The concepts that constitute the explanatory core of psychology are open concepts. They do not form a tight network of concepts exhaustively defined in terms of experience and each other in such a way that one can clearly distinguish what is true by definition from what is true as a matter of fact, or that one can use the network to predict with precision. So, for example, we can define pain as a mental state usually caused by damage to the body and usually causing behavior designed to achieve avoidance or surcease. Odd as it may sound, it is a *necessary* truth that we *usually* avoid pain; but our concept of pain allows for masochists.

The very fact that psychologists concern themselves with construct validity indicates an absence of neatness in their concepts. Consider the validity of a test for hostility, surely something worth testing for. (The example is from Cronbach [1984]; the discussion here builds on the discussion of construct validity in chapter 2.) One could try to measure hostility by counting acts that meet certain criteria of aggressiveness; a naive behaviorist might suggest that. But there is independent reason to believe that some people are under stress because they dare not manifest their hostility in behavior. If that is true, then no test that just counts aggressive acts will accurately measure the construct.

In looking for a valid measure or set of measures of hostility, one is at the same time looking for a clear and adequate definition of the concept. But, as I argued earlier, Newtonian physics does not permit a clear distinction between truth by definition and truth as a matter of fact. Terms like *mass* and *velocity* and others are not defined independently of each other or of the substance of the theory they are used to state, as even some old positivists acknowledged. Over time physics has achieved a precision not found in psychology; but it does not follow that psychology is procedurally wrong or that it should stop trying to refine its measurements (including instrumentation) and its constructs. Or, by the way, that probability can or should ever cease to play a significant role in psychological theory.

"Define your terms," a critic may demand of a theorist, as though the definitions were arbitrary and separable from the theory. In fact the definition indicates causal relations with other postulates that are themselves not readily observable; in doing so it makes certain substantive claims. One might insist on avoiding postulates altogether by defining hostility just in terms of behavior, but that sort of definition would fail for the same reason any definition of a disease purely in terms of symptoms would fail. This is an example of the important truth that some definitions are better than others, as anybody acquainted with the notion of construct validity should know.

Recall that one of the criticisms of psychology was that its theories were tautological. That criticism works better against behaviorism than it does against the notion of mental events as postulates of a theory. Still, there is a trace of tautology here: it turns out to be impossible to distinguish cleanly between truth in fact and truth by definition. But not only here, as I have argued. To object to psychological theory on this basis is to put oneself in an extraordinarily awkward position on the whole question of how science explains.

It must be acknowledged that definitions of certain concepts, particularly in psychology, have ideological implications. Consider intelligence once more. If you believe that the Wechsler Adult Intelligence Scale is a valid test of intelligence, then your belief has significant political implications. You might deny this by insisting that intelligence is simply what the WAIS measures; but if that were true, then there would be no reason to administer the test. Employers and others administer the test because they think intelligence relates significantly to behavior that is of interest to them. What are we to say, then, if WAIS scores begin to correlate less well with certain more direct indices of performance on the job or in college? That the test is invalid, or that one's interpretation of it is invalid, or that intelligence is now less important for getting an A than it used to be? What are we to say if eating a good breakfast before the test adds twenty points to your score? If one racial group consistently does worse than another whose members are wealthier but members of both do better if their parents are wealthier? Testimony in a number of court cases shows how difficult, even ideological, questions like this can be.

These difficulties, more severe than anything a physicist or even an engineer must normally deal with, may make practitioners of psychology long for concepts whose definitions are not subject to this sort of pressure. They provide no reason whatever for its practitioners to give up and go into some other field, at least until they find some other field that either answers psychology's questions better or finds better questions to answer.

4. PSYCHOLOGICAL EXPLANATION AS FUNCTIONAL

The account thus far has not exactly been a ringing endorsement of psychological explanation. I have conceded a certain looseness in the theory, and have suggested that in that respect it is not altogether different from some respectable theories in the natural sciences. What remains is to give a more affirmative account of how psychological explanation enlightens.

Prediction and remediation are just two of the activities in which one's proficiency is increased by the use of valid constructs. In certain branches of psychology these activities are most important, and one finds there causal theories of the standard sort described in chapter 1. But when the topic is cognition, perception, or intention, psychological theory generates functional explanations, whose logic is similar to that of standard organization theory, discussed in the same chapter.[6]

I have argued that defining psychological events, including mental events, goes hand in hand with giving a theoretical account of them and of behavior. Many such events we define in causal terms: a desire is typically a cause of behavior; a pain is typically an effect of damage to the body and a cause of behavior; a state of perception, deceptive or not, is the kind of thing typically caused by observing something; and so on. We fill out the definition to some extent by invoking causal relationships to other states, some of them psychological. That is not an unusual way for scientists to define. But psychological faculties are also subsystems of the person insofar as the person is considered a system: they perform their characteristic functions in support of the whole person. Of course that is not a very precise description, and there is much more than that to be said about psychological states and events. But the same is true of any functional state or event; all have other, nonfunctional descriptions. Pains, perceptions, and desires, all of them functional, typically contribute to the economy of the whole and are defined by reference to their causes as well as by their effects—that is, their contributions.

The very use of the word *contribution* is meant to imply that the system has goals, possible end-states that are beneficial to it in some sense—possibly a much extended sense. A subsystem or functional state normally causes the system to achieve a goal or to maintain itself in existence.

A person, like an organization or a computer, has a complex of interlocking capacities; and that complex can be analyzed into sub-capacities, of which many are psychological capacities. Many of these capacities have functions. That means not only that they have characteristic activities but also that those activities contribute to the survival and flourishing of the whole organism, and so, by feedback, to that of the capacities themselves.

Psychological states are a species of functional state, respectably compatible with the discoveries of physiology and generically familiar to orthodox organization theorists. Any psychological state is a physiological state too, and may be described accordingly.[7] Psychological descriptions are not logically equivalent, nor in that sense reducible, to physiological ones that make no implicit reference to contribution to the survival and flourishing of the organism. On the other hand, in response to a demand for a detailed analysis and causal explanation of the psychological state one may appropriately invoke physiology.

But we must distinguish functional states of the sort plants have from states of genuine intention. Psychological states are functional states insofar as there is survival value and more in pain and sight and similar faculties, and in the ability to reason and use symbols. The explanation of my native ability to reason, which is functional as a turtle's shell is functional, need not invoke anybody's goal-directed behavior. On the other hand, my acquired ability to reason (e.g., to think of these arguments) is in effect an artifact, for it is partly the result of intentional action on the part of my parents and others and me, something created with a purpose in mind.

To describe a person's conduct as motivated by reasons is to offer a functional/causal explanation, as though you were explaining how a turtle's shell protects the animal from harm, but at the same time to attribute reasons for action. The psychological is functional in this sense: there is a functional answer to the question, "Why do people have these faculties or capacities?" That answer indicates how the subsystem in question contributes to the system. In this sense the psychological is not only functional: there is no mere functional answer to the question, "Why did you fire Jones?" In fact, the correct answer to that question may make reference not to any contribution to the intending person, but rather to the company for which Jones worked, or perhaps to Jones.

When I explain some action of mine by reference to my reasons for acting, I am going beyond specifying cause and function to suggest that there was something good about the act or about some actual or probable result of it; otherwise my intention would not explain the action, but would only raise the question why I intended that; and that question itself would suggest that the intention cited did not explain very well.

All this shows one of the important differences between psychological explanation in general and explanation based on intention in particular. The former is a form of functional explanation; the latter includes but goes beyond functional explanation and adds an implicit reference to reasons for action, rather as a computer state described at a certain level makes implicit reference to the rules of logic, or grammar, or mathematics. (Keep this in mind when we discuss intentions as causes in chapter 4.)

There is nothing in functional explanation that is inconsistent with the Hempel-Oppenheim account of causation summarized in chapter 1. The action of the subsystems causes that of the whole system. For example, a group of subsystems in an organization have an effect on the achievement of an organization's goals. But those goals are also causes of the subsystems. By way of a feedback or decision mechanism, achieving the goals keeps the subsystems going. In the case of psychological explanation, the whole system (the person) exerts a causal influence on the subsystems as well as the other way around. That is one of the characteristics of a system: the subsystem contributes to the whole; the whole is thus enabled to continue to sustain the subsystem and, in the case of natural organisms, to produce new exemplars and so maintain the species.

The functional analysis of a piece of intentional behavior would be an account showing how the components of the agent work together to cause the behavior which, if it is intentional, is done to achieve some specific end. If the components are characterized physiologically, this is an impossible task. We seldom know enough about physiological states to see how they cause a piece of intentional behavior. And if we did, the causal laws we invoked would likely not characterize the resultant behavior according to the description under which it was intended. Psychological explanations do permit this sort of analysis; they refer to faculties whose activities are those postulated psychological states (which are also physiological states) that help achieve the intended end.

A system's goals exert a causal influence on what the subsystems do if there is a feedback mechanism. The achievement of a goal may be a necessary condition of the system's continued existence, or it may be less essential. But we should distinguish between a situation in which there is a straightforward feedback mechanism and a situation in which the managers of an organization decide on the basis of the organization's goals to develop or alter the subsystems. In the first situation, achieving a goal (or not) may affect the system's subsequent behavior; in the second, an intention that makes reference to a possible goal causes the system to act in pursuit of the goal, whether or not the goal is ever achieved or even exists. The latter situation may include the former if management makes a decision based in part on its assessment of how well the organization has achieved its goals in the past, but rationality is not reducible to functionality.

As I argued in chapter 1, functional explanation is in some cases a legitimate and enlightening way to explain the phenomena that can be viewed as input followed by output. Criticism of psychology for using this mode of explanation will succeed only by showing that functional explanation as a whole is flawed.

It bears emphasizing, however, that part of the strength of that sort of explanation is that it rests on further explanation of a different kind. At a certain point one may say, Don't tell me what role this subsystem plays. Tell me how the subsystem came to exist; tell me about its components, and what causes them to be in the state they are in. At this point a computer programmer can begin to discuss the electronics of the machine. A biologist may abandon functional analysis and turn to a microanalysis of components of the organism and how they get that way. An organization theorist may turn from saying how subsystems and subfunctions contribute to the activity of the whole and go into detail about how people in the system do their jobs and why.[8]

In such cases we are talking about a phenomenon under multiple descriptions that do not entail each other and multiple explanations that answer questions that are different but may be mistaken for each other because they both ask *why something is the case*. The unity of the phenomenon does not imply that the descriptions or the explanations can be reduced to each other. It is one thing to describe the flowchart, another thing to describe the hardware states. At some point one might ask for the latter description rather than the former.

The same is true of psychology. In answer to certain questions it may be necessary to refer to the physiological basis of psychological states. In fact there is no theoretical reason why, if one knew enough, one could not explain every psychological state by reference to its physiological basis and (very important) the external influences on it, though it would be utterly impossible in practice. Psychological states are functional states, but functionality is not a criterion of the mental or the psychological; for some of the physiological states of an organism (or an artifact, for that matter) are functional too.

Physiology provides a further way of explaining psychological states, parallel to the further way of explaining computer states and biological states and organizational states. And there is a temptation, for some people a particularly strong one in the case of psychological states, to say that the description and the explanation of psychological states in physiological terms are somehow the accurate description and the real explanation.

What is wrong with that view?

5. THE POSSIBILITY OF REDUCTIONISM

It is conceivable that at some time in the distant future advances in physiology may enable scientists to describe the state of a human brain and central nervous system in such precise terms that they can determine what the subject's mental state is by looking at the physiological states. So when certain of the subject's C-fibers are firing, the subject can be counted on to report a headache. In due course people may be taught to report the firing of C-fibers as well as the occurrence of a headache. It is even possible that the term *headache* could either disappear or come to be regarded as a general and not very informative term, like *trouble*. Nothing much would be lost: one would still dislike having one's C-fibers fire, and making other people's C-fibers fire would still be cruel, or at least not very nice. No doubt our vocabulary would still be capable of stating those possibly ideological facts.

From the point of view of future science there are a number of possible commentaries on this situation. One might say that pain is just the firing of C-fibers. Or one might say that there is just no such thing as pain, in the sense that there are just no such things as witches or ghosts. When you gain a new fund of information about some thing or event and find that much of what you once believed about it has proved false, you may express your change of view by saying either that what you thought existed does not, or that it exists all right but is very different from what you once believed.

In some cases there is no sure way of saying which statement is the better description of the situation. When apparently solid objects like tables and chairs turned out to be clouds of particles, nobody persuasively argued that there are no tables and chairs. When the Copernican theory finally took hold, we did not abandon talk of sunsets as illusory.

Psychological predicates are more than crude but handy place-holders to be used until a more detailed and perspicuous set of theories and postulates comes along to replace them. If the day should come when people reliably report physiological states, there would likely still be a use for concepts like headache, as there are uses for functional concepts when their physical basis is no mystery. We now know enough about physics to be able when talking about a bridge to use predicates much more descriptive than ". . . safe to drive across": we can describe its physical state in great detail. But the former description of the state is one worth knowing, and one that neither engineers nor motorists dare remove from their vocabulary—on ideological grounds. The argument of the previous section (and chapter 1) gives us reason for saying the same of software states, biological states, and organizational states as well as psychological states.

As is typical of functional states, mental states can be both described and explained in a number of ways. The functional name or description ("intention to call Fred"; cf. "lubrication of the pistons") fits with explanations that are mostly related to behavior and reasons for it in persons, and, in systems generally, to production of desired output. It makes no sense to think the descriptions and explanations have to compete, or that one does or does not "leave room" for the other. They are compatible, though they do not do quite the same work.

Much of biology has been reduced to chemistry without throwing biologists out of jobs. Physics does not eliminate concepts of civil engineering. Physiology may in due course find ways to reduce much of psychology to physiology, but it will probably give us no good reason to drop current concepts of psychology or medicine. Psychological states are less like the entities countenanced by religious belief than they are like the entities countenanced by organization theory.

It was the philosopher Leibniz (1648-1718) who first compared the mind and a factory. He claimed that if the brain were expanded to the size of a factory so that one could walk through it, one could still not see mental events. Presumably he would now agree that one could walk through a giant computer and not see states described in software terms. But in either case there is no real mystery: neither mental events nor program states are immaterial or ghostly, though the former are reliably reportable. It might be a bit misleading to call a mental state a state of the body, but that is not for reasons having anything to do with ghostliness. We would not say that the state of being in debt or the state of being a native of Norway is exactly a state of the body either, but there is nothing mysterious about either one. (Or about other states not locatable. If Jones dies in San Diego while Mrs. Jones is in Minneapolis, where does Mrs. Jones's becoming a widow take place?)

So psychology is respectable as functional explanations are respectable—hence, as standard organization theory is respectable. Pushing hard on functional explanations may lead to structural explanations; pushing hard on psychological explanations may lead to physiological explanations. ("He is brain-damaged.") But the first of each pair is not reducible to the second. Nor do they correspond one to one, since (for example) different physical states may instantiate a particular kind of mental state. They are both giving causal accounts, but answering slightly different questions.

Now what does pushing hard on explanations in organization theory lead to? In general terms we can say it leads to explanations that respond to demands like this: I know what function these subsystems perform; tell me how they get there in the first place and how they work, in some more detail. And the response to that demand will include—of all ironies—psychological explanations of individuals' behavior.

The notion of functional explanation permits us to save psychological explanation, for psychological explanation differs from physiological explanation and is useful apart from it and not reducible to it. But that same notion of functional explanation, applied to the organization as a whole, shows that organization theory is not reducible to (or replaceable by) psychology or to any other of the ways in which we explain the existence and behavior of subsystems in the organization.

NOTES

1. This view has been developed and elaborated over a period of years by so-called analytical philosophers. Some of the major figures have been Wittgenstein (1953), Sellars (1963), Hampshire (1965), Rorty (1979), and Davidson (1980).

2. Wilfrid Sellars, a longtime associate of Meehl, whom Cronbach and Meehl thank for his assistance on the paper I have cited several times, came to treat not only technical psychological terms but all mental events as postulates; see the previous note.

3. The decision to attribute, say, the capacity to experience pain has some moral implications; for a mistakenly grounded refusal to attribute pain may lead to its gratuitous infliction or some other morally inferior attitude or act. We may not expect a theoretical decision to have these implications if we believe questions of value can readily be separated from those of fact. But we cannot use the moral facet as grounds for ruling the attribution out of court, for the decision not to attribute the capacity for pain has moral implications as well. Consider the abortion debate, in which the "right-to-life" side condemns the "choice" side for refusing to attribute certain protopsychological states to fetuses. This issue recurs in our discussion in chapter 5 of whether organizations have anything like mental states.

4. The famous logician Ramsey (1950) showed a way to get around this problem, but only for a restricted range of cases. See Davidson (1980).

5. A number of points made in these three paragraphs recur. The occasional difficulty of knowing whether certain noises are to be interpreted according to certain linguistic rules becomes a part of the problem of interpretation, discussed primarily in chapter 5. The attribution of belief turns out to entail an attribution of rationality; that critical fact, which comes up in chapter 4, relates to interpretation as well. The linguistic basis of belief provides some further sense to the notion that reality is socially constructed, and that different systems of language and theory are in some meaningful sense referring to different worlds. That we shall discuss in chapter 7.

6. This section is indebted to Cummins (1983), the Block anthology (1980), and Woodfield (1976), as well as Donaldson (1985).

7. Here I adopt a form of materialism, according to which psychological events are a subset of physical events, and so take a broad position on a controversial issue without giving much argument for doing so. Not much of current interest to organization theorists hangs on whether I am right in taking this position; so I omit what would have to be a long argument. A more extreme form of materialism would hold not only that psychological states are identical with physiological states (true), but also that psychological explanations

and descriptions are logically equivalent to physiological ones (false), or in some other unspecified way analyzeable into them (too vague).

To claim that a belief is a physical state of the person seems to do violence to the very essence of belief. But the claim that a spoken sentence is a certain kind of noise is misleading without being false.

8.   Here I concur with one of Donaldson's (1985) major arguments against those who criticize structural-functionalism for "leaving out" the causal bases of the structure. Structural-functionalism is perfectly compatible with any of a number of accounts of how the structures came to be in place.

4 INTENTIONS AND RATIONALITY

Having argued for psychological entities as explaining behavior, we now undertake to show how sound explanations can work by attributing reasons for action. *Rational individualism*, sometimes said to use the *rational model,* holds that one way to explain what a person does is to state the goal of the person's action; then, if the action is one that can be expected to lead to that objective and if the objective itself is the sort of thing that might give a person reason to act, the objective explains the action. A degree of rationality must be assumed in an account of intentional action.

How do we justify the apparent assumption of rationality in attributions of intentions and reasons? In human action there is irrationality, and argument is possible about what counts as rationality; so it is not clear what is gained by postulating reasons to explain behavior, aside from ideological satisfaction. I have claimed that psychology's concepts have a characteristic looseness; Mohr (1982) argues that the law-governed link between motivation and action is so loose that any motive can cause any action, hence that identifying a motivation explains little.

Evidence about the causes of behavior does not undermine the notion of intention; free will and rationality are not about the absence of causality; we do not face a choice between Man as subject for science and Man as rational self-creator. Whether rational cognitions explain individual behavior is a form of the problem of free will, which has little to do with whether science can explain or predict behavior. What threatens free will is evidence that reasoning has so little to do with behavior that the soundest theories a manager can use have no need of it.

Rationality in the classical sense is often absent, sometimes impossible, occasionally not worth attempting. Sometimes the best we can do is manage our desires with an eye on our irrational side. Yet the rational model is presupposed by how we think about ourselves and others. The notion of personal identity presupposes a level of rationality; so to refuse to attribute rationality is to be logically cut off from coherent talk about individual people.

Our discussion will raise the question whether one can reduce certain characteristically philosophical or ideological questions to terms amenable to the results of experiment, perhaps of the kind organization theorists undertake. It is not as easy as empiricists believe. Some of its difficulties reveal how different disciplines define their terms differently according to their characteristic theories.

1. THE STANDARD ACCOUNT OF INTENTION AND SOME OBJECTIONS

1a. Intention and Rationality

Jones acts intentionally if and only if Jones wants to bring about some state, believes that action A is such a state or will produce one, and so performs action A. (A full account would rule out situations in which an intention gets fulfilled accidentally, as when someone prepares to jump from a ledge and, unnerved by the prospect, slips and falls.) An intentional act is one to which it is appropriate to apply the question "Why did you do that?" in a sense that asks what the agent wanted. One way of setting out this sort of explanation is Aristotle's *practical syllogism:*

(1) I like to eat ice cream for dessert.
(2) Dinner is over, and the stuff in this dish is ice cream.
So (3) [Agent eats the stuff in the dish.]

The practical syllogism indicates what causes the action and how the action makes sense. Intentions regularly cause intentional actions; invoking an intention also shows the point of the behavior and by implication defends it as somehow rational.

The example is oversimplified: the agent may need to balance many considerations in making the decision. And superficial: the first premise probably follows from other, general premises, and no covering law is specified. The rational agent may not consciously reason through the steps, and may make a mistake in logic. But the syllogism explains the act and shows the structure of a satisfactory answer to the question, "Why are you eating the stuff in that dish?" or for that matter the question, "Why do you claim the diagonal of this room is the square root of fifty?"

Intention may entail knowledge of the future. I sometimes know what is going to happen not by inferring from available evidence but by forming an intention on the basis of reasons for acting. So I know I am going to have ice cream for dessert because I intend to, not because I have noticed that in situations like this in the past I have eaten ice cream and can now draw the obvious inference.[1]

Intention needs inferential knowledge as well. To know that I shall do A, I must have grounds for believing I can. The latter may include knowledge of myself—for example, whether I am likely to continue in my intention—and of the influences on my behavior. One purpose of psychological explanation is to enable an agent to manage his or her desires more knowledgeably, hence more effectively. For the most part, the more you know about yourself and your circumstances, the more freedom you have. It is misleading to talk about science "leaving room" for choice or autonomy, as though human action were a finite space some part of which is taken up by each of various influences, except for a tiny cause-free corner into which the will can fit. Autonomy is not just another independent variable, nor is it the absence of independent variables. (Section 4 defends these and similar claims.)

A rational agent is one whose preferences are logically consistent and complete, in the technical sense that the agent either has a preference or is indifferent between a pair of alternatives. The agent's beliefs are consistent too, with each other and with all intentional actions. Beyond that narrow sense we usually say the rational person's beliefs are based on the available evidence.[2] This definition of rationality leaves a great deal of room for elaboration and disagreement. By the argument in chapter 2, we cannot finally distinguish between defining rationality and making substantive and controversial claims about it; so the elaboration that will continue throughout this chapter will raise further disagreement.

A truly rational action is one that Jones undertakes on the basis of reason to believe that it will be in his interests, or in the interests of somebody whose interests he has reason to care about. It is therefore possible for reasonable people to disagree about whether an action is rational, according to their differing interests and conceptions of what a good life is.

A kind of rationality characteristic of humans is the ability to think and act strategically in the sense of achieving an objective by indirection or by sacrificing some near-term good to a greater subsequent good. This requires the ability to have a preference between not only present options but possible options. As any cybernetician will tell you, a simple system can be in a functional state or can respond adaptively to feedback. Responding preemptively to possible feedback is another matter. It requires rational deliberation not found in thermostats or in most animals. That these two kinds of capacity are both functional is no reason to assimilate them.[3]

A rational agent will know that there are other rational agents in the world, and that one's own action is the more rational as it takes account of the rationality of others. One's view of the best action ought to take into account how others will react and so create further consequences. (See section 6.)

The best way to determine whether a person is a rational entity is to see whether that person talks and behaves rationally. We do not determine whether an individual has a mind or some mental state or faculty by identifying some internal realm or item or power in it. But the question is a difficult one. Whether an individual is behaving rationally on an individual occasion is not a straightforwardly empirical question (assuming there are any such questions). The broader question whether it makes sense to describe—hence assess, positively or negatively—an individual from the point of view of rationality is even less clearly amenable to evidence. We do not call a sunflower loyal for tracking the sun, or a snowfall cruel, or a newborn child an egomaniac or a boor. Our decision to consider a person the sort of entity that can be rational, clever, or responsible is in part one of attitude, a determination to apply to the person certain expectations and treatment. In that sense, use of the rational model is an ideological act, but not therefore an unreasonable one.

1b. Deliberation and Intention

Although deliberate action is the standard case of intentional action, an action may be intentional but not the result of deliberation. You do not consider the pros and cons; you just do it, possibly on the basis of reasons you do not consciously consider. The ability to gather pertinent evidence and make sound judgments without conscious inference is a valuable form of rationality. Unawareness of one's inclinations and their strength is common, the measurement of inclination strength being difficult. Human actions are not always based on advance rational calculation that issues in knowledge of a future under one's control or influence. Trial and error is a rational procedure on some occasions.

Weick (1979, 194-210), along with many others, claims that rationality is often retrospective: one understands and rationalizes one's action after the fact rather than deciding by reason in advance.[4] Ignorance of one's motives and the presence of rationalization do not show an action to be unintentional or even irrational; nor does the existence of after-the-fact rationalization prove that all explanations by reference to intentions are rationalizations. It is essential to understand whether the intention caused the action (in a sense other than the accidental one mentioned in section 1a). If it did, then the statement of intention is not a mere rationalization. If it did not, it does not follow that no intention at all caused the action. Characteristically (not invariably), mental entities are incorrigibly (not infallibly) reportable, but sincere false reports of intentions are far more common than sincere false pain reports. The intender's knowledge of what he or she intends is sometimes noninferential but seldom if ever incorrigible. It may be only after the fact, if then, that you see clearly with what intention you acted. But such a case provides no reason at all to deny that the intention preceded the act—even if identifying the intention did not—and caused it. (I assume that we are not by definition conscious of all our intentions.)

The discussion so far has presupposed a simple and unified self. That presupposition cannot be taken for granted.

2. RATIONALITY, SATISFICING, AND DESIRE MANAGEMENT

In the past thirty years a number of scholars have argued that the classical model of rationality does not show the only way to be rational. All agree that intention embodies a desire and a belief. You want a certain kind of thing,[5] and you believe a particular action will get it, or at least help get it. Simon (1954, 1957) and others have raised questions about the belief: it may not be well founded. March (1978; I am indebted to this excellent synthesis) and others have raised questions about the desire: what we want is not always a simple matter; and whatever it is, we do not always act on it.[6]

According to Simon, making decisions is often a matter of "satisficing"—that is, doing one's best given constraints and one's inevitable ignorance and inefficiency in calculation and in taking the appropriate aspects of the situation into account. At some point the cost of more information to support the decision exceeds its benefits; so the decision will be an imperfectly rational and optimizing one. It is tempting to respond that Simon has shown only that optimizing is possible but more complicated than it may look, for satisficing is really being rational. But as Winter (1964, 1971, and 1975) has pointed out, in some cases one cannot decide rationally exactly how much information to buy, because one cannot determine exactly what the cost and benefit of the additional information is unless one has information which is itself costly, whose cost and benefit cannot be precisely known unless . . . into infinity. Where one cannot choose a profit-maximizing amount and kind of information, there must be a point where calculation stops and one just exercises something like experienced judgment, at best. And if you do not know what good any given amount of information will do, it may well make sense to exercise this judgment on the basis of minimal information.[7]

As March shows, study of actual choice behavior has also raised questions about the consistency of preferences and the agent's knowledge of them. Preferences may not only change over time, partly as a consequence of choices made on the basis of them, but also be inconsistent at a particular time.[8]

We may modify preferences as we become better acquainted with the nature or consequences of what we thought we wanted, or its cost; as a result, the process of implementing certain desires may cause us to alter or abandon them. We may cultivate some desires that we consider noble. We may expect desire to change, deny them to others and ourselves, and manipulate them. People who know themselves well may take steps to preserve the preferences with which they identify in their cool, rational moments. If I know I am so weak-willed that I am likely to start smoking again within a week after stopping, I may deal with my future craving by boasting to all my friends that I have stopped forever, making a huge bet that I shall never smoke again, or otherwise "binding" myself.[9] Accepting these features of our preferences is a way of staying out of trouble and optimizing in the long run; so self-management—that is, the management of short-term desires by long-term, second-order ones—is preeminently rational.

These exceptions to the classical rational model show that one ought to be as rational as possible all things considered but that trying to be perfectly rational is no way to do it. The arguments about managing one's contending and changing preferences have roughly the same outcome: trying to be a saint may make things worse.[10]

3. REASONS, DESIRES, AND VALUES

A rational desire is compatible with a coherent conception of a good life. That permits a great deal, but it rules out of the realm of rationality short-term desires that undermine long-term objectives, desires to do what is certain to be regretted, that are self-defeating, that on reflection the agent cannot account for and cannot identify with.

A rational agent has values–that is, relatively general, permanent, considered desires, of which a number are usually second-order desires. Asked why I did something, I will probably mention some feature of the act that makes it worth doing. Asked why that feature of the act makes it attractive, I may respond with a statement of a value: because causing pain gratuitously is wrong, or something of the sort. A statement of value may function as the first premise of a practical syllogism, or a principle in support of a first premise.

Most of us cannot state our values and their implications in a coherent and airtight way; hence unanswerable questions arise about whether we really hold this or that value. Most people who are not fanatics hold values with an implicit "other things being equal" clause attached to them. A rule for behavior may be overridden by another. For example, a principled reluctance to lie may be overridden by a principled reluctance to do anything that leads to an innocent person's death. For some easy cases of value conflict one may have explicit rules for choice, but one cannot foresee or formulate—much less justify—rules that will cover all possible conflicts. Skill in dealing with these situations in ways satisfactory to all interested parties is not formulable in principles.[11]

If you determine whether I hold a particular value by noting whether I embrace its implications on specific occasions, then when you attribute values to me you are also attributing a certain amount of rationality. Since I can never act on my values if I never know what they imply in particular circumstances, and since I can have no values I can never act on, attributing values—even quite elementary ones—without attributing any rationality is very difficult. But as nobody is completely rational, we cannot always know whether failure to act on a value is a failure of rationality, an absence of the value in question, or a simple lapse.

If an executive claims to value free competition but consistently demands government protection, there is reason not to believe the claim; but one does not always know what is wrong with it. Maybe the executive is insincere, or has a weak will, or is hypocritical, or holds the value but permits it to be overridden by others. Consider someone who always votes for candidates who espouse law and order and traditional values, but just as consistently defends officeholders who flout these principles in practice; or one who espouses racism and generally acts accordingly, but has intense friendships with a few members of the despised minority. A distinction between claimed values and effective values does not do justice to these situations.[12] But the conceptual difficulties and loose joints do not imply that we must abandon the concept of value. Values can be inculcated and rationally criticized and clarified, as effective managers know.

4. FREE WILL

4a. Towards a Definition of Free Will

A highly rational person chooses actions compatible with a coherent set of values, subject to complications of the sort Simon, Schelling (1984), and others indicate. The ability to act rationally may be curtailed by an absence of options, by ignorance of certain options, by inability to choose the option that maximizes some objective function, or by inability to execute a choice. Clearly rationality of this kind has something to do with freedom.

The traditional view of free will denied that human action is caused. But it is unclear what could count as evidence that any action or event was uncaused, and why uncaused actions would be free rather than random, hence out of control. In the organizational literature, challenges to the rational model (and by implication to free will) advert mainly and properly to the environment's influence on the individual's rationality rather than to materialist determinism.

Free will involves control of one's own actions by one's reason rather than by impulse, ignorance, emotion, constraint, or influence that does not work through one's reason. (See, for example, Hampshire [1965], Frankfurt [1981], Watson [1981], Dennett [1984].) Knowledge of one's options and one's interests and the ability to act effectively on that knowledge is as much freedom as an agent can have, or imagine. A desire for cocaine is antithetical to freedom; a desire for a useful life is not. The distinction has to do not with whether the desire was caused, but with the reasonableness of the desire and the agent's knowledge (of what will create happiness, for example) and opportunity to act on it. Freedom of the will is a matter of degree. It is also an ideological issue, for attributing it involves some idea of what a good life is.

The account of freedom as rationality in unimpeded action is supported by the conception of the agent as having settled, long-term, particularly second-order desires. (Thus Frankfurt, for example.) You can be unfree because you are seldom capable of acting on your second-order desires or because your second-order and other long-term desires—including your values—are incoherent or ill-considered or nonexistent. You increase your freedom by learning to manage your first-order desires according to your second-order desires. Awareness of environmental and other influences on your behavior increases your desire-managing ability.

It is reasonable to tame one's passions and learn to take pleasure in what is available rather than in what is not, or in what will have bad consequences. One might develop a taste for cocaine, but it is a freer person who avoids doing so. It is a high form of rationality to shape one's preferences and one's character to the demands and opportunities life is likely to offer. Unlike retrospective rationalization, an inept form of desire management, this activity of reason is done in awareness of the probable consequences. But there is sometimes a subtle difference between this situation and one in which you let your preferences be shaped by recognized constraints on your options, in effect claiming to prefer to be a prisoner.

March's argument that rationality for unsaintly humans has to do with desire management has a counterpart in our definition of free will. For real people in the real world, the greatest attainable measure of freedom is probably not to have a wholly consistent and static set of second-order desires, but to have moderately consistent and slowly developing desires towards which one maintains a critical attitude. Realistically, free people need to be able to try, fail, make mistakes, and learn what they really want. Few people ever reach the end of this process; most of those who think they have arrived there are victims of a self-deceptive rigidity that has little to do with freedom. The next freest thing to the vanishingly elusive state of self-knowledge is the capacity for self-discovery. (See March [1976].)

4b. The Issue of Free Will in Organization Theory

In the literature of organization theory there is not much discussion of second-order desires. Indeed, if proponents of operant conditioning, social-information processing, and other environment-based theories are right, there is reason not to take second-order desires very seriously. A favorite target of these theorists is the Maslow tradition, which for the most part has followed its founder by postulating needs—in effect, psychic deficiencies. The critics argue that environmental influences either override deliberation or control it. The experimental evidence they offer indicates that not only stated preferences but perceptual claims may be influenced by social factors. The social factors themselves act through the mediation of the agent's perception of them; the perception of the context is what counts, and it may vary independently of the actual context.

Consider, for example, the O'Reilly and Caldwell (1979) experiment: whether subjects considered assigned tasks interesting and meaningful apparently had more to do with cues they received from others than with actual properties of the tasks. Herman and Hulin (1972) found attitude to correlate better with subunit membership than with need. What follows? Perhaps that a theory that predicts attitudes by reference to individuals' needs and values and the properties of states and events that impinge upon them could be a good theory only if the cues one receives from others are counted among the properties of the states and events. In short, one wants to fit in. One wants what the others want. Social psychology is a mine of evidence to that effect.[13]

Interpreted this way, the experiments provide some support for Weick's notion of retrospective rationality: agents often either find out what they want after the fact or develop a want as a result of coaching or social pressure or the common tendency to make the best of a bad situation—or rather to decline to acknowledge that the situation is bad. In many cases one does not know what one wants—that is, one is unable to give an appropriate description under which it is wanted. One may prefer the pleasure of being in accord with one's co-workers to the pleasure of a challenging job. This is the kind of fact about their own desires that many people do not know. There are even pleasures that depend on their not being understood. If what pleases me most is a job that is easy to perform but appears challenging (because I think I like a challenge but I really don't), then my pleasure is contingent upon my not knowing what pleases me—not a state characteristic of a free person.

Social factors, including socialization and roles associated with one's position, may impart values to the agent. A person who works as a prison guard may begin to behave like one even away from the prison, for example. But then all our values and attitudes have some causes. What amounts to a loss of autonomy is one's being unable to see it happening. In that case one cannot manage or even affect the process from the point of view of one's most fundamental (including second-order) values.

Attitudes—a form of first-order desires—may be role-dependent in the sense that one may be brutal in one's capacity as a prison guard but kind elsewhere; that is the phenomenon that Milgram (1974) and Zimbardo and White (1971; discussed in Peters and Waterman [1982]) enlighten. In the Milgram case subjects inflicted what they thought to be increasingly painful and even dangerous shocks on people who had ostensibly forgotten nonsense syllables; the subjects' only motivation was that "the experiment requires that you continue." Zimbardo had people play the roles of prisoners and prison guards, but aborted the experiment when the subjects began to act out their roles with brutal seriousness even though everyone knew it was only an experiment.

To summarize, values are vulnerable in a number of ways. First, we may not know what we really value. Second, our values may be shaped by social and other forces of which we are not aware. Third (hard to distinguish from the others in an individual case), we may traduce our values under pressure.

It is essential to free will that the agent knows what is going on—in particular, knows what his or her desires are. If I am a good manager of my desires, I can step back from my immediate situation and ask myself why I am doing what I am doing and whether it conforms to my second-order desires. (See especially Hampshire [1965] on the phenomenon of stepping back.) To the extent that I do not notice and reflect on what is going on or can do nothing about it, I am out of my own control.

4c. Making the Free Will Issue Empirical

Recent work in organization theory suggests that being out of control happens more often than philosophers and other partisans of the practical syllogism seem to think. Notice, however, that experiments of the kind we have been discussing characteristically do not carry their lessons on their face. There are many possible interpretations we can give when

Jones claims to be pleased with a state of affairs that does not fit with his prior broad claim about the sort of thing he likes, or acts against the claim in a particular case. The claim may be false. Or it may be true, but Jones may be unable to act on it consistently. Or Jones may be misreporting his attitude towards the specific case. Or Jones may be mistaken about the pleasing task (e.g., it may not be as important as he thinks), and that mistake may reflect an unconscious desire to believe it important. But if agents frequently act against what they claim to be their values, then either they do not know what their values are or they can barely be said to have values worthy of the name.[14]

Weick (1979), Pfeffer and Salancik (1978), March (1976), Staw (1974), Weiner (1972), and others who consider evidence that behavior is not value-driven as the practical syllogism suggests appear to be addressing the practical problem of free will: for some people in some circumstances (the scope is a matter of controversy), there is little explanatory power in invoking values or needs. In that sense those people do not have free will. In effect these critics have interpreted the free will issue as an empirical one. They have provided evidence that free will is sufficiently rare that managers ought not to assume that their employees have it.

Pfeffer (1982, especially chapter 3) attempts a somewhat different way of cashing out the notion of free will. He claims that uniformity of behavior among individuals in a particular kind of situation—as opposed to differences in behavior based on individuals' different reaction to the kind of situation—argues against the "rational actor perspective" and in favor of taking external factors as effective influences on behavior. But an explanation of motorists' stopping at a red light need make no reference to their perceiving the light or to their intention to obey it *because they nearly all perceive the same way*. Managers may have the same reason to take the external control perspective seriously and design their organizations accordingly as traffic engineers have to design stop lights without worrying about the different ways in which people perceive and react to them.

Free will has nothing to do with predictability, and uniformity from one situation to the next and from one person to the next has nothing to do with the effectiveness of reason. I can predict that, faced with a choice of drinking spring water or heavily chlorinated tap water, virtually everybody will drink the former. Their freedom has nothing to do with predictability or consistency except insofar as these are based on constraints or ignorance. In saying that eighty-seven per cent of some variance or other is accounted for by social class, we seem to leave the individual at most thirteen per cent of the causal space to maneuver in. But if one hundred per cent of all Yuppies prefer wine to beer, it does not follow that they have no choice as to which to drink. They may choose to drink wine because they prefer the taste.

To make a necessary truth out of the dubious proposition that people with identical tastes cannot choose freely is to distill the question of free will down to manageable size by trivializing it. But there are no clear guidelines on how one cuts philosophical questions down to size. Disciplines proliferate in part because there are so many ways of interpreting the great questions and so many kinds of favorite experiment thought to be decisive in answering them. As a practical matter, these questions get interpreted in a way that somebody finds applicable. For example, what managers care about the question of free will is just whether they have to take account of people's values in making decisions about the structures and processes in the organization.

To the extent that there are different ways of boiling down the profound questions, there will be different experiments undertaken to answer them. So the discovery that a range of cases does not distinguish two theories should not tempt us to the conclusion that they are equally sound, or that the extra entities postulated by one of the theories can always be eliminated. Traffic engineers and economists (see, for example, Stigler and Becker [1977]) theorize adequately without postulating psychological states. Clinical psychologists will not abandon belief in psychological entities because traffic engineers and economists can get along without them.

Some managers ought to proceed as though their employees had no free will. For example, there is evidence that in deciding about job enrichment and performance evaluation, managers should not worry about needs or values. They are justified in adopting local theories that in effect ignore freedom of the will. Others are not so justified, and in yet other cases the matter will not be clear.[15]

In effect, managers have reason to satisfice in choosing a theory. On the other hand, no practitioner should assume that what can be eliminated from a local model can therefore be ignored for all purposes. Evidence that behavior is in certain situations a function of some controllable aspect of the situation is important news for managers. Good local theories are always welcome, and one might have been helpful to the managing director of the British company described in the Introduction. But it is a mistake to extrapolate from that situation without good reason, and worse still to move to conclusions about the Nature of Man.

When an economist or an organization theorist suggests an experiment that in effect gives flesh to the notion of free will, the results are likely to be parochial. Not only that: as I have suggested, there are difficulties in knowing what an experiment proves. So, for example, Pfeffer and Salancik's inability to show that needs make much difference to actions may show only that it is hard to determine what people's needs are—a fact that supports some of Pfeffer's (1982, 75) misgivings (and ours) about psychological explanation. If we satisfice in designing our theories, that is important; but it does not tell us everything we might ever want to know about the efficacy of intentions.

Scholars, if not managers and traffic engineers, typically want to get beyond the purely practical, to find statements and even theories that are not only useful for a certain range of tasks but also true. Granted, the different disciplines have different problems to manage; still they must overlap at certain points. Either the rational model is right or it is not, we want to say. We feel there must be some way to get this question clear and answer it.

What we need in order to make a judgment about the efficacy of intentions and thus about the truth in the rational model is a situation that all partisans can agree is not designed to favor one mode of explanation over another. The area of criminal behavior is promising. A sociologist would argue that people become criminals because they are socialized that way to the norms of their subculture. An economist might try to determine how criminal behavior seems to maximize expected utility for people in certain situations. A psychologist of a certain orientation would look for ways in which their criminal behavior had been rewarded. If changes in a criminal's environment could be shown more effective in altering behavior than manipulating rewards and punishments, that would give grounds for the claim that the sociological theory was better at explaining criminal behavior. An interdisciplinary team might be able to design one or more experiments and state in advance what results would count for or against each of the various forms of explanation. Conclusive evidence against the psychologist's explanations would also argue for a reduced freedom of the will, for it would show that, for this significant range of cases at least, the agent's deliberation made little difference. (See Elster [1984], chapter 3.)

But this just won't work.

One who espouses rational individualism, hence free will, can claim that the sociologist's predictive success shows only that there are many who have little or no free will precisely because they are not guided by an understanding of their own best interests. Proponents of rational individualism usually make no claim about how many people are rational, and might not be able to agree with their opponents about how little rational action there would have to be in the world before using the rational model became pointless. Even if agreement on that point could be reached, there is no reason to think it would be possible to design a set of experiments that all the contending parties would agree would settle matters one way or the other.

The characteristically empiricist claim that large conceptual and methodological questions can be clarified and reduced to testability and manageability if they are worth asking at all shows an undue confidence in the ability of scientists to frame experiments that answer large questions clearly. The opposite error is to hold that apparently empirical questions are actually philosophical ones—that different "paradigms" may generate different and irreconcilable answers to the question at hand. It seems safe to say that answering certain interesting empirical questions may turn out to be anything but straightforward.

Note too, as I have suggested before, that there is some difficulty in deciding whether theories characteristic of different disciplines actually contradict or are answering slightly different questions. It is hard to be certain whether the economist and the psychologist really disagree or are answering different questions because they are in effect defining *free will* differently. But the difficulty cannot be cleared up by an agreement on what the term means, since each discipline has reasons, related to its characteristic rules about what counts as evidence for what, for defining the term in its own way.

But there are ways other than experiment to argue about the rational model and free will. Some of them come into play as we attack the global claim that cognition and desire cannot play a part in anything that deserves to be called a real theory about behavior.

5. CAUSALITY AND TRIVIALITY

In this and the previous chapter we have referred to the looseness of the conceptual link between psychological states and behavior. This looseness creates problems for intention-based causal explanation of behavior. It is informative to say that John Jones ate the ice cream because his mother offered him fifty dollars to clean his plate, or that Jones, Inc. acquired Greenacres to assure a supply of wood; but the theory that seems to lie behind the specifics of the explanation just isn't much of a theory. How could any evidence overturn any theory to the effect that if, everything else being equal, Alice Smith wants, everything considered, to do something and is able to do it then she does it? Any purported counterexample can be rejected as showing at most that other things are not equal. That way of dealing with alleged counterexamples saps the theory's strength. Compatible with anything that happens, the theory excludes nothing and so predicts nothing.

Earlier we identified Vroom's (1964) expectancy theory as an apparent example of the deficiencies of explanation by reasons. The theory that people act to achieve their highest subjective utility appears to be compatible with any conceivable counterexample, and is therefore worthless.[16] But there is serious doubt about whether people work harder on the basis of expectation of better rewards, for reinforcement of behavior is more effective when intermittent than when constant. Work on motivation has found feedback, instruction, difficulty of goals, self-evaluation, expectations, needs, attitudes, job characteristics, and other factors to affect motivated behavior. A reasonable conclusion is that evidence for either expectations or values goes beyond immediate behavior; if so, there is less reason for thinking the theory trivial. One cannot arrange all possible influences into a theory strong enough to bear quantification.[17] Vroom tries to specify the factors in motivation and show how they could be quantified; but he does not cover all possible factors bearing on behavior, and he gives no strong reasons for believing one could measure the factors they do mention.

Mohr (1982) considers theories of motivation not quite tautological, but inadequate because of the multiplicity of "impact parameters" on the process of practical reasoning. There can be no covering law linking a motive and a kind of behavior, for one can never rule out the possibility that something else caused the behavior. He enunciates a principle that, if true, damages any possible theory of motivation: any motive may cause any behavior.

I claim that reason-based explanations are viable, even though theories that invoke motivation are shaky and of questionable relevance to managerial imperatives. To begin with, explanations based on reasons are at least as informative as those based on dispositional properties, since reasons and other mental states have dispositional properties, and others too. Explanations by reference to dispositional states are not all trivial.

If a glass falls to the floor and smashes, you might explain it by saying the glass was brittle. To call something brittle is informative; to say that something broke when dropped because it was brittle is explanatory. It rules out as possible primary causes my having thrown it down, there having been something very hard about the surface it hit, and so on. To say that Jones wept when criticized because he is brittle is to say something explanatory. (It isn't that he was drunk or that the criticism was vicious.) We do not explain the crying by invoking a law that all people cry in this situation: that may be false, as may be the purported law that brittle things break when dropped on a hard floor. It is necessarily true, and important, that brittle things usually break when dropped on a hard floor; but that is more like a definition than a natural law. (Not that the two can be cleanly separated.)

The covering law (though there may be several) that supports our statement that brittleness caused the glass or Jones to break is a complicated one of physics in one case and psychology in the other. As the example in chapter 1 of the line drive breaking the tibia shows, we attribute causes without knowing exactly what the supporting law is, so long as there is reason to believe there is some such law. And as the law does not explicitly connect dropping with breaking—the laws of physics, not confined to observables, are not so crude—there is no puzzle about dropped glasses not always breaking.

So with psychological explanations: for those who are not behaviorists, attributing brittleness to a person is more than saying that the person has a tendency to cry. The attribution implies that the person is in a state causally connected to crying; and the explanation has explanatory power because we know something about how brittleness is causally connected with other states of the person—beliefs, desires, other personality traits, and so on. So it is with most psychological states and events we believe in: we know how they are causally related not only to behavior, but also to other states. But we do not know the actual covering laws in any detail. As states of intention are functional states (and then some), we can again use the analogy of the computer: a computer's being in a certain logical state (for example, printing a problem) causes its being in a certain subsequent logical state (printing the solution). The covering law supporting the causal claim is a law of electronics, and it can be identified.[18]

When we explain what Jones did by stating his reasons in doing it, we are not resting our causal claim on any law to the effect that people, even rational people, do what they have reason to do: that is either false or trivial. In referring to someone's acting on the basis of a desire or a reason or a principle or a personality trait, we are directly implying some informative generalization *about that individual person*—for example, that he or she abhors rudeness or is a sociopath or is brittle. The generalizations that go beyond the individual and link mental states, traits, and events at a general level are only indirectly implied in the causal statement, as the laws of physics that account for brittleness are only indirectly implied in the statement that the glass broke because it was brittle. But they account for some of its explanatory power.[19]

If behavior of a certain kind is evidence for a personality trait or a more transient mental state rather than just being identical with it or in some other way logically connected with it, then it is nontrivial to say that Smith is pursuing what she values most and—by the same token— possible to say that poor neurotic Jones is not pursuing what he (second-order) values most. It is not so different from explaining Smith's sleeping through the sermon by saying that she has narcolepsy, whereas Jones finds sermons boring. Generally, if a certain behavior is evidence for a particular desire rather than the latter being reducible to the former, then there is no problem about a desire causing certain behavior, and there is no problem about the desire being there but the behavior not. So it sometimes goes with causes. Not every line drive breaks a tibia. The laws supporting causal claims are just not laws about desires or line drives.

It is important to establish that desires—that is, reasons plus beliefs— cause behavior. One may have a reason to act, but one may act consistently with that reason without acting for that reason. Citizen Jones may perform the public-spirited act of identifying a criminal to the police; but did he do it from public-spiritedness—out of a desire to benefit the community—or because he wanted the reward? The question is asking whether his public-spiritedness *caused* the action.

Yet a reason is not only a cause: it states some respect in which, from the point of view of the agent, an action is a good thing to do. We can identify a cause without identifying the covering law. When we identify a reason, on the other hand, our reference to the principle on which the reason is based is much more direct. But the principle is not the covering law, and probably not any part of it.

It follows that we can often identify a cause with confidence even if we do not know the applicable covering law, even if pyschological theories often create problems about identifying antecedent conditions and knowing whether other things are equal. There may be a whiff of triviality about psychological explanations if we concentrate on the general rather than the specific, but identification of a psychological cause in a specific case need not be at all trivial, whether it involves a reason for action or not.

We are readier to attribute physical brittleness to a thing than psychological brittleness to a person because we know there are familiar, well-based, quantified laws available to describe gravitation, molecular structure, and other related phenomena underlying physical brittleness. These are superior to loose generalizations about the sort of thing that makes people hypersensitive, and in general about relations among dispositions, desires, and beliefs. They are altogether more readily available and easily applicable than physiological or psychological laws.

Some critics of intention, apparently including Pfeffer (1982, chapter 2) have unduly high standards for theories. As I argued in the first two chapters, most theories cannot be overturned by individual bits of evidence: their fundamental propositions are often well insulated from the data. Sometimes we do choose to reject apparent counterexamples to an established theory; so we are not always prepared to say whether the antecedent conditions hold until we know it is all right with the theory. But this happens far more often with reason-based explanations, because the states and events they postulate are defined so loosely relative to ordinary observation and to each other. There are psychological states, and one can identify them as causes in particular cases, but that is less than most managers want. What good is motivational theory to them? So goes one line of criticism, of which Mohr provides a version.

One might reply that it may be useful to managers who must motivate individuals, each according to his or her own psychological makeup. A civil engineer will acknowledge that we have too little applicable knowledge of physics to be able to determine from a structure's components and their conformation how much weight the structure can support under various circumstances. Yet no engineer will stop using normal engineering kinds of explanation and prediction because they are so crude relative to the physics that underlies them. For some purposes it will be enough to say how brittle the girders are.

What this analogy suggests is that it is useful for a manager to know who is brittle or paranoid and who is not—though the previous section indicates that sometimes one need not know this—and to have available some psychological generalizations about how one can deal effectively with such people. But from time to time, perhaps in choosing among materials, a civil engineer may need to get behind the vocabulary of stress and weight to physics; and it is ready for the engineer's use. Psychological theories invoking motivation do not provide comparable support for the manager's investigation of what is behind the individual's personality and how it could be affected. (This is yet another reason for denying that the manager's job is like the engineer's.)

As the previous section suggests, one appropriate stance for a manager is to try to find and put into practice theories of appropriately limited scope, rather than universal ones. Mohr (1982, 90) claims that one can use explanations based on motivation to explain an individual's behavior in a particular case, and to explain the behavior of a certain group of people within a restricted scope—as, for example, in a particular organization, industry, or profession. In such cases one's modest assumptions about how people think and what they want are far more likely to be true. That they lack the universality characteristic of scientific laws is, as contingency theorists will insist, fatal neither to the usefulness of the theories nor to the accuracy of the causal claims.[20]

From that point of view it is important to recognize the milieu in which Frederick Winslow Taylor motivated workers successfully, and to note that today's employees are not German immigrants living at the subsistence level with few job options and low expectations. The same kind of information will help the managing director and others understand the British workers' reaction to the loss of their tea break. No one has come close to proving that psychology is incapable of finding generalizations of high probability that any manager can use. Even if it is characteristic of the human sciences not to be able to provide all-purpose quantified universal theories using concepts like job satisfaction, attitude, and motivation, there are local and (relative to physics) loose theories that solve problems and occasionally—as with Taylor—revolutionize our understanding of management. (See further chapter 5 on culture.)

The empiricist's criticism of psychology turns out not to be entirely meritless. There are difficulties about observing psychological entities and falsifying psychological theories; and though they are not unique to psychology, they are more severe there than in the hard sciences. The rest of this chapter raises further difficult issues. But in some cases it is the best we can do—and in fact isn't bad.

If intentional action were always rational, understanding action would be a more straightforward matter, just as interpretation of speech would be a more straightforward matter if everybody said only what is true.

Such is not the case, but in those two instances we must proceed on the presumption of rationality and truth.

6. THE PROBLEM OF IRRATIONALITY

An action may be intentional but irrational. It is intentional if it is done for a reason; but as we have seen, people sometimes fail to understand the causal bases of their behavior. People are sometimes self-deceptive; they rationalize; they do not know what they want until they have done it, and can only then look back and make inferences about their preferences. There are intentional actions that the rational model does little to explain. How then can we explain behavior by reference to the reasons and beliefs that in combination cause it?

The problematical cases are those in which people have their eyes open but do not seem to be acting on reasons, good or bad, at all. Can the rational model account for the behavior of the subjects in the Milgram experiment? The same doubts arise concerning behavior shaped by operant conditioning. The instructor whose students reinforce his movements so thoroughly that by the end of the semester he is lecturing from a corner is not acting on deliberation or in accordance with his values. The intentional, the rational, and the deliberate are not identical and may occur apart, though the standard case of each is the same.

The logical relationship between the intentionality of an act and its rationality is subtle. If an agent appeared to act on an objective that had nothing to be said for it or did something unlikely to lead to any remotely desirable state, one would still probably ask, "Why did you do it?"—thus presupposing that there was some reason, however inadequate, for doing it. Intentional action presupposes some minimal degree of rationality. If Smith eats a toad and claims to have done it in order to stop acid rain but freely acknowledges that there is no causal relationship between her eating the toad and acid rain ending, then Smith has not identified any basis for considering the act intentional. In such cases the presupposition is questionable.[21]

For all that, the rational model has so strong a hold on the way we explain behavior, others' and our own, that it is embedded in our language. It is not only psychologically difficult but logically odd to ascribe certain kinds of irrationality to oneself. It is like believing one is mistaken in believing something. Consider the strangeness in these two sentences (cited by Hampshire [1965]):

(1) I have decided to do *A* even though I know it is a mistake.
(2) I believe *p* even though I know the weight of the evidence is over-whelmingly against it.

Common usage presupposes that we normally choose beliefs on the basis of evidence and goals on the basis of reasons; thus the discomfort those sentences generate. This suggests that an implicit theory that presumes minimal rationality in describing behavior is a useful one. And that is a point in favor of the attribution of rationality in some cases, and in favor of making a practice of looking for reasons in trying to explain behavior.

How, indeed, is it possible to decide to do what one knows is a mis-take? Aristotle, the inventor of the practical syllogism, sees a problem here, and he does not solve it very satisfactorily. It is still a controversial issue for the many who take an Aristotelian view of intention. Perhaps the best we can say is this: intention, like preference, pleasure, and allied con-cepts, is defined in part by reference to the sort of action of which it is postulated as a cause, but it does not always cause its characteristic effect. Intention is *necessarily usually* followed by the intended action. That is the way it is with ordinary psychological concepts.

There is another way in which an intentional action, one whose struc-ture the practical syllogism describes, may be irrational. A practical syllo-gism could look like this:

(1) I like to look at things that are orange.
(2) Setting fire to my house will generate orange flames.
So (3) [Agent sets fire to the house.]

An explanation that invokes an intention does not require that the agent be rational: the reason may not be a good one. Identifying the intention here explains the action causally about as well as a ten-foot fall explains some very unfortunate person's death. In both cases a cause is identified, but in both cases there is much more to be said, because the usual pre-sumptions do not hold. In the case of the firebug, since it is under-standably unusual to prefer orange-gazing to having a place to live, one suspects a disorder and therefore overrides the presumption of rational preferences. That presumption has a status similar to that of the presump-tion of the presence of oxygen mentioned in our discussion of causality in chapter 1. Even if the presence of rationality were as thin an explanation as the presence of oxygen—it is not—its absence would be informative because we take a little rationality for granted.

We distinguish between two positions: (1) naming intentions is a way of explaining actions, and all intentional actions are to some degree rational; and (2) all intentional actions are truly rational. The first is true, the second false. Distinct from those but supportive of the first is a proposition not only true but sufficiently reliable and important to be presupposed by discourse about action: (3) people usually act with a significant degree of rationality.

There is one more point to be made against assuming general rationality. Game theory provides games that have no single rational solution—hence, in which there is no such thing as the rational thing to do. In that sense, rationality is not definable perfectly soundly. (See Elster [1984 and 1985].)

Strategists, individual or corporate, must know how others who might be one's competitors or confederates think, perceive, and intend. In a social situation one cannot make predictions or therefore form sound intentions without taking one's stakeholder's intentional knowledge into account, and so cannot make good long-term predictions. Chapter 3 argued that one cannot attribute to oneself any kind of thing one cannot attribute to others. Nor can one consider oneself the only possible rational person in the world. In a competitive situation you must normally assume that whatever techniques are available to you to use against another person are also available to the other person to use against you. One of the lessons of the celebrated Prisoner's Dilemma is that there is no way for either competitor to get enough information to be sure of winning except on the assumption that somehow the other competitor not only cannot get the same information but also learns very little while playing the game. Such a situation is possible, but not for long.

If the competitive situation has the structure of a game without a solution, then there may be no rational way for the strategist to choose the best possible strategy. Given that almost all strategists must play games with many stakeholders, it is clear that detailed and accurate predictions of stakeholder behavior and confident choices of the best possible strategy are impossible. But since determining as best you can what your competitors and others are up to is essential to strategy (that is the core argument of Henderson [1979], for example), it follows that there cannot be a natural science of strategy. Most of us want to manipulate the environment and those that dwell therein while remaining ourselves independent and unpredictable; but others have similar aspirations. Hence in a world of intenders strategy is no science. (See further MacIntyre [1981, especially chapter 8].)[22]

Considering others to be deliberators is necessary for philosophical as well as strategic reasons. Your ability to be conscious of your own acts of deliberation and of the connection between how you reason and how you act implies the ability to attribute deliberation to others; for you could not attribute deliberation to yourself unless you also knew how to attribute it to others. Not to acknowledge grounds for attributing it to others, therefore, is to forgo the possibility of being conscious of your own deliberating. I have suggested it is a sign of rationality that we can not only deliberate about our actions but also attribute to our stakeholders the capacity to deliberate about us.

The kind of rationality you attribute in considering a person capable of intention is like the kind you impute to anyone with whom you communicate. You cannot explain by reference to reasons for action the behavior of a person who is not in the least rational, or whose idea of what is rational is altogether different from your own; for in those cases you have no basis for understanding the relationship between that person's intentions and his or her actions. You cannot attribute a belief to Jones without assuming he is sufficiently rational to act consistently with the belief at least some of the time. For approximately the same reason, you cannot communicate with Smith if she is not in the least rational, for then you have no reason for taking any sounds she makes to be coherent discourse. That is, you cannot know what she means, or even that she means. But of course we do attribute beliefs to people and communicate with them all the time. It involves an assumption of rationality, which is to some degree an ideological assumption; but if you think it is unjustified, your own position makes it impossible to communicate your objections to anyone.

7. PERSONAL IDENTITY AND RATIONALITY

The concept of personal identity presupposes something like the rational model. That is, in order to talk about people, we have to talk about a significant degree of rationality and consistency. It is a necessary truth that people are sometimes rational. The irrationality and inconsistency that we unquestionably find in human experience make personal identity imperfect but do not undermine the concept, nor, therefore, the rational model of explanation.

When an ordinary material object exists over a period of time, it may undergo changes. It continues to exist because its changes do not amount to the destruction of the old thing and its replacement by the new. In fact, attributing changes to something requires the assumption that the same thing persists through the changes. Its essential properties are those that necessarily abide throughout its life; the accidental ones do not.

Individual persons change over time. In addition to physical changes there are some alterations of personality, values, memories, and so on. Ordinarily we assume that the individual is still Jones in spite of these changes. We may modify the assumption in cases of severe psychological or neurological difficulty, and abandon it in the case of Dr. Jekyll and Mr. Hyde. But the concept of personal identity is useful, and not vulnerable to just any change.

What makes us say that Person A (e.g., the boy who could not lie about having chopped down the cherry tree) is the same person as Person B (the Father of his Country)? We attribute personal identity under certain conditions: for example, bodily spatio-temporal continuity, the apparent ability of B to remember things that only A experienced, similarity of personality, and in some cases continuity of intention. But if A's deliberation does not as a rule affect B's action, there is reason to doubt the identity of A and B.

What makes a person a unified entity is the ability to remember the past, make decisions that are effective in the future, and maintain fairly consistent values, policies, traits, and knowledge at a particular time and over a period of time. Some people do this better than others, largely because some people are more rational than others: they have coherent values based on a manageable conception of a good life. In that sense we can say that their ends provide a principle of unity for persons. Nobody is a perfectly unified person, even at a particular moment (see Nagel [1971], who is even more pessimistic than March); but that does not keep us from talking about individual people, and so assuming the presence of some consistency and some ability to deliberate—hence to be at least minimally rational—for ordinary purposes. What is most important about personal identity is a matter of degree, and the degree we normally presuppose is consistent with our experience of irrationality, ambivalence, and changes of preference and values and even character.

Not that questions about borderlines are trivial. To take one example, it is a serious question whether it is just or sound as a matter of social policy to punish someone whose values, preferences, and tastes have radically changed since he or she committed some serious crime. That is the practical question of personal identity. A practical question of rationality is whether to grant some marginally sane person the freedom to make major decisions about his or her life.

The concept of the person as a unified entity presupposes and is presupposed by many concepts we require for coherent discourse. If we did not assume that people are necessarily usually consistent on the whole, our notion of a person would crumble, and with it many other concepts we require in order to talk about knowledge, meaning, and morality.

In the next chapter we shall see how much of this may be said about organizations.

8. A LOOK BACK

There are some lessons yet to be drawn about psychological explanation and organization theory.

We have found two caveats attached to the view that we can explain individuals' actions by reference to their intentions, hence to rationality. First, it is difficult to assign a reason for action because the necessary "other things being equal" clause covers so much as to permit almost any reason for almost any action. Second, experimental evidence suggests that sometimes the best way to explain, predict, and control action is to look to the environment rather than to intentions. The caveats are related: experiments that appear to undermine the efficacy of intention are inconclusive in part because there are no known covering laws tight enough to permit us to know when things are equal.

I infer that it is reasonable to use explanations that invoke intentions as well as those that do not as the need arises, and that there is no sure way to determine which kind is appropriate when. One must be content with the approximation that appears to be adequate, and one may not be able to determine which approximation is in fact best, or how exactly to balance theoretical considerations against practical ones.

NOTES

1. What I know in this case is not just that I intend to eat ice cream or shall try to eat ice cream but that I shall eat ice cream. Jones knows that something is the case (let us say, knows that p) if Jones strongly believes that p, it is true that p, and Jones has good and well-grounded evidence that p. There is no reason for saying that Jones knows only that he believes that p. Knowledge is warranted true belief. Though there are arguments about what constitutes warrant and about how strong the belief has to be, there is no basis for say-

ing that what one knows must be something that could not conceivably be false, or that one knows only one's own intentions and beliefs. (In fact, one does not always know even them for certain.)

2. This definition of rationality is not intended to be technically complete or correct, but it will serve our purposes. Those with more demanding purposes may consult Schick (1984), for example.

3. Recall the discussion in chapter 3, section 5. In all I say about rationality I am much indebted to Elster (1984, 1985).

4. According to the common philosophical convention, to rationalize an action is to give the reasons that actually caused it and that justify it. Weick appears to use the term in the everyday sense, which does not imply that the reasons offered caused the action or justify it—if anything, the contrary. Unless fair warning is given, I shall use the term as Weick does.

5. On technical grounds that are not of immediate importance here, we say that an agent wants that something be the case.

6. In chapter 5 we shall discuss whether it makes sense to think of an organization as being like an individual. March reverses the analogy: an individual is like an organization that can be made to act rationally only by skilled management.

7. Natural scientists satisfice too, as I shall argue again, especially in chapter 7. A scientist could indefinitely expend time and money testing a theory and determining its details and its range. It is not clear that there is a scientific or even wholly rational answer to the question, When does one finally call a halt?

8. March points out the similarity between the difficulty of the intertemporal comparison of preferences and that of the interpersonal comparison of utilities. (Wisely he refrains from pushing the analogy so far as to land him in serious controversy.) If consistency of preferences is one mark of personal identity, as I argue in section 7, then this similarity is what one would expect.

9. Strotz (1955), Ainslie (1975), Elster (1984), and Schelling (1984) are the best-known analysts of "egonomics," the art of strategically managing one's desires and preferences.

10. Edward Freeman has pointed out to me that it may be rational in the long run to be irrational in the short run—for example, in order to undermine a competitor's ability to predict one's behavior.

11. One reason is that any such rules will themselves be subject to being overridden; so one would need another rule, etc. unto infinity, as in the case of satisficing mentioned in the previous section. The point will recur as in chapters 6 and 7 we discuss similar problems with scientific laws and their application.

12. Rokeach's (1973) influential treatment of values seems to take too little notice of people's inability or unwillingness to report their values accurately.

Given the argument of chapter 2, his work is handy for people who write about climate rather than culture.

13. Pfeffer (1982) cites these and a number of other experiments with similar results.

   Consider the famous Asch (1955) experiment, which showed that under social pressure people made grossly mistaken claims about what might have been considered unmistakable factual data. Asch found that antisocial people resisted the pressure better than others.

14. Either case would give reason to predict that talk of values in contexts calling for rigor might go the way of talk of spleen and vapors. Our difficulty in interpreting experimental results of this kind argues for deficiencies in psychological theory. Concepts are never perfectly tight, to be sure; but in this case the concepts at our disposal are so loose as to raise the question whether any experiments, however numerous or cleverly designed, could lead us to a convincing theory about what goes on when people claim to prefer something apparently not consistent with values claimed in advance.

   But the last two sections of this chapter argue that something like the concept of value is essential to our discourse about ourselves and other people.

15. As Mitchell (1982) points out, we could stand to have much more work on questions of this sort: for what kind of job is motivation more important than environment?

16. So, for example, Mayhew (1980, 1981). Of course almost any theory stated at that level of simplicity and generality will be worthless. If all Newton had claimed was that gravity is what makes bodies move towards each other, then his theory would have been trivial too. The trouble with Vroom is at the level of greater specificity, as for example in the suggestion that one can measure "valences" of desire.

17. If one did, ordinary regressions would not capture the richness of the multidirectional causality in play. Pfeffer reviews the literature on expectancy theory, without noting that evidence against it shows that it is not trivial. For more on multidirectional causality see chapter 5.

18. Recall that one may say, "Don't tell me about the function of this state or its logical relation to other states; tell me about its causes and its results."

   There should be no discomfort about resting a causal claim on the existence of unknown laws. We would not want to say that nobody before Newton ever made a justifiable causal claim, since they all had false notions of the appropriate laws. And we do not think people living in the year 4000 A.D. will be justified in making that claim about us.

19. My argument largely follows Davidson's (1980). Mohr's (1982) is similar, but his is led astray by Hempel's (1962 and 1969) and gets wrong what Davidson, who also cites Hempel, gets crucially right. This error does not destroy Mohr's entire account, however. If he had seen more clearly how the laws relating cause to effect need not use the description of either the

cause or the effect, he would have been able to show an even closer affinity between his process explanation and the kind of causal explanation intentions provide of actions. In both cases you can identify the cause without being able to come close to citing the covering law.

20. The importance of this discussion becomes further evident as we discuss interpretation in a preliminary way in section 7 of this chapter and more extensively in chapter 5. It relates also to our discussion of the range of science in chapters 6 and 7.

21. Cherniak (1986) sets out to find how much rationality is logically required for intentionality and other mental capacities. Not as much as has been traditionally thought, he concludes.

22. Pfeffer claims that rational individualism and environmental determinism cleanly separate the agent from the enviroment: one is cause (which one depends on which of the two approaches you adopt), the other effect. He contrasts these approaches with theories that see agent and environment in a reciprocal causal relationship. This seems a major mistake on Pfeffer's part, from two points of view. First, I take perception and rationality to be socially based and in that sense environmentally determined, but still essential parts of the agent's causal arsenal in dealing with the environment. Second, I argue that a particularly subtle form of rationality, codified in game theory, is deciding what to do on the basis of the stakeholder's possible reactions to one's possible moves. The environment, actual and possible, is at the heart of the decision process.

5 CORPORATE REASON AND VALUES

In the last two chapters we have considered psychological explanation, intentions in particular. In this chapter we ask whether organizations, like people, have objectives, values, and even something like psychological states. This requires defending the notion that organizations are entities. My defense is based in part on the view that an organization is a purposeful system: the ends it pursues unite it. Some organizations, like some individuals, can act rationally and effectively in accordance with their values. That is, they have free will, at any rate to a certain degree. Some of the mystery vanishes from this argument if we think of ourselves as discovering, not how organizations resemble rational people, but how rational people, effective managers of their desires, resemble organizations.

The values of the organization find expression not only in its objectives but also in the way its internal life is conducted—that is, in its culture, which has some of the properties of the mind of an individual.

The discussion of culture leads to a further consideration of the social aspect of individual intentional behavior. As some anthropologists have held, to understand individuals' intentional behavior requires understanding the culture that surrounds this behavior and helps determine how it is motivated and how it is to be explained—or, to use the technical term, interpreted. In this way corporate culture helps explain the behavior of aggregates by reference to intentions, but opposes reducing corporate intentions to those of individuals.

Culture homogenizes language. As understanding speech requires presupposing rationality on the part of the speaker, a community or an organization that shares a language shares a basic conception of rationality, for reasons suggested in chapter 4 and elaborated in this chapter. This account gives limited sense and defense to the idea that reality is socially determined and that different cultures have different realities. It also defends the rational model, but makes individual rationality in some ways a social matter.

1. IS THERE ANY SUCH THING AS AN ORGANIZATION?

Weick (1976 and elsewhere) argues in effect that there is no such thing as an organization. If goal-directedness and rationality are criteria of unity, he suggests, then organizations are at best sometimes and in some ways unitary. Reifying organizations is to be avoided. But I argue that, while Weick's criteria are reasonable, his application of them is too demanding.

One extreme view on the question whether there is any such thing as an organization is that we know there are organizations because we observe them, talk about them, work in them, and so on. The opposite is that organizations are ideologically convenient fictions but really nothing other than people behaving in certain organized ways. The first view is usually taken for granted, not stated. Rarely does anyone go so far as the second, perhaps out of deference to the idea that a sufficiently convenient fiction is no fiction; but a milder version of this second view is argued by social action theorists and others who consider organizations symbol systems or political arenas. There are those who see the subordination of individual interests to the interests of the organization, or of its owners and managers, in facile talk about the organization.

There is much to be said for common sense in talking about what exists—ontological issues, to use philosophical jargon. The word *organization* itself is useful enough to communication to have lasted this long. But the question for us is whether it can survive in anything more demanding than conceptually relaxed conversation.

Burrell and Morgan (1979) claim that organizations are not concrete entities. It is difficult to know precisely what they are trying to deny—more, surely, than that organizations are spatio-temporal objects like rocks. Elsewhere Morgan (1981) claims the support of Wittgenstein (1953) in denying that the concept of organization represents reality and asserting that it functions instead as a tool to help us deal with what we perceive. Apparently he is denying that an organization or anything else is a naturally observable entity, a self-evidently unitary building block of a world predivided for our convenience. If so, he is right, for reasons I gave in chapters 2 and 3. One's theory sets the rules for determining what counts as observable, and those rules are no better than the theory itself; so claiming to observe something whose existence is problematical will seldom convince.

Indeed we cannot simply observe organizations; but we cannot simply observe anything else, either. The right question is whether it makes sense to embrace theories that postulate organizations. There are some reasons for thinking not.

One, offered by Burrell and Morgan, is that reifying organizations takes a dynamic world to be static. But theories from the design tradition do take account of change and disintegration, and not casually: organizations must often change in order to adapt, and will disintegrate if they do not adapt. But these changes do not undermine the concept of the organization as unified at any time and persisting as the same organization through time despite changes of strategy, personnel, and so on.[1]

What is required to make good on the claim that a thing exists is an understanding of the conditions of unity at a time and persistence through a period of time. These conditions do not have to be specified in perfect detail, and cannot be, but we know roughly what they are in the case of an organization. Over a period of time the current managers, employees, and stockholders of the organization may completely change while the organization continues. As in the case of the individual human being, there are certain legal conditions governing identity, but they are not unarguably correct conditions for all purposes. If Jones suddenly undergoes a radical change of values, intellect, and apparent memory, we have grounds for saying that there is a different person in this body or that this body is a different person; but the law would not say that. Similarly, though the laws of incorporation govern corporate identity loosely, we have grounds for saying that an organization whose mission, policy, and objectives all suddenly change radically is now a different corporation. (See French [1984].)

Arguably something is lost when our explanations presuppose that there are organizations and that the function of organization theory is to determine what they do and why. Some of the greatest advances in science were made possible because scientists ceased thinking of the world as populated by *things* whose properties were related in a lawlike way (as Aristotle and the medieval philosophers did) and started thinking of it as

populated by *events* thus related. That advance required understanding—
not that there are no individual things, but rather—that those individuals
are not necessarily the only or even the primary subjects of science. To
raise parallel questions about the primacy of organizations is to invite explanations from outside organization theory, from disciplines that propound theories relating individuals, populations, groups, and other entities
that cut across organizations and need not worry about the conditions of
their identity for the same reason Newton did not need to worry about the
difference between essential and accidental change in a material object.

Even if one can talk coherently about organizations, habitually doing
so focuses attention away from the kinds of useful explanation that do not
take organizations as basic, and so misses opportunities to explain events
in possibly better ways. As I argued in chapter 1, broader theories (think
of economics or sociology) are more powerful than narrower ones (think
of organization theory); Newtonian theory joined terrestrial and celestial
phenomena in a way science devoted to the features of terrestrial sub-
stances could not. The underlying issue is whether one should make do
with organization theory or try for something more ambitiously broad. In
short, there is much to be said for both.

However freely one uses theories from outside the field of organization
theory, there will always be good reasons for considering the organization
a single entity. The idea of goal-oriented activity is central to that notion:
the organization's chosen ends make it what it is. That it has some chosen
ends of a certain kind is essential to its being an organization; that it has
these particular chosen ends is essential to its being this organization
rather than some other. But talk about corporate objectives raises problems conceptual and moral. We turn to the first kind of problem right
away, and to the second in section 3.

The conceptual problem is an old one: how do we distinguish between
the goal of a system and just any old end-state? The traditional cybernetic
way is to operationalize the notion by means of equifinality or plasticity,
but too many instances of them are unrelated to goal-directedness. As I
argued in the discussion of functions in chapter 3, what is required is an
end that is in some way—possibly a very broad way—good for the system in question. So it is with an organization: its goals are or are supposed to be good for it. It follows that assigning a goal to an organization
is more than merely a matter of describing it; it has evaluative content.
But is there any reason for assuming that a corporation is the sort of thing
that can have goals? Yes, goals and more besides.

2. THE ORGANIZATION AS A RATIONAL BEING

There is a tradition, going back at least to Plato, of comparing a collective with a person. Organizations plan (and so presumably deliberate and have objectives); they do things for reasons; they have values; and so on. The primary accountability of senior management is to ask the question, "Where are we going?" on behalf of the organization, and then to answer it with a statement of corporate intention. The permanent answer to that question, analogous to the individual's conception of a good life, is the mission of the organization. The organization's objectives are its intentions. The organization's values are expressed in its mission and its policies, and in its culture.

Organizations do not merely adapt to their environments. They are often capable of forgoing an opportunity in favor of a later and better opportunity, using indirection, and actively searching for new opportunities and techniques. In those respects they go beyond the biological mechanism of adaptation.[2] Granted, as Hayes and Abernathy (1980) lament, some organizations cannot choose among possible as opposed to actual options and are therefore incapable of undertaking long-term strategies that involve short-term sacrifice. Still a good many evidently can, sometimes through the corporate equivalent of the kind of desires management discussed in chapter 4.

A highly rational management is capable of taking players in the environment to think, perceive, and intend rationally. Even the effects of the strongest constraints on the stakeholders are to some degree filtered through perception, which in turn is affected by intention. Here too the stakeholders' state of corporate mind may be, depending on the circumstances, more or less important to one's own strategy. I claimed in chapter 4 that it is an elevated form of rationality to be able to deal with an environment that you know itself reacts rationally to your strategy, though game theory shows us that in some such cases there is no unique rational way to act. So for organizations in environments with which it is possible to deal rationally: there stakeholders are an irreducible part of strategy. (Freeman [1984] gives an extended exposition and defense of the view that strategy is essentially about stakeholders, who have their own agendas, which preclude one's own confident predictions.)

There is an obvious objection to all this, however. When we say that an organization can plan, are we not using language metaphorically? Isn't it people who plan? Can't we rephrase talk about an organization planning or deliberating or having values into talk about individuals who really do all this? Are we not taking a metaphor too literally?

We are not. To begin with, if what I have said about mental events and states is true, they are not entities that reside in some immaterial space that ensouled beings like people have and organizations do not. They are postulates of a theory that explains what we can observe.[3] If they are not themselves unproblematically observable, they are in good company.

It is a mistake to say that corporate planning is reducible to a group of individuals making a joint decision. If anything, it is the other way around: what these individuals are doing would not be planning if they were not employees of the corporation. Their position in the organization and the legal, institutional, and conventional contexts that give that position its status are what make their activity planning. You and I cannot do corporate planning for Exxon for the same reason we cannot declare war on Canada on behalf of Norway. And note: no one can simply observe the difference between what a corporate planner at Exxon does and what I do, given that the former but not the latter constitutes planning.

It is in any case possible for an organization to act rationally even if its managers are irrational, if its structure and systems are designed so that selfish acts lead to the achievement of corporate ends somewhat as Adam Smith claims they lead to general welfare in society as a whole. That is what makes the art of organization design a challenge, but sometimes rewarding.

In a reductionist mood, wary of attributing rationality to an organization, you might call it a legal fiction and thereby suggest that it is not "out there," in Morgan's words, whereas a tree is. But in the same sense a marriage is a legal fiction; so is an inauguration, or a sentence of death, or cashing a check. These "fictions" have consequences because they are sanctioned by the very real power of the law and convention. Organizations have consequences by virtue not only of statutory law but also of other institutions and practices, some of them informal or even unconscious. Surely we would not say that a dollar bill is "really" just a piece of paper rather than a medium of exchange.

To some extent many things are what they are by virtue of how we agree, formally or informally, to treat them. Everything we can deal with and talk about is essentially connected with a social context. Marriage and money are examples of highly institutionalized entities. A baseball less so, but it would not be a baseball unless there were the game. Something is a chair because there is a practice of sitting on it and things of its kind.

Chapters 3 and 4 suggest how much of what characterizes people is based on conventions and institutions: rights, language, imposed roles, and less formal treatment that shapes one's personality and view of the world. The boundaries around everything we know, even about our own mental states, are drawn in the public forum.

This is emphatically not an argument for believe-what-you-like subjectivism. To note the importance of convention is not to be a subjectivist. For one thing, some conventions and institutions are more readily acceptable than others. We have no problem in calling a piece of paper money or a wooden object a chair, because the convention does not place demands on our credulity. But your views about religion might be such that you would resist calling a dissident statement heresy, or you might refuse to accept a convention that sanctioned ghosts. The second reason it is not a subjectivist argument is that there really is money because people really do spend it. It is wrong to call something a fiction just because in different circumstances it might have had some different (probably relational) properties or might not have existed at all.

The important point here is that in talking about organizations we should not stigmatize them or any of their properties as fictions because they depend on conventional or institutional arrangements. Nor, for that matter, should we suppose that we can always identify what any entity is in itself as opposed to what social practice makes it.

From a narrow materialist point of view, an individual's decision is a sequence of events in the brain; but what makes those events a decision is that they play a causal role in the economy of the person and that that role is defined by reference to a whole complex of linguistic and other social practices—as are all mental events, by my account. From a similarly minimalist point of view, an organization's strategic decision is a group of people in suits coming to an agreement; but that is not the same as saying that that decision is nothing more than the decisions of individuals. What makes this event a corporate decision is that it is done according to law and corporate rules and other criteria and that it can be expected to have certain consequences for employees and other stakeholders of the corporation.

A corporate decision is a decision in virtue of its context. So is an individual's decision. Each is real and effective. But the analogy goes still deeper.

Decision making is an essential activity for an organization, for several reasons. If there were no organizational decisions, there would be no organization. What makes an organization the same organization from one time to the next—aside from what the law says about charters and so on—is the continuity of policy and mission. The organization's ends make it what it is.

The standard case of organizational decision and organizational identity is one in which management decides everything in advance in full view of all pertinent facts and a clear understanding of the organization's policy and mission, and it happens just that way. Actual cases may be different. Management often has a rough idea of the facts, a warped notion of policy and mission, or tenuous authority over the employees. As Mintzberg (1978 and, with Waters, 1985) shows, a successful strategy may be emergent rather than the result of deliberation.

Decision making is an essential activity for a person, for similar reasons. If there were no individual decisions, there would be no person. What makes a person the same person from one time to the next—aside from what the law says about brain death and so on—is the continuity of values and intentions.

The standard case of individual decision and personal identity is one in which the agent decides everything in advance in full view of all pertinent facts and a clear understanding of values and intentions, and it happens just that way. Actual cases may be different. The agent often has a rough idea of the facts, a warped notion of values and intentions, or a weak will or inadequate resources. As March (1976 and 1978) shows, reasonable behavior may be emergent rather than the result of deliberation.

3. PROBLEMS WITH THE ANALOGY

Even if organizations can make decisions and perform other such actions, it does not follow that organizations and individuals are alike in all other important ways. In fact, the implicit analogy is a problematical one, particularly where it causes the user to ignore important disanalogies, including some of moral significance.

The analogy can lead to two bad mistakes: one can overestimate the ability of the organization to impose its will on the future, and one can miss the importance of events below the top management level by ignoring them as random or insignificant noise. Some organizations resemble arenas of political conflict more than rational men writ large. (See Fischer [1986], among many others.)

Even where they do not, there is something sinister about the idea that the values of the individuals within the organization should be subordinated to those of the organization itself.

We know how to impute intentions to other people, and to ourselves; we could do neither without being able to do the other. When we do impute intentions to agents, with or without the help of commentary by the agents themselves, our attributions have the uncertainty characteristic of interpretation of either language or behavior. There is not always an observable difference between failing to do A and succeeding in doing B. This is not fatal, but it does show the need to interpret, at least to the extent of taking account of the context of the behavior, and it illustrates again the tenuousness of claims about observability and operationalizability. Similarly, whether an organization has been effective or not is a question that calls for some evaluation; but in spite of some questionable cases, we can often identify clear instances of effective and ineffective operation.

Now although intention is a more complex concept than goal-directedness, as we indicated in chapter 4, it may be easier to attribute when the agent can often provide evidence by stating what the intention is. Similarly, the management can state what the corporate policy or strategy is. The authoritativeness of such reports is limited, however. Some agents are not very good at carrying out their intentions. Organizations too can be neurotic, in the sense that management habitually can have poor control over what actually happens after policy or strategy is made. (And in other senses as well; see Kets de Vries and Miller [1984a, 1984b, 1986] on the causal relations between the personality of the chief executive and that of the organization.) An organization's actual as opposed to its claimed objectives are not necessarily what top management decides. In order for objectives to be genuine rather than mere inscriptions in a slick binder, they must have the requisite support within the organization. In most large organizations implementation of planning is an elaborate process of building political support, rather than just telling everybody exactly what to do. (See Quinn [1980] for an exposition of this familiar point.)

Increasingly turbulent environments and independent-minded middle managers will be less amenable to having strategies thrust upon them. This limitation on corporate "rationality" is a counterpart of what the rational person faces. Few of us have the self-control or the control of the environment required to carry out our best-laid plans. But then carrying out one's best-laid plans is not the only way to be rational, as we noted in chapter 4 that Simon, March, and others have argued. Having a clear understanding of coherent ultimate objectives is enough for saints only, and does sinners less good. For individuals and for organizations, the implementation process overlaps with the process of setting goals. Implementation problems may show certain goals to be more trouble than they are worth. Discussing how to reach a goal may stimulate discussion of whether that is the goal we really want to reach, considering the price and the probability of success given the resources available. Nearing or reaching a goal may alter one's attitude towards it. This is neither unusual nor irrational. The March view of how rationality works parallels the Mintzberg-Waters (1985) distinction between strategies formulated in advance and those that appear as a pattern in a stream of decisions. The latter are often perfectly appropriate, even if they fall short of—let us rather say, differ from—rational deliberateness.

So when we address the conceptual problem about individuation of organizations by saying the organization is united by its goals, we confront the very practical problem that the goals do not unreservedly unite everybody, and may not be clear to anybody. The imperfect unity imparted by the goals does not undermine our talk about organizations as entities, for the imperfection is mirrored in the case of the person; but it does show looseness in the concept.

The greatest disanalogy between the intending person and the intending corporation is that the latter comprises persons who have intentions, values, and rights of their own. To subordinate employees' interests to those of the whole organization is not automatically immoral, but it raises some hard issues. Silverman (1971) and others, including Marxists, see exploitation where employees are pressured to give precedence to the interests of the organization as a whole. An employee may be pressured to respond to an obligation beyond any implicit or explicit contract by an appeal to a claim on a firm's employees rather like a nation's claim on its citizens. Or the organization may work on the employee by changing his or her preferences. This is not always a bad thing, but it is morally risky. We discuss it further in section 5, under the heading of corporate culture.

It is very important to understand that these moral issues are little affected by whether organizations have intentions, rights, and obligations. The chief executive is obligated to take into account fiduciary responsibilities of the office along with his or her own personal values in determining what the organization is to do. The executive may therefore make decisions that he or she would not make if there were no duty to consider position-related objectives and responsibilities. But this does not reduce the executive's moral liability for the decisions. Nor does the existence of rationality and values of the organization in itself necessarily abnegate or even reduce those of the employees.

4. RATIONALITY AND DELIBERATION

Most of the complications about rationality in the case of individuals have a counterpart in the case of organizations. Some organizations are in effect neurotic in the same way individual people are neurotic. Even successful companies do not always know where they are going, for the environment may require opportunistic, flexible guerrilla warfare rather than set-piece battles with elaborately defined tactics. In such cases not only means but ends as well may change as opportunities arise. Does this make deliberation hopeless? The question sounds like a profound philosophical one; and while we should now be wary of the temptation to cut the issue down to practical size, we can at least address some of the more practical aspects of it by considering some facts about the environment.

For organizations the problem of free will boils down the practical issue of how to plan and organize given top management's ability to control what happens in the organization and to deal with what happens outside. Organization and planning theorists (see Thompson [1967], for example) address that problem as they develop theories about the value of planning given certain environmental, technological, and other forces.

We can set up a rough hierarchy of forms of organization theory that differ according to the extent to which the organization can "proactively" create its future:

Population ecology in its simplest form is the view that adaptive organizations survive and maladaptive ones do not.

Resource dependence (associated primarily with Pfeffer and Salancik [1978]) postulates variables intervening between organizations and environments that give maladaptive organizations the opportunity to shape up—for example, by doing something about resources—rather than ship out. Resource dependence, a functional theory, shows not only that the organization adapts to its environment but also that there is a feedback mechanism linking the environment to the organization, hence an answer to the question, "How does the environment make the organization adjust?" This theory considers the organization a system; it is a version of structural-functional theory.

Structural-functional theory is not quite a theory. It takes the view that different structures lead to success in different situations, that it is the task of managers to determine the most appropriate structure and put it in place, and that it is the task of organization theorists to determine how that is to be done. This approach is neutral on the details of how an organization adapts, and is on that account sometimes criticized for not taking account of political power or whatever critics think the salient mechanism is. But there is nothing inherent in that approach to keep a structural-functional theorist from discussing the salient mechanisms.

Strategic choice theories, and theories generally that take the notion of strategy seriously, characteristically hold that the organization is a rational entity that can create its future by deliberating and making decisions calculated to achieve its objectives. The organization has free will.

The critical issue here is not which of these approaches is correct. Arguments on just that point rival for futility arguments about whether the house collapsed because it was too weak or because the wind was too strong. What is crucial is to determine in what circumstances which approach is closer to the mark. Lawrence (1981) points out that different combinations of resource scarcity and unavailability or complexity of information have significant implications for an organization's autonomy. An environment may be more or less constraining; the internal constraints, and to a lesser extent the external ones, may be susceptible to the manager's will, which may depend on whether the manager believes the constraints can be affected, as Weick (1987) indicates. It is wrong to believe that the environment cannot be profoundly affected by the organization, equally wrong to suppose the environment is passive in dealing with it. (See Pfeffer [1982, 157ff.].) Both Lawrence and Weick suggest that the right questions about how the organization deals with the environment are specific ones having to do with what makes an organization able to be proactive, and how much of that is within the organization's control. These are difficult questions, but not profound conceptual ones.

In considering explanatory options, however, one must take into account some points that are not straightforwardly empirical. It is very important, for example, that managers see why they should not hastily embrace a theory about the relation between organization and environment that takes the two to be related as dependent and independent variable. The danger here is not a result merely of the kind of strategizing of which humans are capable. Two biologists' (Levins and Lewontin, 1985) discussion of ecology raises questions about theories that make assumptions about the influence of the environment as well as about what discoveries of correlation mean and how they can badly mislead theorists. Levins and Lewontin argue that it may be radically misleading to adopt the standard statistical approach, which looks to environmental factors surrounding a species for main effects with relative weights. The significance of these factors depends on the relationships of these species to other species, and those relationships may be too complex to be captured by standard methods.

For example, a certain kind of harvester ant lives between the eighteen-inch and twenty-four-inch rainfall lines, where the temperature is usually above fifty degrees Celsius. To explain this fact by invoking a statistical correlation would miss some things. To name one, the temperature is usually too high for the ant to forage; if it were lower, life would be easier for the ant—except that it would also be tolerable for the fire ant, a fierce predator who would then wipe out the harvester ant. Aridity too makes life hard for the harvester ant, but also makes plants' seeds less prone to spoil and thus more storable.

Consider also, as Levins and Lewontin do, the relationship between predator and prey. As prey increases, all other things being equal, predators increase. But as predators increase, all other things being equal, prey decreases. Over time there is a spiral situation between the two. Predators follow prey in increase, then in decrease, then in increase, and so on. Depending on where the two populations are in the historical cycle, their numbers may be positively or negatively correlated. The correlation between a pair of variables even in a very simple ecosystem depends at the least on the structure of the system, its history, and the duration of the observation. In these circumstances it is too easy to find a correlation that looks as though it leads to the correct causal story but really does not. It is too easy also to find some factors and assign them weights as if they were independent causes, and to ignore properties of complex wholes and interactions among the parts as random noise. The result is an oversimple theory about how harvester ants thrive in a certain temperature band, and a worse theory about how an increase in prey causes an increase in predators.[4]

Some companies, like harvester ants, can thrive only in environments that are hard for them but hard enough to discourage their competition even more. The predator-prey model could apply to certain new markets for highly specialized products bought once and not replaced for a long time. In many situations causal factors do not have the independence implicit in the use of standard weighting techniques. Managers who think they do may find themselves in the position of harvester ants in a nice cool place: it looks good until the fire ants find out about it. But managers, unlike ants, can often anticipate and thereby avoid the consequencs of taking a position advantageous in the short run but disastrous in the end.

Understanding possible complex relationships of this sort is required for anyone who wants to determine the extent to which and the ways in which the organization can impose its will on the environment—for example, by choosing an environment and adapting not only one's strategies but one's objectives to it—as well as the other way around. As in the case of an individual's free will, this is not a purely philosophical issue.

The organization's will is not, however, always to be identified with that of management. Our understanding of an individual's values and objectives and behavior in pursuit of them can be enhanced by study of his or her style of living and dealing with relative ephemera. In much the same way, we better understand an organization's design and implementation of strategy if we understand its culture, which is the repository of the values that guide the way it operates. When the values that guide the choice of objectives really are nothing more than those of top management and have nothing to do with the organization's culture, they will not be effective, and ineffective values negate free will—that is, they undermine the strategic management of the organization.

5. CORPORATE VALUES AND CORPORATE CULTURES

Sathe's (1985) definition of culture as "the set of important assumptions (often unstated) that members of a community share in common" is a standard one. The community of interest to us is the organization. What makes the assumptions important enough to be cultural ones is not only that they have something to do with the success of the organization and the quality of life within it, but also that they strongly affect the way people in the culture think.

Schein (1985) proposes a tripartite division of culture: its first level is behavior and other observable "artifacts"; the second is what people say in describing, explaining, and justifying what they do and what they produce; the third is people's assumptions, including values. (The second level is the subject of section 7, below.) The first covers what sociologists call social structure; the third is culture in the sense we shall use. Social structure and its components are relatively observable; culture is postulated as a causal basis of the observable aggregate behavior.

There is a parallel between social structure and culture on the one hand and behavior and mental or psychological entities on the other. Chapter 3 argued that our commonsense view of the world believes in mental entities as a causal basis of the relatively observable behavior of individuals. Psychology systematizes common sense into a theory by postulating its own kind of event, which largely overlaps and elaborates on the offerings of common sense, to explain behavior. Corporate culture, a relatively unobservable entity whose variants are not defined very sharply, is perceived and defined through its effects on behavior in this way: it affects how independently people work, and the intensity with which they work; what priorities they act on; how they treat and are treated by the boss; often how they dress, talk, and address each other. Culture is also defined by reference to other states and properties of the organization—strategic ones, for example—to which it is claimed to bear a causal relationship.[6]

A distinctive culture is often said (by Brown [1978] and Weick [1979], for example) to give meaning to the lives of employees and managers. They appear to be claiming that those who work for the company have the sense of participating in an enterprise that is worthwhile as a whole, a good community whose sense of virtue and success is passed on to its participants. So the employees of the much-studied Lincoln Electric Company identify with the company's success and with its reputation as a progressive and ethical but at the same time no-nonsense organization. But culture gives meaning in more senses than that, as I shall argue in the next two sections.

An organization's culture, like an individual's values, is difficult to describe precisely and with confidence. The influence of both on human behavior is filtered through many other factors; neither is always fully coherent, and there may be some dissonance between language and the behavior it describes. Can we call a particular culture intensely work-oriented if most people work very hard but those who do not seem to suffer no sanctions? How consistent and widespread must a form of behavior be in order to qualify as essential to the culture of the organization? How much deviation from the norms is permitted before we are prepared to say the norms do not exist? There is no firm answer.

In chapter 2 I noted that some consultants and scholars prefer to deal with management climate, which operationalizes culture in terms of management opinions. Gordon and Cummins (1979) take a position on climate that resembles that of Rokeach (1973) on values, though the former's position is more explicit. An organization's climate by definition reduces to managers' perceptions of the company's vitality, openness, generosity, and so on. It is easy, too, to see the management climate of a particular organization as being more or less pervasive and consistent. When managers are asked questions about climate, their responses cluster in certain ways or do not. Embracing climate in preference to culture has all the advantages of embracing behaviorism as an analysis of the mental. Disadvantages may appear when one ventures beyond diagnosis to try to fix what is wrong with the organization, not just the symptoms.

6. CULTURE AND INDIVIDUALS' VALUES

It is important not to assume that organizational culture is essentially about what the individuals in the organization value. Sathe's standard account of corporate culture somewhat misleads in claiming (1985, 12) that it is a matter of what people really value, as opposed to what they espouse. The values in force are not necessarily those of the individuals doing the acting; they are rather the values that the individuals accept as attaching to their roles in the organization. (Recall the argument in section 2 that rational managers may make an organization rational, but that the organization is itself then rational.) Individuals in a strong culture may swallow hard and play by rules they do not much like, for some of the same reasons good citizens have for obeying laws they regard as foolish, even if failure to comply is not unsafe. In accepting these assumptions and values, individuals may be buying into a culture that is not as they would like it to be. The assumptions and values may not be held consciously; individuals do not always think through the implications of the role-related values that drive their actions.

In many organizations there is tension between culture and people's private views and aspirations. DiTomaso (1987), following Parsons, argues that in a strong culture people must take for granted prevailing norms that would not survive close examination from the point of view of self-interest. If this is true, then organizational values are not only not reducible to people's values but potentially antithetical to them. A strong culture may be a means of managerial control that undermines free will and exploits people by rendering their own values ineffectual in generating their behavior.[7]

If this does not sound plausible to you, consider the Zimbardo experiment mentioned in chapter 4. The outcome of the prison simulation showed the extent to which individuals can voluntarily yield their personal values to those in charge—unless, as seems implausible, they set great value on obedience. The artificial culture Zimbardo generated did not originate with the participants, nor did it represent what they valued in any ordinary sense; but they accepted it, and it did not take long. Here is strong evidence for the distinction between personal values and corporate culture, and the latter's potential for overriding the former.

Paradoxically and very significantly, a culture may fulfill the employees' interests by overriding them. In claiming that an aggregate of individuals acting on self-interest will generate a Hobbesian war of all against all, DiTomaso seems to be assuming, what is probably true in most organizations, that there is no stable solution (in game-theoretic terms) to the problem of meeting the desires of each individual. But by imposing certain rules that might seem oppressive in themselves, a culture may do what a good government does: it may force interdependent or cooperative action that would not be possible if each agent were unconfident of the others' cooperativeness.[8] DiTomaso suggests that a culture works best when the individuals in it do not know they are being guided away from pursuit of their own individual interests. It would be useful to determine under what circumstances individuals will accept a culture that they are aware imposes a stable and broadly advantageous solution that each individual's separate calculation of self-interest could not achieve. But since building such a culture depends on management being highly skilled and having the employees' full confidence, it would seem risky for management to disguise its tactics in imposing a solution.

From all this it follows that a strong culture never merely aggregates individual preferences: it transforms them, in one of two senses. It may transform them in a weak sense, making the consequences of apparently narrowly self-interested behavior unacceptable—or in a strong sense, by causing people to consider the good of all the people in the organization as itself an object of personal desire. Neither transformation need involve a contravention of the interests of the most ardent egoist, but either could amount to exploitation. The distinction has something to do with whether the employees know what is being done to them and whether they can do anything about it. Clearly, a strong culture may either reduce the employees' free will or, in a few cases, enhance it.

Whether an organization can have interests of its own is a more difficult issue, since there is reason to deny that organizations as entities have any moral standing. Often, managers who invoke "corporate interests" to justify actions that are not in the best interests of employees are acting primarily in their own interests. Managers who fend off takeovers that would improve the company but put their jobs at risk, thus putting their personal interests above corporate interests, appear to be traducing their fiduciary responsibilities. One might argue that corporate interests are those of the stockholders, but that is not compelling. When an organization plans for the distant future, as some oil companies do, it is undertaking actions that most current stockholders will not live to see.[9] Certain interests attach to people insofar as they have certain relations to the corporation, as responsibilities attach to individuals by virtue of their positions in the organization. By virtue of something akin to patriotism, one may identify with the organization's success. In that case, more common in Japan but not unknown in this country, it is individuals who have responsibilities and interests, but the collective entity is an irreducible factor in the attribution of them. (For a thorough argument see French [1984]).

Now although corporate culture is not the aggregate of individuals' desires, the view at the opposite extreme, that corporate culture is just the principles of behavior that management requires of people in the organization, is false too. Culture is internalized to the extent that it guides even unscrutinized behavior. It gives people in the organization some reason, not wholly extrinsic, to behave as they do. Making people obey rules that they have not internalized is not building a culture. As the analogy of patriotism suggests, even scoundrels take refuge in organizational values.

Consider a lawyer who defends a client who is evidently guilty. The usual justification is what ethicists call rule-utilitarian: it's a dirty job, but somebody's got to do it because there has to be a consistent practice of lawyers doing this sort of thing in circumstances of this sort, for the sake of the long-term good of the greatest number. But the feeling of moral discomfort as one brings to bear all one's skill to achieve an unjust verdict is not always assuaged by what appear to be rule-utilitarian considerations but may be shared self-interest thinly disguised as ethics. (See Abbott [1983].) The principle is effective, but the professional neither wholly internalizes the principle nor feels literally compelled to follow it.

7. THE SECOND LEVEL OF CULTURE: LANGUAGE

As mentioned earlier, Sathe, Schein, and others think of culture as having three levels. The first level is observable social structure; the third level is culture strictly speaking. The second level of culture is linguistic. Adopting a language entails some commitment on the issue of how to view the world, for meaning is inextricable from substantive commitment on facts. Note the implications of having words like *space-time* or *heresy* in your vocabulary.[10] Adopting a language also requires enough rationality to speak—hence think—coherently.

People within a linguistic community share a language (by definition), hence some concepts, hence some beliefs. Among the beliefs they share are beliefs about what concepts mean—that is, how they connect, logi- cally and causally, with other concepts. For in order to communicate, people must come to some fundamental agreements about which infer- ences are to be permitted and which are not. They must share standards of justification of words and actions, and these are not mere linguistic standards.[11]

A linguistic community requires only a limited consensus on the facts and on what is reasonable. Beyond what it requires, however, it does en- courage uniformity; so we can expect that within a linguistic community the area of agreement on what is the case and what is reasonable will nor- mally be broader than what the very existence of the community requires. Insofar as that happens, we have what amounts to not only a linguistic community but a culture. The symbols characteristic of a culture go be- yond linguistic ones; the shared beliefs go beyond what is needed for clear communication; the shared values go beyond the rules of inference embedded in the common language. So with corporate cultures. But at the core of the culture is its language.

Suppose that, knowing nothing of baseball or any other team sport, you came upon two baseball teams playing a game. You would not under- stand what they were doing, and would not much increase your under- standing by trying to describe their behavior in as neutral and noncommittal a vocabulary (behavioristic, perhaps) as you could. You would need to understand the significance of the players' action in this sense: you would need to know what counted as a base hit, a run, an out, an inning, and so on. Not only would you need to have these concepts yourself, you would need to attribute them to the players. For the players do not merely act according to the rules as some natural phenomenon obeys the laws of nature: they follow them in a way they could not if they did not undertand them. So you acquire the vocabulary, as the players themselves did, in the course of understanding the game, its rules, and its point.

This is part of how culture gives people meaning. It provides not only something to identify with and strive for, but also a context, somewhat like the rules of baseball, that gives significance to people's words and acts. Just as people who speak a common language do so by assigning a common meaning to certain noises and inscriptions generated under cer- tain circumstances, so people who share a culture tend to interpret certain behavior similarly. Baseball's rules make a certain set of bodily movements a successful pickoff play; in the same way, the rules defining a corporate culture make a certain way of addressing one's subordinate a low-priority order, or a certain way of responding to a policy an act of flagrant insubordination. In the case of baseball the rules generate a vocabulary for describing the action: triple, cutoff, balk. So in the case of religion: blasphemy, sacrament. So in the case of a society: insult, gaffe. So, less distinctively and uniquely, in the case of an organization: comptroller, black eye, innovation. (One organization's innovation is another's insubordination. On such matters the rules of conduct inform the rules of language.)

Observation is not theoretically noncommittal; hearing what a person says is even less so. To characterize a noise as an act of speech is to bring to bear a language, hence a complex set of rules and practices. To characterize it as a directive or an offer or a commitment is to presuppose still more that lies beyond the range of immediate observation.

The characterization of the organization as a system of shared meaning is supported by what we are discussing here. Organizations are under control partly because participants take on a language and a way of viewing events, at least those that affect the organization. Understanding the language and the behavior in the organization requires knowing the rules that embody that organization's culture. Those are not as different from the usages of everyday intercourse as are the rules of baseball, but understanding them usually aids in understanding the participants' behavior and language, for they much affect what people believe and what they think rational.

The employees' vocabulary is a social product, and it influences and sets limits on how they understand themselves and others. Whether or not it is helpful to say that their world is socially constructed, as scholars like Berger and Luckmann (1967) have argued, these employees could not talk and think and react the way they do without the concepts they learned and continue to sharpen in the public forum. As chapter 3 argued, it is in this way that people learn the basic concepts that we share: size, color; pain, embarrassment; and since learning the concepts is not wholly distinguishable from learning what they apply to, one acquires opinions as well. Different social milieus may lead us to react differently, to find different events humorous, threatening, insulting. The environment of the English working class has its effect, as does the work environment of a particular English company, on how individuals react when they are faced with the loss of a tea break.

If organization theorists are to explain, predict, and help control behavior, they often need to understand the individual organization's environment. Often, too, a significant degree of interpretation is required.

8. INTERPRETATION AS ESSENTIAL TO THE SOCIAL SCIENCES

Since organization theory and other kinds of theory in the social sciences involve people, we have to deal with some complications not found elsewhere. In determining the effects of certain events and states on people, and vice versa, we must at the very least take into account how they perceive and intend. If workers do not notice a change in their working conditions, or if they decide it is all for the best, the change will have little effect. How they perceive and react to the change will play a large role in determining its results. Now a theory that covered workers' perceptions and intentions would be a psychological theory, with all the attendant difficulties; but, in some ways to be discussed now, it would be something more as well.

Consider again the English workers who rebelled when they lost their tea break. An explanation of the workers' behavior would have to answer questions like, What does the elimination of the tea break mean to them? How important do they take it to be? But a thorough psychological explanation of a complex event may involve discovering or postulating states and events in the social realm: possible effects of past experience and training, social and economic class, corporate culture and custom, expectations about the owner and about owners in general, and many other factors that do not fall within the usual purview of the organization theorist or psychologist. All this may be part of the *interpretation* of the workers' behavior—a form of explanation that takes into account the agents' shared view of the situation, motivation, and therefore beliefs and rationality. In fact, it may involve attributing interpretation to the workers themselves, who will probably try to understand the owner's behavior.

The task is a complex one, but interpretation is more difficult in some cases than in others. If the interpreter shares the workers' attitudes, then there will be no difficulty at all in seeing that the workers have certain attitudes and perceptions. The danger there is that the interpreter will take these attitudes and perceptions for granted in precisely the way behaviorists take for granted that the monkey sees the light and wants a banana. (You can see that even a behaviorist does a little interpretation. It is hard to escape.) Where the interpreter understands these attitudes and perceptions and knows how they operate in various circumstances, there are no special problems about explaining the workers' behavior.

Where the culture in question is alien to the interpreter, however, the task is more difficult. Then one can know little and assume less about how the subjects perceive and what meaning they put on events. Hermeneutics is the scare-word for the most intricate kind of interpretation, where the subjects' view of the world is so different from the interpreter's that it would be difficult for them to communicate about it. Hence some recent exponents of hermeneutics have been anthropologists.[12] These take their task to be the understanding of aggregate and individual behavior of a social group by reference to their common expectations and common understanding of the significance of certain crucial words, events, and facts. The star example of this sort of interpretation is Geertz's (1979) explanation of the institution of cock-fighting in Bali. Certain customs, actions, and motives made sense to the outsider only when Geertz showed how they looked to the insider by explicating their context of practices and expectations.

We cannot rely solely on what the subjects of interpretation say about why they behave the way they do. When Geertz talked to Balinese men who owned fighting cocks, they did not and could not volunteer the crucial information about why they took the practice so seriously or why its rules were made as they were: much of it had to be inferred. To a lesser extent the same is true of the English workers. Their account is a part of the evidence, but it must be supplemented by an awareness of some facets of the situation that they did not mention, either because they were unaware of them or because they took them for granted.

We are unlikely to find universal laws relating social or organizational structure to culture. But it may be possible to construct a sort of mini-theory based on motivation for people within a culture. Recall Mohr's (1982) suggestion that for restricted populations we might construct explanations that assume uniform motivation across all inhabitants. Culture permits just that kind of explanation, the more so the more thoroughly institutionalization has sunk in. (I infer support on this point from Zucker [1977].) Managers could profit from universal theories about how employees are motivated; but in the absence of such theories, they can profit from knowledge, based on an interpretive analysis, of how people in a particular culture are likely to be motivated.

Better understanding of an organization, particularly one with an unusual culture, may take the form of "thick descriptions" (one of Geertz's terms) of certain practices in the organization: that is, descriptions that relate events to the cultural context—the rules—and so indicate its meaning in the sense we are discussing. A good case study could illuminate what goes on in an organization by providing a description that indicates some features of the particular cultural context rather than invoking universal principles of organizational behavior.

A large issue between psychology and sociology has been whether collective behavior can be explained by reference to the behavior of individuals in the collective. That issue comes up again in chapter 6. But it is clear that the explanation of individual behavior through interpretation requires an understanding of the rules of the collective that give words and actions their meaning; so we have grounds for saying that psychological explanation makes essential reference to the collective, much as talk about meaningful speech makes reference to collective rules of meaning.[13]

9. INTERPRETATION, LANGUAGE, AND BEHAVIOR

There is one more way in which interpreting behavior is rather like interpreting words. In order to know what Smith intends, we must make some assumptions about what language she is speaking and about whether she is using the words in that language in a standard sense or some other. The best evidence that our interpretation of her words is faulty is that she appears to be making false statements so systematically that we can make better sense of her—that is, regard her as rational and her words as true—by interpreting her differently. But how do we know she is not extraordinarily irrational or in the grip of a great many beliefs we consider false? There is no way to be absolutely certain. Any evidence is compatible with more than one conclusion, and sometimes different conclusions are equally plausible. So with behavior: in interpreting it one must normally assume that it is to some degree rational and that there is some purpose to it, and one tries to find out what that purpose is. But behavior may be irrational or based on some false belief, or rational by a different set of values and standards of rationality; so one often cannot be sure one has correctly identified the intention with which the act is done.[14]

This should remind us of the claim that explaining someone's reasons for action entails attributing not only beliefs and desires but a measure of rationality, without some amount of which desire could not cause action. If an action is totally unreasonable, there is no basis for considering it intentional. If a statement is totally unreasonable, there is no basis for thinking the speaker means anything by it: in fact, it is hard to see how it is a statement. So to call anything intentional is to call it to some degree reasonable and thus to go beyond description to evaluation. Again the presumption of rationality seems unavoidable.

It follows that any community, including an organization, that shares a language necessarily shares a certain conception of what it is to be rational. Anyone who does not know what a community considers rational will not understand its members when they speak and will have difficulty explaining what they do. Let us not overstate the point: organizations are not exotic cultures. Nor need organization theorists or consultants be anthropologists, but they may learn something about understanding organizations from noting what anthropologists do. This point shows the pervasive importance of the rational model of human behavior, and gives additional sense to the notion that our understanding of reality is socially determined.

This version of the social construction of reality does not deny a reality distinct from what people believe. It is compatible with theories that emphasize the environment's effects on the organization, though it implies that the influence of the environment is mediated by the culture of the organization.

Interpreting may include attributing interpretation. Suppose we try to interpret a situation in which person A utters a string of phonemes and person B responds by walking briskly away. On a subsequent occasion person A utters an indistinguishable string of phonemes, whereupon B strikes A. What makes the two situations different may be that the two strings of phonemes, indistinguishable in themselves, are taken to be sentences in different languages; or the relationship between the two people may be such that what is appropriate behavior in one context is a horrendous gaffe in the other. So the actors behave differently because they interpret differently, and the outside interpreter will need to know their interpretation. The kind of feature a natural scientist is likely to notice in such a case—a feature that can be detected fairly readily by the inspection of the current scene on certain standard assumptions—is not a feature that makes any difference.

If interpretation is so chancy, why do it? Why undertake an activity that makes attributions of indeterminate accuracy and pollutes description with evaluation? Those questions suggest, what is not true, that the decision to take an interpretive point of view is an arbitrary one. In the case of the baseball game, the unfamiliar society, and the organization with a distinctive culture, the good reason is that understanding, prediction, and control are increased by doing so—indeed, in some cases precluded by not doing so. We often have the same reason to try to interpret behavior as we have to try to translate a foreign language. Anyone who tried to understand German by designing a "scientific" theory that bypassed linguistic rules and took sounds as variables would be dismissed as a crank. Some of the same considerations would apply against anyone who would reject in principle the interpretive approach to understanding what goes on in organizations. It is perfectly true that interpretation rests on no sure foundation. But neither organization theory nor any other kind of theory should be a search for sure foundations of knowledge.

NOTES

1. This argument accords with Donaldson's (1985) defense of what he calls traditional organization theory, or the design tradition, or structural-functionalism, or the contingency approach. Recall that the term *contingency approach* is more frequently used differently, to refer to the use of local theories rather than global ones.

    We should not be taken in by any argument that seems to rest covertly—as I suspect Weick's does—on the view that there is something contradictory about an organization (or anything else) being unitary in space and time while its component parts are multiple at any given time and change from one time to another. Still less does reifying organizations or anything else imply that their components do not exist. (Recall the last section of the previous chapter on spatio-temporal continuity.)

2. See Elster (1984), chapter 1. Among other services, he undermines various economists' attempts (e.g., that of David [1975]) to reduce the search process characteristic of rational beings to something like the process of natural selection. For one thing, he notes, the former requires short-term sacrifices for long-term advantage.

3. To put it crudely, whatever consistently acts as if it had a mind has a mind; so much was suggested in the first section of chapter 4. That is not a behaviorist position. Properly elaborated, it is a position that applies to any postulate. Of course there is an immensely difficult and morally significant problem about what counts as acting as though one had a mind.

    In order to state whether something has a mind it is not necessary to know the causal basis of the activity that constitutes its candidacy for having a mind, whether the entity in question is an individual or an organization.

124 CONCEPTUAL FOUNDATIONS OF ORGANIZATION THEORY

4. Roberts et al. (1978) make some similar points about postulating causes in organization theory; see especially their chapter 5. The problems in deriving explanations from correlations make what Mohr (1982) calls process explanations look all the more attractive.

5. This and following sections are not meant to exhaust or even fairly to summarize the rich topic of corporate—or, more precisely, organizational—culture. As will be clear, I am interested primarily in the cognitive aspects of culture. I do not spend much time on organizational symbolism, for example. The Pondy, Frost, Morgan, and Dandridge anthology (1983) goes into those issues and others, including the ones I discuss in this chapter.

6. Insofar as culture is the repository of collective values, which govern not only the style of work within the organization but also long-term objectives, there is reason for saying that culture unifies the organization somewhat as the mind unifies the person. The coherence and pervasiveness of the culture are matters of degree; so is the unity of the person. No one's values and long-term desires are wholly consistent; but as I argued in chapter 4, a significant level of consistency is a necessary condition of personal identity.

7. Zucker (1977, 1983) and Meyer and Rowan (1977) claim that greater institutionalization—that is, standardization of behavior and language—correlates with reduced effectiveness of the individual's reasons for action (and other states as well, including structural ones) as causal bases of behavior. A company with a tradition might have a powerful culture that most managers accept while at the same time not personally identifying with it. Some religious organizations, fraternities, and not a few universities are that way.

By an argument parallel to one in chapter 4, section 4c, we can raise questions about whether these experiments prove what the experimenters claim they prove. In this case, however, no other plausible interpretation is available.

8. Elster (1984, 1985) and Sen (1973, 1974) discuss how a government may provide a stable solution to an otherwise unstable game. In so doing, they suggest that it is indeed possible for an organization to be both a rational entity and a political arena (contra Pfeffer [1982, chapter 4]). What is needed is a set of political rules that make it in everyone's interest to cooperate in the achievement of the collective. I do not claim it is easy.

9. Managers may claim they are doing such planning in the interests of current stockholders, whose stock would lose value if potential buyers of it had reason to believe that in the long run the company would be dead. But it is not at all clear that that is the reason why real managers do long-term planning.

10. Here is a technical point. The last two sentences give us grounds for calling a belief a mental sentence rather than a mental proposition: a proposition is what synonymous sentences (possibly in different languages) mean. But we have been raising questions about whether sentences in genuinely different languages can be genuinely synonymous.

11. This raises a question notoriously difficult for moralists but recently trouble-
    some for others as well: How do we justify the standards of a community as
    a whole? Can we apply some other community's standards? In Chapter 7 I
    shall argue against the view that there can be no justification at all.
12. See especially Geertz (1983). Gadamer (1976 and 1981) is perhaps the pre-
    eminent modern expositor and practitioner of hermeneutics.
13. These sections bear on the long-lived argument between those who coun-
    tenance organizational climate, which is similar to culture in the sense we
    have been discussing, and those who hold that it is no more than psychologi-
    cal climate, that is, the sum or average of the psychological states of the in-
    dividuals in an organization. (James, Joyce, and Slocum [1988] and Glick
    [1988] represent opposite sides of the argument in a brief exchange.) James
    et al. deny a separate organizational climate largely on operationalist
    grounds. Glick attacks the operationalist grounds for reasons similar to those
    I adduced in chapter 2, and describes organizational climate in part by impli-
    cit reference to interpretation and explicit reference to Geertz.

    Gordon and Cummins define climate operationally, but they avoid the
    problems that beset James et al. by not trying to eliminate organizational cli-
    mate or culture from our vocabulary on operationalist grounds. They just do
    not deal with it.
14. See Quine (1960). The point Mohr makes about any motivation being able
    to cause any action is pertinent here too.

6 REDUCTION AND INCOMPATIBILITY

The immediate issue in this chapter is the claim that organization theory is at some fundamental level really psychology; but our larger target, in this chapter and the next, is what that claim presupposes—namely, the characteristically empiricist view that all sound theories are potentially part of a unified network of theory, and that the mission of science, including organization theory, is to work towards developing that internally consistent body of theory. That view implies that sound theories must all be compatible, and that moreover sound theories about the components of things—for example, psychology—must be related to sound theories about things themselves—for example, theories about organizations—in a way that faithfully reflects the part-whole relationship. It suggests too that, because psychology covers individuals, it is more basic than sociology or any other aggregate-based form of explanation and hence closer to the unvarnished truth, which is the empiricist's Grail.

To anyone who takes this point of view seriously, it is an important question whether sociology and corresponding views of organization theory are reducible to psychology, or whether organizations and other aggregates are "emergent"—that is, in some coherent sense more than the sum of their parts. To focus on this question is to suggest, as empiricists do, that the postulates of psychology are naturally individual events, direct objects of mere observation, whereas in fact there are no nonemergents, no natural and preconventional parts of things. A theory about the parts need not be a part of a theory about the whole. Sometimes theories about parts and theories about wholes are designed to answer the same questions; often not. When they are not, there is no reason to assume they will complement each other in any way.

This chapter attacks the view of organization theory as being basically psychology and the implication that a unified science is possible. Natural scientists, like behavioral ones, must use theories that are incompatible and do not tell the strict truth about the world. In a sense not so different from the one familiar to organization theorists, they sometimes content themselves with local theories.

The first step in the argument is to consider some of the various ways in which apparently different theories may be related.[1]

1. RELATIONS BETWEEN THEORIES

A theory claims that certain lawlike relations hold among things, states, and events of certain kinds. It thereby invites us to think of the world as populated by entities of these kinds, and does not invite us to divide these entities or aggregate them further in the interests of explanation. The entities may have parts or material of a certain sort or may cluster in ways that have consequences beyond what the theory claims. In that case there may be another theory about the parts or the clusters.

There are a number of possible relations between these theories.

1. The second theory may follow logically from the first; or
2. It may follow from the first with the help of natural laws that connect the two theories; or
3. The two theories may be logically compatible but not connected, so that one accepts or rejects them separately and on separate grounds. (This relationship is an interesting one where two theories appear to be incompatible but are in fact answering different questions.)
4. The theories may be compatible, but one of the theories may assume that certain conditions permitted by the other theory never obtain. Or
5. The theories may be incompatible, so that if one of them is true the other is false. Or, finally,
6. The theories may be incommensurable, so that they cannot be compared to see whether they are compatible or not.

To say that organization theory is reducible to psychology is to say that either (1) or, much more likely, (2) from the above list describes the relationship between some theory about organizations and a psychological theory.

In fact, the relationship between a psychological theory and a theory about organizations will usually be a (3), a (4), or a (5), with (4) perhaps the more common case. When organization theorists argue, their dispute is occasionally a (4), but usually a (5), and in some interesting cases a partial (6). In chapter 4 I argued in effect that it is sometimes impossible to distinguish cleanly among (3), (4), and (5). One may not be able to establish whether certain key terms in the two theories are synonymous, with the result that it may not be clear whether the two theories actually contradict or just make distinct claims because the theorists cannot agree on what would count as disconfirming evidence. That is, we cannot say for sure whether they are talking about the same thing. In that case there is an element of (6) in the situation.

Sometimes we make progress in the natural and social sciences by introducing new theories that do not elaborate on old theories but instead replace them. If the new theories recommend themselves by permitting better prediction, explanation, and control, we accept them and abandon the old ones. In some such cases the new theories do not make new claims about old entities but instead (a subtle distinction) postulate new entities. Then we claim not that As are reducible to Bs, but instead that there are no As, only Bs. The old theory and the new one may be just incompatible; so (5) often describes the relationship between them, but occasionally (6) does if the new theory is a sufficiently radical departure from the old.

A number of scholars, most notably Kuhn (1970), have held that (6) is often the relationship between the two bodies of theory; we consider that possibility further in chapter 7. It is the theories in our field that cannot be compared on a common measure that justify talk about paradigm differences in the fullest sense.

Two claims about reduction are of particular interest. The first is that things are in some nontrivial way, probably best captured by (2) above, reducible to their parts. Understand (e.g., predict) the parts and you understand the whole. The second, almost opposite, argument is that some things are what they are in large part by virtue of relations to something else. The first argument sounds more akin to natural science, the second to the behavioral sciences. I mainly support the second, on the grounds that we should believe in and reify and regard as irreducible or only trivially reducible the entities into which a sound theory or some perspicuous vocabulary divides the world.[2]

Theories at the organizational level are not normally arrived at by being built up from combining theories about individuals. We theorize at both levels. The separate theories that result may turn out to overlap, or to complement each other, or to have nothing to do with each other, or to be incompatible. Newton's triumph in finding theories that united terrestrial with celestial phenomena may be a misleading example for organization theorists. How sound theories designed for various levels and kinds of explanation are related is something to be explored in the individual case, rather than assumed.

One way—oversimple and misleading but nicely provocative—to frame an argument about reductionism is to say (or deny) that a thing is more than the sum of its parts.

2. WHOLES AND PARTS

It is plausible to say that a thing just is the sum of its parts; but a thing can persist through time in spite of a gradual but total deterioration and replacement of parts, and what lasts while its parts do not surely cannot be identical with its parts.

If individuals are the parts par excellence of organizations, then psychology is the essence of organization theory. One reason for doubting that organization theory is reducible to psychology, however, is that, as chapter 5 has argued, organizations themselves exist irreducibly: there are statements we can make about organizations that are true irrespective of what is true of their parts, in the sense of (1) or (2). Recall that an organization can be (say) aggressive when there is not an aggressive person in the place.

But one objects: if we can predict what the parts of something—all the things that ever were or will be parts—will do, can we not predict what the whole thing will do? Yes, but that is misleading. Sometimes what some of the parts do depends on their relations to other parts, so that the actions of individual parts cannot be predicted or explained in isolation from the whole thing.

More important, there is no way of determining what the real parts are. It is not clear that individual people are in any privileged sense the parts of organizations. We can divide the world in an infinite variety of ways.

Perhaps the ultimate parts of organizations are not persons but instead parts of bodies, or atoms, or events, groups, roles, or systems.

A theory explains events by picking them out under a certain description. An event fits into and is explained by a theory by virtue of one of the infinite number of descriptions true of it. Any theory privileges certain descriptions because for theoretical purposes states and events are described by those descriptions rather than by any of the other descriptions true of them. Theories similarly privilege certain ways of dividing the world into individuals and the individuals into parts. To undertake to explain the world by explaining its parts is to risk getting things backwards. We do not even know what the parts are until we have found the right theory for explaining the whole.

The fact is, there is not one theory that covers all causal explanation. Even on specific occasions there may not be one theory that is best from every point of view or for every purpose. So, for example, for the purposes of most of our conversations we say there are individual people, because our discourse would be impossible if we did not presuppose individuals' existence. But a biochemist's theory may not recognize individual people.

In any case, the notion that the parts explain the thing suggests, what is clearly false, that reduction is primarily about whether one thing is the same as another thing. Any thing, state, or event will have a number of distinct descriptions. If we are discussing one and only one entity, there may still be questions about the logical relations among the descriptions and explanations of it. As I argued in chapter 3, it is one thing to say that a certain physiological state is identical with a certain mental state; it is quite another to say that psychology is reducible to physiology. A single computer state may be accurately described in programming language or machine language, but the programming language does not permit statements that are the logical equivalent of those in the machine language.

I have used this analogy previously in discussing functional states. Beyond knowing what functions certain subsystems of the system perform, one might want to know how they get there in the first place and in some detail how they work. Answering those questions about computers may lead to discussion of hardware states; in the case of individuals, questions of that sort may lead in the direction of physiology. In the case of organization theory, one might explain an organization's adaptation to its environment, or in some cases its rational and proactive dealings with its environment, by reference to the way it and its subsystems function; but how the organization happens in the first place to develop the structure of subsystems it has is a different matter calling for a different kind of explanation, probably including some psychological explanations of individuals' behavior.

You might object that the computer analogy favors reduction of organization theory to psychology in sense (2); for if you are a computer engineer thoroughly familiar with a computer and the program it is running, and you know its machine-language state, then you know the software state as well, even if a different machine-language state would also be a sufficient condition of that software state. So you do; but in just that sense a computer is not analogous to an organization. For in the latter, an inference of this sort is not possible precisely because an account of where the subsystems came from and how they work is not a wholly psychological account. There are no laws relating how people behave to how the organization as a whole behaves. The former is not a sufficient condition of the latter. The structure of the organization makes a difference too.[3]

Not only that: psychological states are affected by organizational states, and by social states in general. Still more: insofar as they are functional, psychological states are defined by reference to their results, but the description of the results characteristically makes reference to the social context of behavior.

3. COMPOSITION LAWS AND EMERGENCE

A truly hard-nosed nominalist reductionist will claim that any talk about aggregates will have sufficient conditions in talk about the aggregates' components. Collins (981), a sociologist who has no doubt heard a great many objections from colleagues to his unabashed nominalism, comes close to adopting the hard-nosed position[4] in the course of arguing that states, economies, cultures, and classes do not really exist, that they are "only collections of individual people acting in particular kinds of micro-situations" (1988).

For this view he claims the support of empiricism: "Sociological concepts can be made fully empirical only by grounding them in a sample of the typical micro-events that make them up. The implication is that the ultimate empirical validation of sociological statements depends on their microtranslation." (*Ibid.*; italics omitted.)

This argument has at least three problems. The first is that it carries an unacceptable empiricist assumption about the kind of thing one knows primarily: not surprisingly, that kind of thing turns out in Collins's account to be what psychologists and sociologists take as evidence. The implied claim that sociological statements are sound only if they are translatable into statements about the evidence for them is clearly unacceptable. As I argued in chapter 2, evidence—however "micro"—that a thing of some sort exists is no better than the theory in which that sort of thing plays a role. Collins regards "cognitive/emotional processes" as the subject of "direct micro experience" (1981, 986f.). But there is no such thing as direct micro experience.

The second difficulty, the less obvious and more important one, is that his attempt at microtranslation cannot be made out. What goes on in a culture or an organization does not amount merely to the effects of psychological events and of how the people are arranged and aggregated. This problem is related to the first: if Collins had not been taken in by empiricism, he might have seen that psychological theories and many descriptions of individual behavior presuppose an understanding of collectives.

Collins goes on to discuss what he regards as the genuine microevents, which are psychological events. He is not clear on the nature of the rules of "microtranslation," but they must be substantive rather than true by definition in the thinnest sense, and must include reference to relational properties that apply to individuals in groups. If this is what Collins is getting at, then there is precedent for his position in discussion of aggregation in organization theory and reduction in the physical sciences.

Some recent work on organizational climate (for example, Glick [1985]) argues that we cannot draw inferences about climate as a feature of an organization without additional warrant from what we know about climate as a property of the individuals in the organization. Roberts et al. (1978) and Mossholder and Bedeian (1983) argue that the warrant for inference from individual-level to aggregate-level theories must be in "composition laws," which in turn are associated with causal connections from one level to the other. I take Collins to be calling for microtranslation based on such composition laws.

This is the kind of relationship numbered (2) in the first section. Composition laws that link part and whole are a special case of so-called bridge principles, which link one theory to another. The argument about whether one can explain the whole by explaining the parts is a special case of the argument about when one explanation can supplant another by virtue of laws showing what statement is true in one theory given the truth of some statement in the other. When organization theorists argue over the appropriate level of explanation of certain states and events—for example, whether one should be talking about individuals or the organization as a whole—it is worth asking whether any explanation at one level bears a lawlike relation to some explanation at another. The latter argument is a special case, in turn, of the argument about what makes one sort of explanation as good as or better than another.

A standard—though misleadingly simple—example is the reduction of Boyle's Law, which is about temperature and pressure, to certain principles of statistical mechanics. The science of statistical mechanics is about particle velocity; it claims that to increase temperature is to increase particle velocity and that to increase particle velocity is to increase pressure. The bridge principles in this case link statements about temperature to statements about particle velocity. Statistical mechanics is the more basic science, for its statements plus the bridge principles imply but are not implied by all those of the other science. With statistical mechanics and no Boyle's Law one would lose no predictive power.

The relationship between particle velocity and temperature that the bridge principles state is identity; but that the two are identical is an empirical claim. A similar, clearly causal, law relates the ingredients of something to the whole: put copper and zinc into sulfuric acid, and you get electricity. Roughly, the combination of the parts causes some event or state that is impossible if they are not combined. The term *emergence* is often applied to this situation, which happens both in the laboratory and in organizations.

Among the more interesting cases of emergence, from the point of view of the social scientist and the organization theorist, are those in which the component actions are intended but some of the results are not. Schelling (1984) has shown how a group may share some intention and then by joint action in pursuit of it frustrate it. The results of collective intention are shaped by certain regularities more familiar to economists than to moralists. In these instances the individual intentions alone, not the environment, are sufficient for the (unintended) collective intention. But Schelling does not suggest that it is always that way.

Where there is reason to believe there are unknown composition laws, we usually say that something is "in principle" reducible to something else—engineering to physics, for example. But even if it is possible to reduce engineering to physics, whether it is worthwhile to do so is another matter. As noted in chapter 3, we have not stopped training and employing engineers, and organization theorists need not fear the loss of their jobs to psychologists, because they do not do the same jobs.

Even if it were true that adequate composition laws were just laws about organizational structure, and if the point of organization theory were to use those laws, given knowledge of individuals' psychological makeup and the structure of the organization, to predict organizational effectiveness, it would be a mistake to claim that Collins had been vindicated and that organization theory was reducible to psychology because these laws permitted microtranslation from one to the other. For in that case one could still hold that the individual's state of mind makes little difference to organizational outcomes in comparison to environmental states and events, which overwhelm individuals.

Collins does not agree. He argues that what individuals do is first motivated by the individuals themselves. The "'*mechanism*' by which conditions—certain arrangements of microsituations—motivate human actors to behave in certain ways" (1981, 990) comes in at the level of the individual.

". . . All macroconditions have their effects by impinging upon actors' situational motivations. Macro-aggregates of microsituations can provide the context and make up the results of such processes, but the actual energy must be microsituational." (*Ibid.*; italics omitted.)

Although the experiments discussed in chapter 4 proved not as easy to interpret as they might appear, they do seem to provide considerable evidence that macroconditions may impinge upon actors' perceptions, their ability to reason, and their ability to act on what is most important to them, not just on their "situational motivations"—unless by that term Collins is referring to such a breadth of states as to make the point too vague to support his argument.

With his talk about "actual energy" Collins may be trying to argue that a good explanation is one that gets into the details of what goes on. ("Don't tell me about its function; give me a detailed story about how it got there.") Explaining what the components do may not be a sufficient condition of a sound explanation, but it is sometimes a necessary one. But then why, if Collins wants to be a reductionist, does he not go all the way and hold that the most "micro" parts of things—atoms, perhaps—are real? He might answer that atoms are not observable, and that observability is the measure of what is basic. But we know that that answer is inadequate, for it is based on an unsound notion of what observability is and what it proves. One might say that Collins acknowledges that there are emergent entities; but he has not understood that all entities, including entities postulated by physicists, may turn out to be emergent from some point of view.

In short, we have so far found two problems with Collins's view that sociology—and, he would be happy to add, organization theory—is about a quantity of small entities arranged and possibly aggregated in space and time (1981, 1989). First, it rests on an untenable empiricist view of the kind of thing one knows. Second, his only defense against the view that environment is of overwhelming importance in determining behavior is that real causation happens only at the microlevel. But the argument for that seems to be that causality must relate only observables, never theoretical entities. That is hardly plausible.

There is a third argument against Collins, and against the notion that with the right bridge laws added to psychological theories about behavior, you get organization theory. The case is not like the relationship between Boyle's Law and statistical mechanics because psychology is not more basic than sciences that take aggregates as the subject of their investigation. The reason is the same as the reason why individuals uttering sentences are not more basic than languages, why the latter are not mere fictions dependent on the former.

The reduction of Boyle's Law is possible because statistical mechanics requires no reference to Boyle's Law or to any of the states or events it postulates, and it covers much more territory than does Boyle's Law, which is in effect a special case of it. The relationship between psychology and any science that deals with human behavior in the aggregate is not like that. Psychology is not more basic in the required sense because the social and organizational context of behavior to a great degree determines what behavior it is, as our discussion of culture showed. No individual physical movement is by itself a sufficient condition of cashing a check or giving an employee an instruction.

4. THE REDUCIBILITY OF CULTURE

Psychological events are the building blocks of aggregate behavior no more than meaningful words are the building blocks of language.

The James et al. vs. Glick argument (1988) mentioned in chapter 5, note 13 is pertinent to this discussion. Like Collins, those who argue that there is no organizational climate (roughly, culture) other than psychological climate argue from a base of empiricism, even operationalism. I interpret Glick and his allies as defending organizational culture as an irreducible state—connected to no other more basic states or events by any bridge laws—on grounds that apply with similar force against the argument that organizational states generally are nothing more than psychological states. The key to Glick's side of the argument, which is also mine, is the inevitably and irreducibly communal nature of meaning. Much of my argument in Chapter 5, sections 7 and 8 applies here, but it might be useful to make the point in a slightly different way this time.

We sometimes explain behavior in an organization by indicating that there are cultural or linguistic rules people follow. Discovering these rules is not quite like discovering laws that support causal explanations, because people do not always follow the rules. On the other hand, there must be a general practice of following the rules of the culture, or there would be no reason for saying there really are cultural rules in force. Two conclusions follow. First, to claim that these rules exist is not the same as claiming that the people in the organization always act in a certain way. Second, it is sometimes difficult to determine what the rules are, because on some occasions it is impossible to distinguish between succeeding in following rule A and failing to follow rule B.

The reductionist might argue that this shows that there is no good reason to believe there are rules: there is simply behavior, which we should explain by considering the psychological states of the actors. There is no point in postulating a set of rules when there is no way to pin down exactly what they are and when, even if you know them, you do not thereby know what people will do. This argues against postulating organizational climate or culture as anything separate from psychological climate.

There are two similar responses we can make to the reductionists. First, we can point out that their argument works equally well against believing that there is any such (social) phenomenon as language. In consistency they would have to hold that we explain what people say not by translating or by interpreting but by psychological explanations that do not at any point countenance language. This would not be a wholly impossible argument to make: in fact, a remotely similar position is taken by Quine (1960, for example) and others, who argue that the traditional notion of meaning has no explanatory force. But the no-language position seems at best implausible, and the explanatory task they set themselves is an extraordinarily difficult one.

The second response is conclusive. We can point out that the shortcomings of explanation that refer to organizational climate or culture also afflict psychological explanation. As I acknowledged in chapter 3, there are no covering laws linking psychological states, and the concepts are so loosely defined that on a particular occasion it may be impossible to identify a psychological state. We define pain, for example, by reference to its typical but not invariant causes and effects. But James and other reductionists embrace psychological states; so they cannot in consistency attack organizational climate for doing what psychological explanation does too.

The same argument applies against any claim that psychology is the basis of organization theory and that any aggregate-based explanation can be reduced to it by bridge laws.

When Smith signs a contract or cashes a check or gives somebody an order, what makes her action the action it is is the institutional framework. That framework encompasses widely shared understandings and expectations to the effect that certain bodily movements under certain circumstances constitute the action. Without this framework, which makes essential reference to the beliefs of a collective that outlasts today's component individuals, the bodily and psychological events do not constitute the cashing of a check or an order. The institutional framework not only affects and is affected by behavior in extraordinarily complex ways; it also makes the behavior what it is, somewhat as a baseball game makes a certain journey of ninety feet a stolen base.

No explanation that confined itself to psychology could do justice to the ways in which institutional roles and social rules influence behavior and give it meaning. Some statements that relate individuals to collectives (e.g., "Her native language is English") are more important than most statements about them that do not.

The absence of composition laws relating individual to organizational behavior has no implications at all for the legitimacy of either psychology or organization theory. There are microtheories and macrotheories, and there is no necessity that they imply each other or otherwise have anything to do with each other or even that they be compatible. They are ordinarily assessed according to whether they succeed; and if they have different tasks to perform, then the criteria of success will differ.

In some cases the competing theories are incompatible, and in spite of their incompatibility they may both be worth using. How do we determine whether theories are incompatible? And if they are, what are we supposed to do about it? The answer is disappointing: there is finally no general way to proceed in any of these cases. In some cases we cannot determine whether the competitors are incompatible. In some cases there is no sure way to know which theory to use. We have to satisfice—that is, choose a theory that gives most bang for the buck, even though we cannot be sure we are making the right choice even on that criterion.

5. INCOMPATIBLE THEORIES

If, in the manner of empiricists traditionally, you believe that the unification of science is possible, then you will embrace some corollaries of that view. One of them, as the discussion of Collins suggests, is the notion that microtheories are more accurate than macro; the latter may appear to be the cruder approximations. Another, closely similar, is the view that between micro- and macrotheories about the same entities there should be some sort of connection: if they are explaining the same state or event (assuming, what is not always the case, that one can tell whether they are) and are consistent, then one of them should be somehow reducible to the other. If we have a psychological theory that explains what people in an organization do and an organization theory that explains what organizations of this kind do, then it seems intuitively obvious that there should be some lawlike relations among the theories, unless one of them is wrong. But in fact there is no basis for that view. If the theory about the components and the theory about the aggregates are compatible, fine. If they compete, we may or may not finally be able to compare them.

We are no closer to having that unified science than to being perfectly rational. Recall the view, associated with Simon and March, that under normal circumstances attempting to be perfectly rational—not that one could ever precisely define such a state—is not always the best way to be as rational as possible: better to understand one's limitations and manage one's desires realistically. As we talk about consistency among our theories, similar considerations apply. As satisficers we have reason to accept the theories that best suit our actual and possible long-term purposes rather than to hold out for the ones that best replicate the world—as though we could ever find the latter, or know it if we did—or even for perfect consistency among the theories we use.

Recall Friedman's (1953) argument that an economist does not systematically describe what goes on in the world, but rather describes how a model operates and then says the model resembles the world sufficiently closely that explanations and predictions about it adequately explain the world. So, for example, in Friedman's monetarist model interest rates do not affect the demand for M1, whereas in fact there is some small causal relationship between interest rates and the demand for cash. Friedman wants to be taken as saying, not that there is no causal relationship, but that (1) certain accurate predictions are possible if there is no causal relationship, and (2) those predictions are close enough to serve the purposes to which the model is usually put.[5]

Similarly, in some disputes among organization theorists, as for example between needs theorists and those that focus on external factors, we might effect a reconciliation by interpreting each side as saying something like this: take this as your model of what organizations are like, and be prepared to make exceptions in some cases if necessary, since we know organizations are really not exactly like this. The advice from the various sides does not conflict, exactly, for each can be accurate given certain assumptions—hence, for a certain range of application. Even where the theories are related as micro and macro, as for example in the case of psychological theories and aggregate-based ones, there will be situations in which one or the other is more appropriately used. In these cases we are arguing for relationship (4) from the list in section 1, rather than (5).

In some cases the theories do conflict. Some theorists adopt the model of the political arena to explain what goes on in organizations; others claim that an organization is a complex network of explicit and implicit contracts between and among legal persons; others consider the organization an optimizing organism. It is unlikely that these theories can all be true if taken literally. But where this happens, we make our choices among them according to which one approximates this or that area of the world usefully.

When first designing corporate strategy, a manager thinks of the organization as a unified entity. In choosing among strategic options, the manager invokes value considerations that may involve reference to implied contracts with employees. And when considering implementation of a strategy, a manager has reason to think of the need to gather support for the strategy and so considers the organization a political arena. To such a manager the question whether the organization really is a political arena or a network of contracts or a maximizing machine is not worth pausing to consider. Nor should this manager feel required to choose among these models once and for all even if they are incompatible.

The sponsors of needs-based, social information processing, population ecology, and other theories for the most part claim a wider scope for their own theory than the sponsors of the others would allow, and incompatibility results. But a manager can pick one theory or another depending on the problem to be solved. Let the human resources people read Maslow while the people designing the organization read Asch. General managers should read both; and if they have to make a choice about which to believe—that is, whether to improve performance by working on employees' attitudes or by altering their environment—they should choose what is most cost-efficient (including the cost of information) under the circumstances.

Those (like Pfeffer [1982]) who argue that psychological states like needs and deliberation are of little causal importance would deny that there is so little basis for choice between a microtheory and a macrotheory. They would claim that they have shown needs and rational cognitions to play a vanishingly small causal role in a theory that gives good prediction. But I have already argued that experiments designed to prove that point fall short because the partisans on both sides cannot agree on what experimental results would falsify their respective theories. Their theories cannot be lined up against each other and compared.

In any case, whether two competing theories are really incompatible or just applicable under different circumstances, there remains a practical question for which there is no definitive guidance: in a real rather than ideal situation, how does the manager know which theory to use? One can do no better than to use the theory that gives evidence of working best in local circumstances, without being able to decide precisely what its scope of application is. When a theory does not duplicate the world exactly, there is no systematic basis for deciding when to abandon it or how much more accurate to try to make it.

Perfect accuracy is certainly not a reasonable objective. Science is not in the business of explaining or even taking note of all the complexities of the world. If scientific theories did not oversimplify the world by taking certain features of situations into account and ignoring others, they would have no explanatory power. One may be inclined to wish the behavioral sciences enjoyed the precision and power of the natural sciences, so that satisficing and localizing would not be necessary; but that wish is based on a mistake. Natural scientists too sometimes use incompatible theories and in applying theories make some assumptions that ignore the complications of the real world. In the use of models and theories there are additional complications that make theoretical satisficing a sound policy.

The incompatibility of the social sciences is particularly offensive to empiricists, who take the unity of the sciences as a reachable goal and therefore take the incompatibility of disciplines as a sign that at least one discipline is seriously out of touch with reality. But the following section shows that being in touch with reality is a more difficult matter, and not being in touch with it a less serious one, than we might suppose.

6. KINDS OF MODEL

To this point I have distinguished between theories and models without defining the concept of model. It is time to do that, and to raise doubts about the distinction, and about the distinction between models in the social sciences and those in the natural sciences. Though significant, these distinctions are not so sharp as they may appear to be.

Models cause some misunderstanding because there is no widely shared agreement about what they are. People who write and talk about models seem to have in mind something between an analogy and a theory. There are several different uses of the term, but two of them are of particular importance.[6]

In the least formal sense, X is a model of an entity Y if X is a replica of Y, like a scale model, as of an airplane made for experiments in a wind tunnel. Typically there are physical similarities between the model and the entity modeled (in this case, a full-sized airliner).

Slightly more formally, we may say that X models entity Y if there is some identity of structure, or isomorphism, between them, so that the relations connecting the items and properties in the model are the same as in the entity. A standard example is the relationship between Poiseuille's law of fluid dynamics and Ohm's law governing the flow of electricity through metal.

More formally yet, logicians call a model a set of things that satisfy some axioms and theorems. Models are called interpretations of the axioms and theorems if they reproduce the relationships specified in the axioms and theorems. For example, a diagram may be a model of a set of geometric theories and axioms.

Some models are mathematical models whose variables and constants are related in a way that certain observables turn out to be. In this case we say the mathematical expression is a model and some part of the world is modeled. Natural scientists claim isomorphisms like this; so do economists and operations researchers.

Two kinds of model are prominent and useful and not always sharply distinguished in the organization theory literature.

The first of the two is the analogical model, which is an analogy. It is characteristic of an analogy that it is similar to that to which it is an analogy, but different from it as well. To some extent all analogies are false analogies, but the bad ones are false in ways that mislead, while the good ones make a point or guide research. An analogical model may be simpler than what it models. Once understanding is achieved, complications are introduced.

A picture of a skeleton is an analogical model of a body. An organization chart is an analogical model of an organization; a work-flow chart is probably a better one. You might view an organization as a political system, and as a result might be inclined to look for evidence of coalition building or log rolling. If you view the organization as an organism, you look for patterns in the movement of information. If you view it as a culture, you look for myths and rituals.

It is not always helpful to find a few similarities between two systems and infer that one of the systems as a whole can serve as an analogical model for the other. It is one thing to believe that an organization can plan; whether it has moral responsibilities is another, far more controversial matter.

A theoretical model is normally an interpretation of some theoretical system. That is, it reproduces the relationships among items specified in that system, and in so doing uses a more familiar system to explain a less familiar one. For example, a geometric model illuminates the way in which the universe is said by a particular theory to expand. Theoretical models, unlike analogical models, typically have no part that is to be discounted as false or misleading. A theoretical model differs from a theory in that the model has certain implications that go beyond the phenomenon to be explained. The model suggests, in effect, that certain empirical tests be undertaken to confirm or disconfirm those implications; so it has heuristic value. If the implications are confirmed, the model then qualifies as a theory, though it may retain its maiden name of model for a time. But the terminology is so loose as to give reason to say that theories too have implications beyond the phenomena and that there is no significant difference between a theoretical model, in that sense, and a theory.

We are talking about theories that, by adopting different models, work under different assumptions. They say, in effect, that the theory is true on the assumption that the world is like this or like that. Do theories directed at different models contradict? They do if each claims that its model is the best available approximation of the world.

A natural scientist might propound an analogical model and then by refining it develop it into a theoretical one. So goes the legend of Kekulé, who dreamed of snakes chasing their tails and thereafter postulated the benzine ring. Sometimes the natural scientist is aware that the model is only an approximation of some part of the world, and that it therefore requires a "commentary" to complete an accurate picture. So a theory is a good analogical model plus a commentary; and some commentaries add very little to the model.

The commonsense view of natural science and behavioral science is that social scientists are more likely than natural scientists to use analogical models, and natural scientists are more likely to use theoretical models.

The behavioral sciences, according to this view, deal with subject matter so complex—not perhaps by its nature so much as by its scope—that our models are never more than approximations. It is characteristic of models in operations research, organization theory, and economics to bear the warning label, "other things being equal"; and other things never are. There is no such thing as perfect competition or perfect information; there is no feedback loop that operates without extraneous interference. The organization is not quite like this or that. One model is better than another not because it is true and the other false—all analogies are false, unless there is a complete commentary—but because it permits better predictions or better understanding in some other ways. In fact, a model that approximates the phenomena in greater detail might for that very reason be an unwieldy predictive device. In this respect, one might suppose, the behavioral sciences differ from physics, though not from meteorology or seismology.

But that is not quite right. Against this account I want to argue that models in certain of the hard sciences have many of the features of analogical models as described so far, and that those shared features give us reason to be hospitable to varieties of models, each different, none perfect, all valuable to those who want to understand organizations.

The contrast between the models of natural science and those of social science is overdrawn.[7] Natural science just does not so easily settle upon models whose accuracy qualifies them to be considered established theories.

Consider the following situation. An ordinary radiometer rotates under the influence of radiant energy in a way roughly predictable by Maxwell's theory. The prediction can be only approximate, however, since the radiometer will not satisfy certain ideal conditions. As the circumstances depart from the ideal, we cannot predict the rotation accurately because nobody knows any laws that link the ideal situation to the one that obtains. Nobody can even show that there are any such laws.

When closely examined, this and other models in science begin to look more like those used in organization theory and related fields. Often in the background lie words like "other things being equal," or even "in fact it is never like this." The similarity has been noted before, however; and it does not lead all who have noticed it to assimilate the natural and behavioral sciences. Hollis and Nell (1975, 43-46), for example, distinguish the two in this way: in the case of an economic ideal like perfect competition the exogenous factors ruled out of consideration by "other things being equal" are not clearly definable and measurable as they are in the case of frictionless motion. We can define and measure friction; so it is not the end of the world if cases of genuine frictionlessness are hard to come by. The factors excluded by the economist are not; so you never know whether you have a case of perfect competition.

The point is an extraordinarily important one; if correct, it marks a clear distinction between the natural and social sciences. But the point is not correct for all cases, nor therefore is the distinction as sharp as the authors appear to believe. Consider how natural scientists explain the movement of the radiometer. Maxwell presents a function that he states is the probability distribution of the velocity of molecules in the medium in question; but the medium he is describing accurately is an ideal medium, not the medium for the radiometer sitting on the desk before us (or for any other actual radiometer, so far as we know). We cannot precisely define or measure all the parameters that cause Maxwell's function not to apply exactly to this situation. They are not like friction. If a radiometer does not act precisely according to Maxwell, one can always claim that other things are not equal. In this way a scientist can keep a theory intact in spite of apparent disconfirmation.

What natural scientists do about disconfirming evidence blurs the difference between analogical model and theory, and so between the natural and social sciences. Strictly speaking, a theory is wrong if disconfirming evidence turns up. But in practice, as we know, disconfirmation does not usually burst the balloon: it may merely force a slight adjustment in the theory, or it may raise doubts about the alleged observation. As I argued in chapter 2, it is always possible in principle to maintain the essentials of a theory against any evidence if one is creative in adjustment or in explaining away refractory experience. What happens eventually is that, as in the case of Ptolemism, a certain pragmatic instinct (or a distaste for epicycles) leads the theorist to abandon the theory as a whole; but there is not always a clear sign of when to do it. Not only social scientists are acquainted with such resilient models.[8]

In fact, natural scientists sometimes use false models. A model in quantum mechanics, for example, may be adopted even though the theorist knows it to be wrong. Any competent physicist can tell you that a helium-neon laser is not a van der Pol triode oscillator, but the assumption that it is permits the scientist to predict its behavior *as nothing else does*. If a physicist wants to describe as accurately as possible the state of a helium-neon laser at any given instant, he or she will abandon the triode oscillator model; but the most accurate description does not fit any proposed law of nature that predicts satisfactorily. Something like this happens every time a mathematical theory is applied to reality in order to explain; and while a commentary may disavow the model's perfect accuracy, it cannot close the gap by saying exactly what is the case.

What scientific theory explains and predicts exactly is not the behavior of things in the world, but that of fictitious items in models. The theory is true if the model accurately reflects the world, but it seldom does.

Physicists not only use models they know are false: they use different and incompatible models of the same phenomena— some having to do with lasers, for example—depending on their purposes and on the questions at hand. The models cannot all be true; maybe none is true. But the scientist can explain and predict just because each of the different models accommodates its own range of cases. That is, locally it is a good model.

Scientists do not all countenance the notion that we require possibly incompatible models to mediate between them and complex reality; many scientists believe instead that science is converging on the truth; so the Copernican revolution seems to show. The original Copernican formulation had some serious problems. It mistakenly postulated circular orbits for the planets, and it could not explain the absence of evidence for the annual parallax. Hence it was not just on ideological grounds that the Ptolemaic model survived for some time: it had certain advantages. Eventually the postulation of elliptical orbits and data confirming the parallax helped round out an acceptable model that could be called a theory, and a broadly confirmed and useful one. The usefulness of Ptolemy, according to the partisans of convergence, was ephemeral and based on scientists' ignorance.

Kuhn (1970) reads the Copernican story differently. Copernicus formulated what proved to be a generally correct though in some respects inaccurate conception of the universe, and Copernicus's theory has guided an activity now popularly (since Kuhn) called "normal science," one of whose functions is to smooth away the residual epicycles and so get the currently accepted model closer to predictive correctness.

But we have no good evidence—we do not even know what would count as evidence—that natural science has its revolutions and its proliferations out of the way and is on a normal path to the truth. Kuhn suggests that for all practical purposes natural science is always where Ptolemy was: unwittingly setting the stage for some further revolution. To a social scientist there is something heartening about this: even natural science turns out to be always a journey rather than a destination, and perfect truth eludes even the most devoted pilgrim. In fact, the journey may not even be in the right direction. One may be tempted to reply that, while natural science is not unified in the required way, nature is but we have not yet learned the rules. But there is no basis for saying that in natural science—or in organization theory.

In spite of the differences between the natural and the behavioral sciences it is clear that they have much in common. In particular, both generate models and therefore theories incompatible with each other and limited in scope. The scientist can predict exactly the movement of (ideal) entities in a model, and only closely the (real) movement of a radiometer. Organization theorists do not come so close in their predictions as do physicists, though they rival meteorologists. Both will shift from one model to another, very different one in order to explain different events.

In some cases of incompatible theories there is a clear winner: chemistry over alchemy; Newton over Aristotle on certain questions. In other cases there is no clear winner, as each theory or class of theory has a kind of question it handles better than the other does, and a kind it handles worse.

There is no guarantee that a new and superior theory will be superior in all possible respects. In some cases we embrace the new one in confidence that eventually the available evidence will favor it in all respects; in others, not knowing which of competing theories is best, we use each for different purposes, as we now use the Ptolemaic framework for celestial navigation.

We are inclined to think that managers are interested in what is useful and that theoreticians are interested in what is true. What I am suggesting is that the distinction is not as sharp as it looks. A true theory is one that describes the world as it actually is; but we cannot check on this by comparing the world as it actually is to our theory of what the world is like. We can only try to propound a theory that past and future experience vindicates. The features of a theory that make it capable of being vindicated are often the very features that make it useful to someone who has to predict or manipulate some part of the world: a manager, for example. Behavioral scientists should feel no embarrassment about using incompatible models to solve different problems or to answer different questions. Whether there is some further, overarching Theory towards which we move is not an issue worth spending much time discussing.

Here we get a sense of why the case study method is such a valuable and effective way of teaching business-related courses. In effect it provides models from which students can extrapolate, rather than rules they can apply. No case study resembles in every particular any situation with which the student will subsequently be confronted, nor are there any known rules for determining precisely how to apply the case to situations from which it differs. Yet this is not so different from situations natural scientists face. Applying a scientific law to a particular situation is a form of extrapolation as well; and there are no scientific laws to guide the scientist's decision on which scientific law to apply.

The use of a model causes trouble when one extrapolates carelessly from the clear similarities between it and the modeled system, and so imputes to an organization properties it does not have. For example, using the individual person as a model for an organization, one can teach lessons about strategic planning or about moral responsibility; but to go on from there to infer that (say) the organization, like any organism, has rights that necessarily transcend those of its components is not only a bad extrapolation but a moral offense. The problem is not that the model is bad, but that it is being used to answer questions it was not designed to answer.

The power of a theory derives in part from its generality, but there is a tradeoff: the more phenomena there are to which a theory applies approximately, the less exactly it applies to anything. Inevitably there is a gap between theory and world, some room for unsettleable argument. By now you know what I recommend in cases of this sort.

Sometimes, it is alleged, there is a radical incompatibility between statements in one theory and those in another because they are expressed in languages that do not even translate into each other. One cannot even see whether the theories conflict, since (as the point is sometimes expressed) they come from different conceptual frameworks, or paradigms. This claim, (6) on the list, is a prime topic of discussion in chapter 7.

NOTES

1. I shall not discuss all the various senses in which one kind of entity may be said to be reducible to another. There are too many, they raise substantive

issues in the guise of semantic disputes, and most of them are not relevant to the present discussion.

2. What I say about theories will normally apply to unsystematic and implicit but organized ways of explaining events. Paradigms are groups of related theories, typically characteristic of a particular discipline, or a shared approach within a discipline; but the word may be used to refer to the conceptual and methodological background shared by theories that differ to some degree. Conceptual schemes are broader: they are the most basic and general views about logic, theory, and methodology shared by speakers of a language, natural or technical. These characterizations—they hardly qualify as definitions—are meant to match actual usage in their vagueness.

3. Precisely because different initial conditions may create identical results, identical functions as well as things and events defined identically from a functional point of view may be instantiated (in the sense of the term outlined in chapter 1) differently.

4. One of empiricism's charms is that it can be used by the proponents of very different, even incompatible theories. So Collins uses it to get rid of sociological entities in favor of psychological ones, and Pfeffer (1982) appears to use it to get rid of psychological entities in favor of organizational ones. I chose Collins's nominalism as an example of a standard move largely because Pfeffer identified it as the enemy. Far from taking sides, I aim to attack what the two approaches have in common. A time-honored way of solving an intractable dispute is to deny a premise common to both contending positions.

5. As it happens, Friedman believes there is no causal relationship, and is virtually alone in his belief.

6. My distinction among kinds of model closely follows the famous treatment by Hesse (1966).

7. The discussion in this chapter reflects a great controversy about explanation in the philosophy of science in recent years. See especially Cartwright (1983), who is the source of several of the examples; also Hacking (1983) and Joseph (1983). For a different point of view, see Van Fraassen (1981); but he too has a strong pragmatist streak and no apparent illusions about theories mirroring reality.

8. This is not to say that economists and physicists are equally well placed with respect to knowledge of relevant laws. No scientist can predict whether a line drive off the pitcher's leg will break a bone, but in this case the crucial ignorance is of the conditions and not of the laws. The point is only that even in physics there is sometimes justifiable doubt about whether it is the conditions or the laws that one is getting wrong. Physics can offer, as economics and organization theory cannot, many cases in which predictions are so accurate that one can without great harm speak of having a law of

nature in one's grasp. With such cases and such laws under one's belt, one is justified (by the principle of conservatism mentioned in chapter 1) in being confident on other and more difficult occasions that it is the conditions and not the law about which doubt is justified. Social scientists can seldom afford to be so confident.

7 SUBJECTIVITY AND SATISFICING

To this point I have argued that, while it is not always easy to tell whether two theories are compatible, it is sometimes a good idea for organization theorists to countenance not only distinct theories but incompatible ones. This chapter raises the ante by suggesting still greater difficulties for the alluring idea that the sciences should or can be unified. Far from recommending subjectivism, however, I shall hold that arguments can be made, and sometimes settled, across paradigm boundaries.

We have built a case against the notion of science as unified. This chapter goes on to show that theories worth using can be not only incompatible but *incommensurable.* That is, there is no easy way to measure one against the other to see which is closer to accurate, or even to state the theories in question in a common language. The various kinds of theory available to the organization theorist are not altogether incommensurable; but the differences among them are sufficiently deep that the task of choosing among them requires the exercise of judgment rather than the invocation of a rule for choice.

Natural science has an enviable track record, and anyone concerned with theory has something to learn from it. Scientific method is by no means inappropriate to the study of human behavior; but the idea of Scientific Method that some philosophers and organization theorists have laid down for the guidance of scientists is another matter. For scientists have not succeeded and progressed by first determining what constitutes proper scientific method and then proceeding accordingly. Whatever we say about scientific method that is worth saying comes from understanding what successful natural scientists actually do, which is not just following nonscientists' a priori rules.

Yet in defending criteria for theoretical soundness by reference to what successful scientists do, we need a way to distinguish successful from unsuccessful science. Doing it by example is not very difficult: particle physics is one; alchemy is the other. There may be some ideological disputes about Copernican and Darwinian science, but history suggests they will die out. But consensus on what counts as successful behavioral science is inevitably harder to reach, because taking a position on the issue requires having a view about the purpose of behavioral science, and that involves moral and political values. I shall not try to provide definitive answers on this issue. For the moment I only observe that it is a mistake to draw one's criteria from an empiricist view of natural science and apply them to the behavioral sciences, then claim that any deviation from them is ideology run amok. (Pfeffer [1982, 37-40, 293f.] claims something like this.)

One fact about science requires emphasis. Whatever else may be true of science, it is a human enterprise. Scientific theories therefore operate under conditions that govern communication within a linguistic community. So a critical understanding of these theories requires considering the ways in which meaning and rationality are community matters: it requires considering interpretation.

Nowadays no critical discussion of theories can avoid mentioning different *paradigms*. There is a great deal said about different paradigms, and much of it is inappropriate and misleading. I cannot curtail paradigm talk, but there is reason to use other terms wherever possible. There is no consensus on exactly what a paradigm is, and to assimilate the several ways in which theories may differ under the label of "different paradigm" is to oversimplify complex issues, to encourage unwarranted subjectivism, to obscure crucial differences of degree, and to stifle discursive argument.

Subjectivism and despair about argument owe something to empiricism. If you have been trained in the methodology of empiricism, your idea of epistemological justification will probably be a foundationalist one. If you then convince yourself that there is no foundation, you are likely to doubt that there can be any justification. Disillusioned empiricism leads to skepticism or, what is nearly the same thing, the view that so far as we can tell one view is as good as another. If you do not come from a foundationalist tradition in the first place, you may have other ways of adjudicating among theories. You will not mistake pragmatism for subjectivism any more than a manager will mistake satisficing for making wholly arbitrary decisions.

There is room for a variety of theories, but we do have ways—more ways than paradigm-wielders usually acknowledge—to show that some theories are good, others not.

1. THE BUILDING BLOCKS OF OUR WORLD

Where different theories divide the world differently into components, the purported laws of nature that form an essential part of each theoretical network will differ significantly. Possibly certain networks of relationships can be compared because the theorists will be able to agree on composition principles permitting translation from one theory to the other, but that is not always the case. Chapters 2 and 6 attacked the proposition that differences among theories are just differences about how the elements of the world are arranged. One difference may be over what counts as an element.

A theory generates knowledge and enables prediction by representing the world as more neatly organized and less complex than it actually is. To say that the world conforms to a finite list of laws is as valuable and as misleading as to claim that, since the most accurate possible television picture is made up of small, isomorphic, individually monochromatic components, it follows that the things in the world that can be televised are themselves a certain configuration of tiny monochromatic hexagons or circles or whatever shape makes up the best picture. But as some television pictures are better than others, there are systems of law that are better than others in the sense that they are less often overturned by experience without being less useful, or are easier to use, or more coherent, or have some other desirable feature.[1]

There is no naturally fundamental level of experience. At experience's most immediate level we are already processing its raw material into some organization. Even to talk about it is to presuppose something about its structure; for any coherent discourse presupposes some relationships, logical and otherwise, among sentences and therefore among the things the sentences are about.

Against any claim to have found *the* perspicuous language for describing organizations, one should consider whether there are others different but no less well qualified. With due respect to the efforts of Roberts et al.

(1978), one should always critically examine the assumption that there are ways of combining and comparing the theoretical options if only we can identify their common components. This assumption is not generally safe.

2. INCOMMENSURABILITY

2a. What Incommensurability Is

Incommensurable bodies of theory are related so that the sentences that express one of them cannot be determined to be either compatible with or contradictory to those that express the other, for there is no means of translating sentences of one such theory into those of another. The proponents of incommensurable theories or groups of theories may be unable to understand each other, hence unable to agree on tests for determining whose theory is true, for such tests would form the basis of translations. If such tests appear to be available, the opponents will probably describe both the tests and their results differently.[2]

Kuhn's (1970) examples of incommensurable theories are usually separated in time. He argues that successive bodies of scientific theory owe some of their differences to their asking different questions and having different purposes. But contemporaneous theories too, particularly those in different disciplines, may address some of the same issues but postulate different things to talk about.

This goes on in organization theory largely because it is interdisciplinary. A particular discipline will encompass a set of interlocking commensurable theories and definitions that help define it as a discipline; other disciplines will have their own characteristic theories, probably commensurable with one another. Theories in disciplines whose assumptions and theories differ discuss different things in the sense that they define certain terms differently—inevitably, as definitions overlap with theories.

I argued in chapter 2 that theories say not only how the things in the universe act and are put together, but also what things are basic. In the case of incommensurable theories, the definitions not only differ but cannot be compared on a common scale or expressed in a common language; so there will be no rules of translation from propositions in one theory to those in another. The important point here is that certain theories of interest to organization theorists are to some degree incommensurable.

A first step towards establishing that view is to show how hard it is to have consensus on language when there is significant disagreement on facts.

2b. Problems about Essential and Accidental Properties

Our discussions of identity and reification in chapters 2 and 5 showed how there can be knowledge and discourse about things in the world in spite of change. A thing has certain essential properties that remain even if certain other properties change, so that we can talk about an individual—the same individual—even if it changes as we talk about it. This distinction between essential and accidental properties, familiar since Aristotle, is handy too for cases in which different speakers make incompatible statements about a particular individual. Comprehensible contradiction and falsehood are possible because you and I can refer to an individual thing and make incompatible statements about it either at a particular time (in which case somebody has said something false) or at different times. When a thing changes, its essential properties remain and some accidental ones do not. When we speak falsely of a thing, we get the essential properties right (in referring to it) and one or more of the accidental ones wrong (in describing it). The extinction of the thing comes when it loses an essential property: so if you cease to be a human being, you no longer exist. There is no *you* to refer to.

This account does not claim that conversation requires natural essential properties, or that we must know the boundaries of the properties we consider essential. Convention and convenience, which are not arbitrary, provide not very rigid guidelines for our choices of essential properties, hence of what we reify. But convention and convenience change with circumstances and purposes. And even when they are stable, they can be criticized on the basis of their ethical or political consequences. So you and I can disagree about exactly what the essential features of a company are—that is, about the definition of *company*—and our disagreement may have ethical weight; but we can still talk fairly clearly about companies.

Not only can we not distinguish cleanly between essential features and accidental ones: we cannot easily distinguish sentences true by virtue of the meanings of their component words from those true by virtue of describing the world correctly. Newton's theories, for example, do not take this distinction seriously. It follows that different theories may make distinct claims in part because they have different definitions of certain common terms, with the result that there are no rules of translation from propositions in one theory to those in another.

Why does this matter? Recall that one of the reasons for distinguishing between essential and accidental properties is that we can agree about the subject of our conversation while disagreeing over some of what we say about it. Rules of translation based on the distinction between what is true by definition and what is true as a matter of fact perform a similar service: they let us know what some proposition means independently of whether it is true. Without the essence-accident distinction we cannot readily distinguish one sentence or one theory from another by saying that each makes different claims about the same thing(s). How then can they contradict each other? How can either of two claimants know what the other is talking about? What the other means? Without the necessary-contingent distinction, how can incompatible theories communicate?

In this situation the best we can say is that knowing the meaning of a sentence is a matter of being prepared to judge whether it is true or false. Within a theoretical context, knowing the meaning of a word is a matter of knowing what role it plays in a theory. Yet we can still usually judge whether a proposition is true.

Recall the cases, discussed in Chapter 5, in which it is difficult to tell whether to interpret a statement as meaning "p" and being false or meaning "q" and being true. The normal practice is to give a statement whatever interpretation makes it true, but people do make false statements. There is similar uncertainty about whether two scientific theories are incompatible or are simply using different languages to make points that do not contradict.

Think of a theory as a network of propositions that form a coherent whole. The meanings of even the most basic propositions are a function of their relations (logical and evidential and in between) to other propositions. The clearest and most manageable arguments, those that generate a minimum of misunderstanding, take place within and presuppose a network of related theories and methods, as of a discipline. Such arguments can be settled by observation or experiment if the discipline has progressed from its philosophical origins far enough that its rules encompass agreement about what counts as evidence for what. (But no discipline ever becomes the philosophy-free science of the empiricist's fantasy.)

The more the disputants agree about the easier it will be for them to see where their disagreement lies because, to put it crudely, the more nearly alike will be the meanings of their words and sentences, the more they can say they are talking about the same things but saying different things about them. If they disagree narrowly about certain facts and not about theory, they can argue clearly. If they disagree about logical principles, they will fail to understand each other well. Those are the extreme cases.

Between the extremes are cases of people who have very different theories in their networks and who consequently have significant difficulty in conversing. Collins (1981) and Mayhew (1980 and 1981) appear to be related in this way; and Mayhew suggests his awareness of the nature of his argument with his opponents in titling the first section of his two-part essay "Shadowboxing in the Dark." Their definitions will be different, and those differences will not be resolved by agreeing on how to use a term or two. This indeterminacy helps explain why we have trouble talking across disciplinary lines, hence within organization theory, which is interdisciplinary: the theories in question are systematically different, as therefore are the meanings of the terms and propositions each side states. These differences cannot be straightened out by mere clarification, for definitions even of observable entities embody some of the substance of the respective theories.

We might put the point by saying that theories do not clash because their terms have different meanings, but that suggests that we know how to pick out the meaning of a term apart from saying what it does and does not apply to, and it is clear that we sometimes do not. Let us say that there is no method agreed to by holders of both theories for determining which statements are true.

For familiar reasons we cannot always use predictive ability, verification or falsification, to show one theory superior to another. For one thing, the winner in one case might predict less well in another case. Or the theory that predicts the event correctly might be inferior on one of the other grounds, mentioned in chapter 1, for evaluating theories. Again, one of the theories might be sound as a whole, while some other proposition, assumed for the purposes of testing it, is false. In chapter 4 I argued that there is sometimes indeterminacy as to whether the sentences in two theories have the same meaning when in the crunch neither theory must admit that the facts are incompatible with it.

2c. "Paradigm" Shifts and Gulfs

Immediate deflation by counterexample is as rare in the natural as in the social sciences. If little goes wrong, you conclude that your theory is a good one and that the occasional anomalies are the fault of observational error or of other things not being equal in the environment. When a lot goes wrong, then you start to think your theory needs minor adjustments—or, eventually, more than minor ones. But how much is a lot? When is it time to stop patching the leaks and abandon ship?

This is the scenario most people have in mind as they consider the notion of the paradigm shift: you stop trying to improve on your old theory and scrap it in favor of a radically new one. But, particularly in the behavioral sciences, we are aware of cases in which the competition between two theories is far from one-sided. Each may have its characteristic difficulties, problems it can solve better, areas in which its predictions are better. There is not always a neutral arbiter to lay down standards for determining which is closer to the truth.

These are not the hardest cases, however. The Copernican revolution is a case in which the theories in question are not so radically incommensurable that the opponents cannot talk to each other; the differences between the theories were never such as to bring conversation to a standstill. The Einstein theory of general relativity as compared with the Newtonian framework better illustrates how definitional change may be part of the replacement of one theory by another. But even here, where definitions as well as lawlike statements will differ greatly, a speaker of Newtonian language can learn Einsteinese fairly readily. No less important, Einsteinian theory predicted a number of observable events that Newtonian theory excluded; and the correctness of the predictions was a decisive blow to Newton, though not fatal for all purposes.

The relationship between Aristotelian and Newtonian science is a better example of deeply incommensurable systems. Translation is a serious problem. The systems pose different questions, and neither answers the other's very well. They talk about different things. Each of the two systems carries with it its own rules for the assessment of theories. So, for example, Aristotle's final cause cannot be cashed out into Newton's kind of causality; Newtonians consider that a problem for Aristotle. Each is a better theory on its owner's criteria than the other is. But in the absence of the foundation for knowledge and meaning that empiricists dream of, who gets to decide what the right criteria are, and how?

The comparison is important because our commonsense view of the world even today is largely Aristotelian. The world is populated by individual objects, some of them purposive, that persist through change; and things happen for reasons. Whether our outlook on human matters should be irreducibly teleological as his is a matter of controversy among organization theorists.

Roberts et al. (1978; see especially 64ff.), in order to build a foundation for reconciling disciplines that explain human behavior, propose a vocabulary that all these disciplines can share, from which each can build up in its own characteristic way. But no noncommittal vocabulary can be found to describe the basic pieces of behavior or anything else. The vocabulary that Roberts et al. propose clearly presupposes at least as much as the behaviorist description of the monkey pressing the bar to get food.

I used the example of the monkey in chapter 3 to show that behaviorists do not have a noncommittal observation language that cancels out any suggestion of teleology and mentality. Here the point is related, but different: there is no way to translate the language that includes bar pressing into the language that mentions the movement of particles of matter. There are no bridge laws. No statement that anyone could make in either language could be a necessary or a sufficient condition of any statement in the other. To that extent the languages, as well as the theories stated in them, are incommensurable.

The same is true, as I argued in chapter 6, of all kinds of description of characteristically human activity, from talking to cashing a check. They just do not map onto each other. They are not wholly incommensurable; for we must define intentional behavior partly by reference to ordinary causes; and that is important, for it shows that the notion of causation and implicitly of scientific law is an ineliminable part of the concept of intention. But any account of intention makes explicit or implicit reference to purposes, which cannot be defined in any language of natural science. A language of natural science is not incompatible with a language that countenances human purposes: it does not deny the existence of ends, nor does it affirm them. It has no way of doing either, since the term *purpose* is not in its vocabulary and does not translate anything that is.

The standard move for theorists more attuned to natural science is to seek an analysis of purpose that reduces it to something amenable to traditional scientific vocabulary, by trying to operationalize the concept or by some subtler means. (Rosenblueth and Wiener [1968] can be read as an attempt to do that by identifying function and human purpose.) If this attempt succeeds, the inference is that various kinds of teleological state can all be assimilated to the state of a physical system with a feedback mechanism that keeps it going. If the attempt fails, the inference is that there are no purposive states, because the rules forbid them. Heads, the approach based on natural science wins; tails, purpose loses. This is not surprising, because this approach, like any other, is characterized by its rules about what gives a statement legitimacy. And where shall we find rules to evaluate those rules? Before addressing this question by invoking theoretical satisficing, we have to get clear on some other things.

2d. Degrees of Incommensurability

At several points I have suggested that some pairs and groups of statements are more incommensurable than others. That is true: incommensurability is a matter of degree. There is in fact a continuum ranging from full incommensurability to ordinary factual dispute. At the limit, partisans of neither theory will even recognize the other as a theory.

Radical incommensurability, in which communication between theories is altogether impossible because all the rules for the use of all terms are radically different, can never be recognized; for recognizing it would require the kind of understanding of both the incommensurable frameworks that is by hypothesis impossible. The Ptolemaic and Copernican theories are incommensurable only in the sense that, for a period of time, the partisans on each side could not find any tests that they could agree would solve their disputes, in part because of methodological differences. But they could talk to each other, and in due course they found evidence that settled the case for most of the disputants. (The others died.)

We have grounds for attributing a strong form of incommensurability where theories accept the same laws of logic but postulate theoretical networks so different that the fundamental terms that each theory defines have little in common. Some things that can be said in the language of one theory cannot be said in that of the other. Arguably psychology and physics stand in this relationship, as do the organizational theories based on psychology and sociology.

In a similar but slightly weaker case of incommensurability the theories' crucial terms have roughly the same connections with other terms and in that sense have similar meanings. But where the theories have different consequences, the proponents of one of them may take a position that can be stated in this way: I have no way of knowing for certain whether I am misunderstanding some things my opponent's theory says (that is, whether my opponent is using words in a different sense), or whether I am understanding correctly and the theory is false. From the point of view of a certain psychological theory, are economists or expectancy theorists wrong in what they say about utility and its effect on human behavior? Or are they both right given a definition of utility the psychologists do not share? To answer that question by operationalizing the concept of utility trivializes the concept, as operationalizing would trivialize Newtonian physics as well. The right way for the theorist to defend a concept is, as our discussion of construct validity showed, to indicate how it fits into a viable theory. The definition of utility and the theory in which it plays a central role are no more separable than the definition of phlogiston and alchemical theory. Insofar as one cannot separate a statement of meaning from a purported statement of fact, these cases generate situations in which I cannot give an account of the difference between my misunderstanding some things my opponent's theory says and my understanding correctly a theory I consider false.

There is a still less radical difference, but one that creates some problems, between theories that are loosely enough designed or carefully enough hedged with conditions that neither of them can defeat the other on the basis of one apparent counterexample, or even a few. The competing theorists cannot agree on what their respective theories mean in the narrow sense that they cannot agree on whether certain bodies of evidence count for or against one theory or the other, as with the theories discussed in chapter 4.

Incommensurability is the essence of paradigm difference. It has always been unclear exactly what constitutes a paradigm, perhaps because the relationship of paradigm *difference* is what really counts, and that relationship is just incommensurability. Theories united by common background assumptions, methodology, and favored problems may be said to constitute a "paradigm," and to be commensurable. The relationship of incommensurability may hold between two theories, as well; but in that case the theories are not necessarily paradigms. Where a relationship between theories is at issue, we are better off talking about incommensurability.

In fact we have been doing so all along, and in a way that provides evidence that incommensurability is not necessarily a barrier to discourse. Contrary to increasingly popular opinion, proponents of one paradigm can sometimes criticize another.

This requires some proving.

2e. What to Do in Case of Incommensurability

There are disputes in the literature of organization theory about how theorists and managers should deal with different paradigms. Should paradigms be reconciled, chosen between, or both used as each is useful? My view is that except where there is radical incommensurability there is reason for theorists who intend to produce something useful to managers to be hospitable to multiple paradigms. But this is not to say that any old paradigm will do.

Burrell and Morgan (1979) (cf. Silverman [1968 and 1971]) argue that reconciliation is impossible and that using different paradigms according to local usefulness involves one in self-contradiction; so they push for a choice. But they do not well explain what constitutes a paradigm difference, and their examples suggest that they are discussing a variety of distinctions. We should handle different relationships differently.[3] For example, Burrell and Morgan regard certain functional approaches as paradigmatically separate from approaches that focus on causal influences at the component level. I have argued that there is no contradiction here. On the contrary, functional explanations depend on causal explanations; so do explanations that invoke intentions. Again, Burrell and Morgan take the "nomothetic" (roughly, standard causal or hypothetico-deductive) and hermeneutical approaches to be characteristic of different paradigms; but they do not show that one of the approaches excludes the other. So they are not in a good position to advise, in general or on a case-by-case basis, how to deal with approaches they consider different paradigms.

Distinguishing the degrees of incommensurability is one step towards dealing appropriately with distinct theories; but even after we have established the degree of incommensurability between two theories, we may still be uncertain about whether, how, and when to use each. Here are two more points to assist us in considering the possibility of paradigmatic reconciliation: first, some of what Burrell and Morgan consider paradigm differences distinguish kinds of explanation that go together quite well; second, the fact of contradiction between theories does not rule out our using them both.

Certainly the literature of organization theory includes some undue strictures on the use of clearly different kinds of explanation, particularly where each bears the mark of a different ideological tradition. The result may be a failure to appreciate cases in which—to take an example from chapter 5—a statistical-causal approach neatly complements an interpretive one. For example, no anthropologist or anybody else could understand a baseball game without imputing rationality, purpose, and the awareness of rules to the players; but events in baseball are subject to statistical-causal explanation, and any such explanation presupposes a taxonomy that incorporates the rules of the game in much the same way behaviorism presupposes the organization of movement into pieces of behavior. Organization theorists of all stripes would be in a bad way if they could not look for causal relations among human actions defined—as I have argued most human actions are—in ways that presuppose rationality, purpose, and awareness of one's surroundings. They would be no better off if they had to choose between reasons and causes in explaining behavior.

The argument of chapter 6 also tells against trying to confine oneself to a single paradigm. Scientific progress depends on scientists' continuing attempts to make their theories coherent as well as predictively powerful. But it would be an equal mistake to try to standardize the vocabulary and line up the assumptions across all one's theories before using any of them.

Where the competitors are not individual theories but groups of theories, each group united by broad assumptions and methodology, deciding between them may be difficult. But the proponents of one set of theories may criticize those of others by finding incoherence or contradiction or unwarranted assumptions or unwelcome implications or undue imperviousness to fact in one's opponents' theories. Nearly all the scholars I have cited argue that way, as I have done—for example, in attacking empiricism. That is the kind of thing philosophers do, but surely philosophy—specifically, conceptual work in organization theory—is too important to be left to philosophers, particularly in a discipline that is still far from reaching agreement about how it should define, measure, etc.; that is, that has not escaped philosophy.

Now a radical empiricist will not countenance this sort of argument, but will claim instead that genuine differences must finally be resolved by reference to experience. If you have accepted the empiricist's view of meaning, you will probably see no way to decide between competing paradigms, in the unlikely event you believe in paradigms and incommensurability at all. But there are arguments other than those involving simple reference to some definitive experience: we rely on parsimony, conservatism, coherence, and so on.

Where different criteria generate different evaluations it may be appropriate to use incompatible theories. In some cases, as with Ptolemy and Copernicus, a decision one way or the other may be possible and necessary. In other cases it may be impossible, or not worth the cost; but additional information might later make a decision possible and economical.

An argument we have discussed before provides a revealing case study of a form of incommensurability. Writing of psychological and organizational climate, Glick (1988), an advocate of the latter, states that the difference between his view and that of the proponents of psychological climate who deny that there is any organizational climate is a paradigm difference; he writes that "it is time. . . to agree to disagree" (135). If my arguments in Chapters 3, 5, and 6 are right, then Glick is giving up too easily. The two sides are indeed using different definitions and different postulates; we are to that extent dealing with incommensurable theories. But telling criticism from Glick's point of view is altogether possible. As he indicates, James (1988) and others who will not countenance organizational climate are operationalists. As I argued in Chapter 2, there are fundamental problems about operationalism, and those arguments apply against the Jamesian position. It is wrong to identify a concept with the evidence for it; it is wrong to believe that we learn how the world is divided into states and properties just by looking at statistical clustering. And of course if their operationalism were right, then, as I argued in chapter 3, James et al. would have trouble defending even psychological climate. Like many arguments between incommensurables, that is essentially a philosophical argument, but it is conclusive.

The question whether organizational climate can be a robust concept is a legitimate subject for argument. We do not have the equivalent of valid psychological tests for the construct. Possibly the theory that best answers questions about what we now call organizational climate will turn out to use concepts far removed from anything Glick would recognize. But it would be a mistake to deny the possibility that a concept similar to what we now call organizational climate may some day be both clearly separable from psychological climate and in some respects more useful to managers. Trying to find evidence on organizational climate is the same enterprise as trying to define it; it is a legitimate enterprise for an organization theorist, as it is for psychologists to do the same for—say—paranoia.

But the proponents of organizational climate are already vindicated insofar as the anthropologist's technique of interpretation proves to be a useful way of understanding what goes on in organizations. As I argued in chapter 5, to say that there is never any use for any such technique is tantamount to saying that the notion of meaningful language is a bankrupt notion. But any empiricist who takes this line abandons the possibility of discourse, and thereby undercuts the empiricist argument—and a great deal else besides. Any theory that makes use of the notions of thought and speech does seem to be incommensurable with radical empiricism; and thus we refute radical empiricism.

The essentially philosophical argument that crosses the barrier of incommensurability in this case does so by bringing in the notion of interpretation. One might respond that interpretation just is not in the empiricist's paradigm. But that is a problem for the empiricist, who is thereby deprived of the concept of meaningfulness, which has traditionally been crucial for empiricists as well as others.

Interpretation is called for when scientific theories that are seriously incommensurable look critically at each other. Think of a scientific community as being defined, like a culture, by a shared language and a corresponding consensus about what is rational—that is, what situations call forth what behavior, and what inferences are permitted from what evidence. If one scientific community (call it the Martians) is sufficiently different from another (call the latter the Earthlings), then we can expect that as a first step towards assessing the Martians' views, the Earthlings will try to interpret what the Martian community does and says by describing the rules Martians follow—as opposed to the laws of nature they conform to. (The two communities may also have a different notion of what counts as following a certain rule, but that complication is of no importance just here.) You understand ballplayers' behavior when you understand the rules and the objectives of the game. You may learn what the rules are by being told; otherwise you must infer them, and in doing so assume (charitably but necessarily) that most of the time people obey the rules. Over a period of time you learn to detect infringements of the rules, perhaps even to account for lapses. So in the case of an unfamiliar culture you try to figure out what their rules are, and you assume they are usually followed (or they aren't the rules). So for a linguistic community: you infer the rules governing what is evidence for what, and under what circumstances people say what they say; you assume people are following the rules most of the time.

I claim much the same is true when you look at a theoretical framework that is wholly different from any you are used to. If it does not map directly onto your framework word for word and concept for concept, then you learn the rules about how to describe present reality and how to move from experience to theory by paying attention to what the practitioners do and how the practitioners describe what they do, and by interpreting them as obeying the rules of the framework unless there is good reason to interpret them otherwise. In this case, however, there is the question whether the framework is true, or adequate. The difficulty of answering that question is obviously greater if our words and concepts do not correspond one to one with those of the alien theorists, for they and we are not going to have the same rules about what to say in what circumstances, or what experience justifies what statement and what inference. (Remember, these are not just semantic rules.)

In trying to figure out the rules of their language, however, we must assume that most of the time what they say is true, at least in circumstances that are not very complicated. The anthropologist finds out what people in this culture are supposed to say in a certain situation by seeing what they do say in that situation—or at any rate, in what appears to be that situation. The anthropologist must assume that the members of the culture usually see the situation as he or she does. The interpretation could never get off the ground if the natives usually said the equivalent of "It's raining" when it was not raining.

It follows that understanding the natives' sentences and judging whether they are true are not wholly separable enterprises: you cannot do the former without doing some of the latter, at least by implication. So if people in this culture see the world altogether differently, it is hard to see how one could interpret their language. If we cannot find a translation according to which what they say is governed by a minimally coherent theoretical framework that serves a purpose, then we have no reason to say they have a theoretical framework at all. If we can find such a translation, however, we can criticize them whenever they violate the rules of that framework.

Consider a theoretical framework that generates predictions that keep going wrong. Its owners may find themselves often and unpleasantly surprised. But must we assume that their purpose in having such theories was to reduce surprise; and if not, how can we criticize their theories? We might see whether their theories were meant to serve any of the other purposes we think theories have. If not, we would have no basis for criticizing them. But once again, we would also have no basis for identifying anything they said as a theory or for translating any word in their language as "theory."

This attack on the view that we cannot communicate across the paradigm gulf—on the view, in fact, that it makes sense for us to talk about other paradigms or conceptual schemes so far from our own—fits neatly with the discussion in chapters 3 and 4 of the need for the assumption that other agents are rational. That should not be surprising, since a paradigm is rather like a set of rules for deciding what is rational.

Interpreting a conceptual scheme that one does not entirely share is possible only if it explains behavior by reference to standards one does share with those in the conceptual scheme under interpretation; otherwise it fails as an explanation. Explaining anyone's reasons for believing something, including a scientific theory, or for taking a certain action entails attributing not only beliefs and desires but a measure of rationality; for without some rationality, evidence could not cause belief or desire action or thought speech. If you are to identify Jones's evidence or motive or meaning, you must assume that to some degree Jones is acting reasonably from your point of view. You may not agree with his reasons, but you have to recognize them as reasons.

If I have no basis for thinking Jones's action reasonable, then I have no basis for considering it intentional. If a statement is literally totally unreasonable, there is no basis for taking the speaker to mean anything at all by it—that is, no reason for considering it a statement. I may be misinterpreting it; but in that case I have no grounds for considering it a statement. So to attribute a theory or a language to a community is to attribute some measure of rationality, and in that sense to go beyond description to evaluation. To understand a community's language is to share to some degree its view of what is rational. To some degree, that is: invoking a principle of charity, I interpret certain words as coherent, but not as wholly reasonable. (There is at least this much to be said for the "rational model.")

Possible reply: But perhaps the alien whose words and actions I can make no sense of is speaking or acting according to what he or she or it, unlike me, considers reasonable to some extent. Response: Perhaps so; but if I can make literally no sense at all of them, I have no reason to think the alien is acting intentionally or speaking meaningfully. This means that the explainer and the agent whose action is being explained must share a notion of rationality to some degree.[4]

So when Geertz (1979) essays an explanation of Balinese cockfighting practices, he must assume that these practices are not totally deluded but instead make sense from the point of view of the Balinese—a point of view whose analysis is Geertz's purpose. If Geertz could not make any sense of the sounds the Balinese make or of their behavior—let us rather say, of their movements—he would have no reason to say that their conceptual scheme is so profoundly different from ours that we can make no connection. For in those circumstances there would be no reason to say they have a conceptual scheme at all, any more than to say that a stone has a conceptual scheme but of course one that bears no similarity to ours.

It is not possible to specify exactly what the aliens have to say and do in order to justify our claim that they have a conceptual scheme. The least that is required is some evidence that they hold to the law of non-contradiction most of the time and that they perform acts that lead to consequences they give evidence of anticipating and welcoming. But even without being able to answer that question we know this: if you can interpret someone else's conceptual scheme, you can criticize it, for being able to interpret requires sharing with it certain notions of rationality and other assumptions, which serve as points of reference for criticism. If you cannot interpret it, then you have no way of recognizing it as a conceptual scheme. But if the conceptual schemes share any rules or theories at all, then they can assess each other to determine possible violations of the rules or assumptions they do share. In the most radical possible cases, the shared rules are logical ones, and criticisms are made on grounds of incoherence.

If there is a small degree of incommensurability, so that it cannot be shown that the competitors operationalize their concepts in the same way, it will be impossible to settle matters between the competing theories by producing the results of a few experiments. There is that much incommensurability between most competing theories; if not, the competition would soon be over.

In the large area between radical and small-time incommensurability lie theories and groups of theories that differ on certain basic propositions connected with experience but somewhat insulated from it, and perhaps on methodology as well. In these cases one has to use other agreed criteria to adjudicate between the theories. This is difficult, since there can be controversy over how to weight the criteria, about how to apply them, even about what they are. Here an attack on an opposing theory usually identifies certain unsupported and implausible assumptions or unwelcome or inconsistent consequences. So, for example, my criticism of empiricism did not identify the fatal counterexample but instead raised questions the empiricist cannot answer (in my opinion) about the justification of certain knowledge claims. My limited defense of the rational model argued that to abandon it is to abandon the notion of the person; and that I assume nobody wants to do or can consistently do. Some attacks on rational individualism (including Pfeffer's [1982]) have shown how difficult it is to state that position so that it is true but not trivial.

Those arguments have something to do with interpretation. Very broadly speaking, interpretation is a technique of charity: one understands a theory or conceptual scheme only by taking it to be true: meaning and truth are here inseparable in that sense. So the arguments against empiricism and the elimination of the rational model are interpretive in the sense that they point to an incoherence in those positions that makes it impossible to define them consistently. They fail to be true because they fail to be coherently meaningful.

Arguments about psychology are similar. Its difficulties have to do with definition—specifically, with construct validity. The complaint about psychology is that its theorists have not been able to agree on a set of valid constructs. Criticisms from outside psychology have extended essentially this challenge: provide a set of definitions that are coherent, understandable in their own terms.

This criticism is one that methodologically self-conscious psychologists themselves make: certain definitions do not meet the standards that both psychologists and those outside the field agree on. It would indeed be a mistake to demand that the theories and definitions of psychology resemble those of physics: that is imposing the canons of one paradigm on another. But there is nothing parochial about assessing psychology as still having much more work to do in developing a network of valid and useful constructs. In other words, psychologists have reason to try to move in the direction of the precision, completeness, and predictive power of physics, but not to become discouraged if progress slows or stops.

It is surprising that scholars like Burrell and Morgan (1979), who appear to see the importance of interpretation, should be so skeptical of criticism from one paradigm to another. If the argument of this section is correct, the interpretive point of view is not just another paradigm; for the very notion of paradigm presupposes the notion of incommensurability, which in its extreme forms calls for interpretation—and, if what I have just argued is correct, in its lesser forms calls for techniques that have something in common with interpretation.[5]

It should be clear that we have been talking all along about a subject of concern to theorists and managers alike: on what basis should one choose a theory? Anyone who has read this far will be able to guess my answer: choose one—at least one—that gives satisfactory answers at a satisfactory price.

3. THEORY CHOICE AND SUBJECTIVISM

I have been arguing that we can rule against what are sometimes called paradigms by identifying incoherence, false or gratuitous and implausible assumptions, unwelcome consequences, and other problems of inference and methodology, some of which attach to empiricism. Identifying unsound and unconscious assumptions may be a perfectly decisive attack on a way of theorizing. That is how we show certain arguments against psychological explanation to be unsound.

Some of the most difficult choices are among theories that are not profoundly incommensurable, but also not subject to adjudication by careful attention to observable data. For example, the view that organizations can have something like psychological properties can neither be overturned by counterexample nor verified; nor can it be eliminated by empiricist fiat, as I argued with Glick against James.

Differences among theories, commensurable or not, may be a consequence of differences among criteria for choosing among theories. There is at least as much difficulty in choosing criteria for theory choice as there is for choosing theories, and any method for doing so is subject to an infinite regress of demands for justification. The criteria are not arbitrary: they have proved successful in explaining what some discipline sets out to explain. But surely, we are tempted to say, we can find criteria that apply to all sciences, and that allow us to rule out alchemy and astrology?

In fact we do have such criteria. They are listed in chapter 1. The problem is that one of two or more disputed theories may be superior according to one criterion but not another. For example, population ecology theories score very well on simplicity and are attractively isomorphic with certain biological theories; but there is a whole range of organizational phenomena of interest to most managers that they do not predict or even acknowledge. Organizational climate appears to be a superior diagnostic concept in the hands of an experienced practitioner, but less useful than psychological climate in other hands and for other purposes.

Experimentation, accident, trial and error, and argument may in due course lead to a theory that makes organizational climate as respectable as manic-depression and psychological climate just another of its symptoms. We do not know what additional hypotheses or information will be available, or needed. We are in the position of people who have doubts about alchemy but as yet know nothing about chemistry. In the natural sciences there is usually reason to believe that a difficulty like this will eventually be cleared up, to be replaced by others. In the behavioral sciences new difficulties replace the old ones more slowly, or never. In neither do we get rid of all competition between theories whose relative scores differ from one criterion—or one purpose—to the next.

The inability to agree on which criteria to apply and how to weight them is most serious where the theories in question are incommensurable to a significant degree—in other words, where there is a paradigm difference. For it is characteristic of incommensurable sets of theories, as of different disciplines, to have different criteria for theoretical soundness, or different ways of applying or weighting criteria. This absence of ultimate authority over our theoretical models tempts us towards subjectivism, which may involve the claim that adjudication among incommensurables is not a rational enterprise.[6] But that point of view ignores the fact of scientific progress. Within disciplines there are successful arguments for fundamental change in theories and definitions. Kuhn is famous for arguing that progress in a science may be explosive rather than gradual, as when a new point of view represents not a sharpening of old tools or an addition of information but a significant and desirable departure from accepted theories, definitions, and methods. Conservatism relative to other accepted theories being one criterion of soundness of theory, such departures are and ought to be rare, for some of the same reasons radical changes of product line are and ought to be rare; but both should happen sometimes.

And they do. Kuhn, who is not the subjectivist he is sometimes made out to be, aims to explain how and why we abandoned alchemy and Ptolemism and other genuinely inferior theories, and he gives no indication whatever that we ought to bring them back. Progress in science is neither as smooth nor as easy as we might have supposed, but it is progress all the same: the new collection of theories is better than the old.

A new theory gains support in a discipline when it turns out to be better at solving the problems the discipline has set for itself. New theories may therefore arise in part because the problems change, usually by becoming more sophisticated and demanding. When approaches differ between disciplines, the differences may therefore reflect the different problems the two disciplines try to solve; and each discipline will probably stick with the theories that work best on their characteristic problems. There is little incentive to change one's theories to deal with problems of other disciplines, and there is reason to stay with the kind of theory that has solved one's own problems.

So, for example, when dissident economists object that orthodox theories quite systematically ignore psychological reality or that they define value by reference to price in a way that depreciates what is traditionally women's work, orthodox economists can ask whether problems of this kind justify significant changes in fundamental models or can be covered by the phrase "other things being equal," which in effect rules out certain possible counterexamples as something like random noise. The same can be said in defense of organization theories that are criticized because they cancel out the states of individuals, especially others than top managers.[7] You can see how the question is an ideological one.

The tendency to stay within the limits of one's paradigm while assimilating information and critically assessing one's theories is one way of honoring conservatism, which is one of the criteria of theoretical soundness. It says, in effect: I will embrace the new theory—or the new way of looking at things—if you make it worth my while. The old theory has its uses, and an adequate reason for discarding it is not that it could be better in some respects but that there is available a theory sufficiently better to offset the costs of switching theories. Where the theories are very different, both the costs and the benefits of the switch may be large. Costs may include some loss of explanatory power in certain areas—this may or may not be repaired as the new theory is improved—and cost increases associated with the new theory's demand for more precise information. In the long run, we are inclined to believe, a theory is more economical the wider its scope; but there is no way of telling how long the long run is. Here again we have reason for following the equivalent of Simonian satisficing in the choice of a theory; and conservatism puts on the new theory the burden of proving its worth. In thus satisficing we are not in the least assuming that there is no difference between good and better, or true and false, but only that it is an open and sometimes unanswerable question whether the better is worth attempting.[8]

A natural scientist with the right kind of grant support might say, Never mind what it costs; we want a theory that is true. But in arguing for their theories against others, natural scientists have reason to use the familiar criteria, which include conservatism. The criteria are a guide to successful scientific practice only in the sense that they are the distillation of lessons from past success. Respecting them all, with their distinct and sometimes conflicting messages, creates very practical problems. In particular, carrying conservatism too far—for example, by holding slavishly to the rules and methods characteristic of one's discipline—stifles progress and reduces the probability of profiting from different points of view. In an interdisciplinary field like organization theory, that is a more serious matter than elsewhere.

So I am in the position of claiming, in apparent opposition to Burrell and Morgan and others, that arguments from one paradigm to another are sometimes worth undertaking, but that it is hard to know when they are worth the trouble. This is a vague statement, but it cannot be much improved. As Winter (1964, 1971) pointed out in discussing Simonian satisficing, we are in an area in which there are no rules to guide one's choices. Judgments about how to interpret, weight, and apply the rules of scientific method cannot be made in accordance with those rules. Scientists cannot avoid all situations in which they must decide whether to pay the price of a radically new theory without knowing exactly what its benefits will be.

Consider again psychological and organizational climate. It is in part because theorists have different priorities for criteria of theoretical soundness that there is disagreement on whether there is any point in doing research into organizational climate in the hope of developing strong theories with construct-valid tests. Those for whom verifiability and falsifiability are paramount will have little patience with such an effort. Those who take clarity seriously will be reluctant to countenance a concept as vague as organizational climate. On the other hand, those who place greater weight on conservatism will prefer to explain phenomena like meaning rather than to eliminate them; and proponents of coherence will attack the empiricist position as incoherent.

Disagreements of this kind are ideological in that each viewpoint embodies a consensus about what is reasonable and what is not, and about which problems are important and which considerations are worth preserving. The viewpoints have moral significance because people have moral reasons for deciding what is important. But judgments at this level are not purely subjective or arbitrary. In the way the criteria for theoretical soundness conflict and override each other and create controversy among the serious and well-intentioned, they are rather like moral principles. Experience in making these judgments and living with the consequences may lead to a fairly reliable skill at it. This practical wisdom, as it has been called in the Aristotelian tradition (see Bernstein [1983], for example), is similar to what an intelligent manager develops through experience. Such a manager can tell you the principles of good management; but the trick, less easy to state, is applying them.[9]

The intellectual faculty required to choose among competing theories, or among models all of which are wrong for different reasons (the organization as a system; the organization as a person; the organization as a polity; the organization as a culture) is essentially the same one that enables managers to extrapolate from particular situations to other and similar situations. It includes the ultimately moral capacity for choosing among the different objectives that competing theories may have. It is developed through experience; but where pertinent experience is hard to arrange, the case study method is a possible substitute even if it does not teach principles applicable to all cases. So perhaps we should not be urging managers to act more like textbook theorists; instead we should understand that, at least when they are making choices among very different theories, successful theorists occasionally act like successful managers.

For a number of reasons the past few paragraphs apply better to the social than the natural sciences. For one thing, natural scientists more often deal with problems that are isolated from certain imponderable complications or little affected by them, while social scientists—and organization theorists more than most others—face problems that characteristically ramify over the territory of a variety of disciplines, and so call for the application of different theories and different methods. Hence the problem of choosing among very different theories is more likely to arise, and less likely to be soluble by straightforward reference to falsifiability or predictive power. To the extent that new theories arise in response to new problems, a discipline that covers a wide range of problems is likely to be faced with a wide range of candidate theories.

Theoretical satisficing is a matter of dealing effectively with this fact: the very best theory you can ever get, no matter what theory it is, will be an oversimplification and may at some points simply be untrue. And here is another fact to deal with: for the inevitably fallible, to try always to get as close to the truth as possible may be self-defeating, as in the case of rational behavior. In any case, closer is not always better for all purposes, and what closeness is is not always clear.

We are better off letting a thousand flowers bloom and making best use of the most useful ones. Distinguishing them from weeds is not a straightforward matter, though it can be done in many cases. But one of the attractive features of science is that there, if nowhere else, in the long run the flowers often choke out the weeds. Given how science proliferates in all directions, no garden worth cultivating will ever have only one flower in it.

Yet some theories are better and some discourses more privileged than others. It was Otto Neurath, usually considered a positivist, who wrote the line that philosophers of almost all schools, beginning with Quine (1960), quote with approval: "We are like sailors who must rebuild their ship on the open sea, without being able to tear it down in drydock and construct it anew from the best components." But in some boats you can sail to your destination, and in others you cannot. Unfortunately, the trip is often well under way before we find out whether the ship will float, or can be repaired.

NOTES

1. I am not attacking the notion that "there exists a single reality external to the mind and that this reality is copied in perception" (Bourgeois and Pinder [1983], 610), in part because I am not sure I understand it. It has been many years since any serious philosopher tried to make sense of the notion that perception copies reality. As to the claim that there is a single reality external to the mind, I can think of several distinct interpretations of it. In fact, given that a claim of unity demands an answer to the question "One *what*?", it is hard to make sense of the idea of one reality. Better, surely, to talk about one or many adequate theories. And rather than to say, melodramatically, that we can never truly be in touch with reality, let us say that we can never know everything.

    In this chapter there are a number of statements that could with a little imagination be interpreted as implying that we cannot talk about reality, but putting it that way just increases confusion. For example, something like the essence-accident distinction seems to be required if we are to identify individuals as opposed to making statements about them. If that distinction is at best relative to a particular theory, as I suggest in this chapter and elsewhere, then there is some sense in saying that different theories must be talking about different things, and that consequently either theories do not talk about the world or there is one world per theory. But such a statement inevitably conjures up misleading associations and apparent implications.

    In any case, talking about perception is probably barking up the wrong tree. It is not self-evident that there is any such topic as epistemology, as distinct from discussion of what justifies formal and informal theories. In particular, talk about how we infer from the evidence of our senses to facts about the world outside them predisposes one to believe that justification of our knowledge claims has to rest on our first knowing what our senses tell us; and that, as I have argued, cannot be right.

The analogy of the television picture misleads if it suggests that truth is a matter of our senses or our theories copying the world as a television set copies what is televised.

2. The doctrine of incommensurability is usually credited to Kuhn (1970), but there is controversy about just what the doctrine is. See also Doppelt (1978), Hacking (1983), Rorty (1979), and Bernstein (1983). I do not find in any of them exactly the view I put forward here, though I am in debt to them all, and to Quine (1960).

3. It may be unfair to make targets of them alone, given how many other authors are in the same position. But they are clearer about what they are doing.

4. One could also discuss communities that differ with respect to their views of what a good life is rather than with respect to factual beliefs. In that case the principle of charity would assume that their preferences were significantly similar to ours. If they were not, then there would be no way to explain their actions by reference to reasons and no basis on which to attribute preferences or values to them at all.

5. This whole discussion of how different paradigms can communicate may appear to involve a bit of overkill. Arguments within organization theory are indeed more difficult because the various disciplines in play are sufficiently far apart that there are problems of communication that cannot be resolved just by defining one's terms more carefully. But the James-Glick argument and the competition among certain schools of theory mentioned in chapter 4 confront us with incommensurability that is about as serious as any we find in organization theory. We do not have to communicate with aliens: most of our interlocutors have comprehensible theories, and the cultures of most organizations we study are based on values sufficiently similar to ours that we find them reasonable if not entirely congenial.

Yet this point is important as support for a form of argument I have used throughout the book. For example, in talking about psychological states and events I have argued that we cannot make sense of personal identity and other fundamentals of our discourse unless we presuppose a certain level of rationality. One might reply that our inability to conceive of a world without psychological entities does not make such a world impossible so much as it shows the limitations of our ability to conceive. But I am arguing now that it is pointless to speak as though there could be many totally unrelated conceptual schemes of which we happen to be trapped in one. To show that a world without pains, intentions, and thoughts is inconceivable for us is to make a conclusive argument against the possibility of such a world. At some future time organization theorists, armed with a more perspicuous vocabulary for discussing states of persons and organizations, may recall with amusement the crude ways in which people once discussed hostility, paranoia, and corporate culture; we are today similarly patronizing about the old science that invoked spleen and vapors. But we can have no reason to believe the future's refined concepts will be wholly unrelated to ours. After all, we still understand that talk of spleen and vapors, and we have good reasons for criticizing it.

6. The Burrell-Morgan suggestion that in criticizing a theory it is good practice to stay within the guidelines of its paradigm—a call for normal science—seems particularly inappropriate for organization theory. As the field has not sufficiently established its independence from philosophy by reaching a productive consensus on concepts, there is no normal science in organization theory.

7. This is not to acknowledge that standard structural-functional theories cancel out individuals' psychological states. They are instead compatible with many possible facts and theories about psychological states. There is little justification for claiming a paradigm difference between structural-functional theories and those that concentrate on the causal bases of structure.

8. Gradually over time, theory users find the comparative costs and benefits associated with a particular group of contending theories change; but for a long time the change may not be noticeable, because it has not been worthwhile to calculate the costs. But at a certain point, perhaps as a result of a new discovery or the proposal of a new hypothesis like that of Kepler, a number of people realize that the costs and benefits must have changed; so a reassessment is made, and a change of theories proves to be called for. It would be an oversimplification to say that the cost-benefit change (which is gradual) has brought about the theory change (which is sudden): it is rather the fact of the change reaching a threshold where it cannot be ignored. In this way theoretical satisficing causes the suddenness of paradigm shifts. It is clear, too, that for people who have different uses for the theory, the cost-benefit equation will differ and so therefore will the point at which the new theory takes over, if it ever does.

9. Most people who think about morality would agree that one of its essential purposes is to increase the happiness in the world and see to its fair distribution with due regard for individual autonomy and desert. There is not much agreement on how that essential purpose can be translated into rules for behavior. The usual way to test candidate rules is to consider their consequences; and moral philosophers and others have been able to criticize candidates effectively in that way. We are not puzzled about whether Canada has a more just government than Chile, and we do not hesitate to criticize Chile for failing by the standards by which Canada succeeds. On the contrary: we (including economists and politicians) may argue by starting with our agreement that a certain practice is bad because it leads to the kind of situation one finds in Chile. When the topic is proper scientific method, we might similarly object to a certain principle by noting that some accepted and successful scientific theory violates it.

BIBLIOGRAPHY

Abbott, Andrew. 1983. "Professional Ethics." *American Journal of Sociology* 88, 855-885.

Ackoff, Russell L. 1978. *The Art of Problem Solving*. New York: John Wiley & Sons.

Ainslie, George. 1975. "Specious Reward." *Psychological Bulletin* 82, 463-496.

Andrews, Kenneth R. 1980. *The Concept of Corporate Strategy*. Revised edition. Homewood, Ill.: Dow-Jones-Irwin.

————. 1981. "Replaying the Board's Role in Formulating Strategy." *Harvard Business Review* 59, No. 3, 18-19, 24, 26.

Asch, Solomon E. 1955. "Studies of Independence and Conformity: A Minority of One against a Unanimous Majority." *Psychological Monographs* 20. Whole no. 416.

————. 1960. "Effects of Group Pressure on the Modification and Distortion of Judgment." In *Group Dynamics*. 2d ed. Edited by Dorvin Cartwright and Alvin Zander, 189-200. Evanston: Row Peterson.

Astley, W. Graham, and Andrew H. Van de Ven. 1983. "Central Perspectives and Debates in Organization Theory." *Administrative Science Quarterly* 28, 245-273.

Behling, Orlando. 1980. "The Case for the Natural Science Model for Research in Organizational Behavior and Organization Theory." *Academy of Management Review* 5, 483-490.

Berger, Peter L., and Thomas Luckmann. 1967. *The Social Construction of Reality*. New York: Anchor Books.

Bernstein, Richard J. 1983. *Beyond Objectivism and Relativism: Science, Hermeneutics, and Praxis*. Philadelphia: University of Pennsylvania Press.

Block, Ned. 1980. *Readings in Philosophy of Psychology*. Vol. 1. Cambridge, Mass.: Harvard University Press.

Bourgeois, V. Warren, and Craig C. Pinder. 1983. "Contrasting Philosophical Perspectives in Administrative Science: A Reply to Morgan." *Administrative Science Quarterly* 28, 608-613.

Bridgman, P. W. 1927. *The Logic of Modern Physics*. New York: Macmillan.

Brown, H. B. 1978. "Bureaucracy as Praxis: Toward a Political Phenomenology of Organizations." *Administrative Science Quarterly* 23, 365-382.

Buckley, Walter, ed. 1968. *Modern Systems Research for the Behavioral Scientist*. Chicago: Aldine.

Burrell, Gibson, and Gareth Morgan. 1979. *Sociological Paradigms and Organizational Analysis*. London: Heinemann.

Cartwright, Nancy. 1983. *How the Laws of Physics Lie*. New York: Oxford University Press.

Cherniak, Christopher. 1986. *Minimal Rationality*. Cambridge, Mass.: MIT Press.

Collins, Randall. 1981. "On the Microfoundations of Macrosociology." *American Journal of Sociology* 86, 986-1014.

Cronbach, Lee J. 1984. *Essentials of Psychological Testing*. 4th. ed. New York: Harper & Row.

————, and P. F. Meehl. 1955. "Construct Validity in Psychological Tests." *Psychological Bulletin* 52, 281-302.

Cummins, Robert. 1983. *The Nature of Psychological Explanation*. Cambridge, Mass.: MIT Press.

Daft, Richard L., and Karl E. Weick. 1984. "Toward a Model of Organizations as Interpretation Systems." *Academy of Management Review* 9, 284-295.

David, Paul A. 1975. *Technical Choice, Innovation, and Economic Growth*. New York: Cambridge University Press.

Davidson, Donald. 1980. *Essays on Actions and Events*. New York: Oxford University Press.

DeGeorge, Richard T. 1983. "Social Reality and Social Relations." *Review of Metaphysics* 37, 3-20.

Dennett, Daniel C. 1984. *Elbow Room: The Varieties of Free Will Worth Wanting*. Cambridge, Mass.: MIT Press.

DiTomaso, Nancy. 1987. "Symbolic Media and Social Solidarity: The Foundations of Corporate Culture." In *Research in the Sociology of Organizations*, vol. 5, edited by Samuel B. Bacharach and Nancy DiTomaso, 105-134. Greenwich, Conn.: JAI Press.

Donaldson, Lex. 1985. *In Defence of Organization Theory*. New York: Cambridge University Press.

Doppelt, Gerald. 1978. "Kuhn's Epistemological Relativism: An Interpretation and Defense." *Inquiry* 21, 33-86.

Elster, Jon. 1984. *Ulysses and the Sirens: Studies in Rationality and Irrationality*. Revised edition. New York: Cambridge University Press.

———. 1985. *Sour Grapes: Studies in the Subversion of Rationality*. New York: Cambridge University Press.

Fischer, Frank. 1986. "Reforming Bureaucratic Theory: Toward a Political Model." In *Bureaucratic and Governmental Reform*, edited by Donald J. Colista, 35–54. Greenwich, Conn.: JAI Press.

Fiske, Donald W. 1978. *Strategies for Personality Research*. San Francisco: Jossey-Bass.

Frankfurt, Harry G. 1981. "Freedom of the Will and the Concept of a Person." In *Free Will*, edited by Gary Watson, 81-95. New York: Oxford University Press.

Freeman, R. Edward. 1984. *Strategic Management: A Stakeholder Approach*. Boston: Pitman.

French, Peter A. 1984. *Collective and Corporate Responsibility*. Columbia University Press.

Friedman, Milton. 1953. "The Methodology of Positive Economics." In *Essays in Positive Economics*, part 1, 3-43. Chicago: University of Chicago Press.

Gadamer, Hans-Georg. 1976. *Philosophical Hermeneutics*. Translated by David E. Linge. Berkeley: University of California Press.

———. 1981. *Reason in the Age of Science*. Translated by Frederick G. Lawrence. Cambridge, Mass.: MIT Press.

Geertz, Clifford. 1979. "Deep Play: Notes on the Balinese Cockfight." In *Interpretive Social Science: A Reader*, edited by Paul Rabinow and William M. Sullivan, 181-223. Berkeley: University of California Press.

———. 1983. *Local Knowledge: Further Essays in Interpretive Anthropology*. New York: Basic Books.

Glick, William H. 1985. "Conceptualizing and Measuring Organizational and Psychological Climate: Pitfalls in Multilevel Research." *Academy of Management Review* 10, 601-616.

———. 1988. "Response: Organizations are not Central Tendencies: Shadowboxing in the Dark, Round 2." *Academy of Management Review* 13, 133-137.

———, and Karlene Roberts. 1984. "Hypothesized Interdependence, Assumed Independence." *Academy of Management Review* 9, 722-735.

Gordon, George G., and Walter M. Cummins. 1979. *Managing Management Climate*. Lexington, Mass.: Lexington Books.

Hacking, Ian. 1983. *Representing and Intervening*. New York: Cambridge University Press.

Hambrick, Donald C. 1980. "Operationalizing the Concept of Business-Level Strategy in Research." *Academy of Management Review* 5, 567-575.

———. 1981a. "Environment, Strategy, and Power within Top Management Teams." *Administrative Science Quarterly* 26, 253-276.

————. 1981b. "Strategic Awareness within Top Management Teams." *Strategic Management Journal* 2, 263-279.

————. 1982. "Environmental Scanning and Organizational Strategy." *Strategic Management Journal* 3, 159-174.

————. 1983. "Some Tests of the Effectiveness and Functional Attributes of Miles and Snow's Strategic Types." *Academy of Management Journal* 26, 5-26.

Hampshire, Stuart. 1965. *Freedom of the Individual*. Princeton: Princeton University Press.

Hanson, Norwood Russell. 1958. *Patterns of Discovery: An Enquiry into the Conceptual Foundations of Science*. New York: Cambridge University Press.

Hayes, Robert H., and William J. Abernathy. 1980. "Managing Our Way to Economic Decline." *Harvard Business Review* 58, No. 4, 67-77.

Hellriegel, Don, and John W. Slocum, Jr. 1974. "Organizational Climate: Measures, Research, and Contingencies." *Academy of Management Journal* 17, 255-280.

Hempel, Carl G. 1962. "Rational Action." *Proceedings and Addresses of the American Philosophical Association* 35, 5-23.

————. 1965. *Aspects of Scientific Explanation*. New York: The Free Press.

————. 1969. "Covering Laws are Presupposed by Any Adequate Rational Explanation." In *The Nature and Scope of Social Science*, edited by Leonard I. Krimerman, 308-316. New York: Appleton-Century-Crofts.

————, and Paul Oppenheim. 1948. "The Covering Law Analysis of Scientific Explanation." *Philosophy of Science* 15, 135-174.

Henderson, Bruce. 1979. *Henderson on Corporate Strategy*. Cambridge, Mass.: Abt Books.

Herman, Jeanne B., and Charles L. Hulin. 1972. "Studying Organizational Attitudes from Individual and Organizational Frames of Reference." *Organizational Behavior and Human Performance* 8, 84-108.

Hesse, Mary B. 1966. *Models and Analogies in Science*. Notre Dame: University of Notre Dame Press.

Hollis, Martin, and Edward Nell. 1975. *Rational Economic Man: A Philosophical Critique of Neo-Classical Economics*. New York: Cambridge University Press.

————, and Steven Lukes, eds. 1982. *Rationality and Relativism*. Cambridge, Mass.: MIT Press.

Hughes, Marie Adele, R. Leon Price, and Daniel W. Marrs. 1986. "Linking Theory Construction and Theory Testing: Models with Multiple Indicators of Latent Variables." *Academy of Management Review* 11, 128-144.

James, Lawrence R., William F. Joyce, and John W. Slocum, Jr. 1988. "Comment: Organizations Do Not Cognize." *Academy of Management Review* 13, 129-132.

James, Susan. 1984. *The Content of Social Explanation.* New York: Cambridge University Press.

Joseph, Geoffrey. 1983. "The Many Sciences and the One World." *Journal of Philosophy* 77, 773-790.

Keeley, Michael. 1983. "Values in Organizational Theory and Management Education." *Academy of Management Review* 8, 376-386.

Kerlinger, Fred N. 1986. *Foundations of Behavioral Research.* 3rd ed. New York: Holt, Rinehart and Winston.

Kets de Vries, Manfred F. R., and Danny Miller. 1984a. "Neurotic Style and Organizational Pathology." *Strategic Management Journal* 5, 35-55.

————. 1984b. *The Neurotic Organization: Diagnosing and Changing Counterproductive Styles of Management.* San Francisco: Jossey-Bass.

————. 1986. "Personality, Culture, and Organization." *Academy of Management Review* 11, 266-279.

Kuhn, Thomas. 1970. *The Structure of Scientific Revolutions.* 2d ed. Chicago: University of Chicago Press.

Lawrence, Paul R. 1981. "Organization and Environment Perspective: The Harvard Organization and Environment Research Program." In *Perspectives on Organization Design and Behavior,* edited by Andrew Van de Ven and William F. Joyce, ch. 7, 311-337. New York: John Wiley & Sons.

Levins, Richard, and Richard Lewontin. 1985. *The Dialectical Biologist.* Cambridge, Mass.: Harvard University Press.

Locke, Edwin A. 1968. "Toward a Theory of Task Motivation and Incentives." *Organizational Behavior and Human Performance* 3, 157-189.

MacIntyre, Alasdair. 1981. *After Virtue: A Study in Moral Theory.* Notre Dame: University of Notre Dame Press.

March, James G. 1976. "The Technology of Foolishness." In *Ambiguity and Choice in Organizations,* edited by James G. March and Johan P. Olson, 69-81. Bergen, Norway: Universitetsforlaget.

————. 1978. "Bounded Rationality, Ambiguity, and the Engineering of Choice." *Bell Journal of Economics* 9, 587- 608.

Mayhew, Bruce H. 1980. "Structuralism versus Individualism: Part I, Shadowboxing in the Dark." *Social Forces* 59, 335-375.

————. 1981. "Structuralism versus Individualism: Part II, Ideological and Other Obfuscations." *Social Forces* 59, 627-648.

Meehl, Paul E. 1986. "What Social Scientists Don't Understand." In *Metatheory in Social Science: Pluralisms and Subjectivities,* edited by Donald W. Fiske and Richard A. Schweder, 315-338. Chicago: University of Chicago Press.

Meyer, John W., and Brian Rowan. 1977. "Institutionalized Organizations: Formal Structure as Myth and Ceremony." *American Journal of Sociology* 83, 340-363.

Milgram, Stanley. 1974. *Obedience to Authority: An Experimental View.* New York: Harper & Row.

Miner, John B. 1980. *Theories of Organizational Behavior.* Hinsdale, Ill.: The Dryden Press.

———. 1982. *Theories of Organizational Structure and Process.* Hinsdale, Ill.: The Dryden Press.

———. 1984. "The Validity and Usefulness of Theories in an Emerging Organizational Science." *Academy of Management Review* 9, 296-306.

Mintzberg, Henry. 1978. "Patterns in Strategy Formulation." *Management Science* 26, 934-948.

———, and James A. Waters. 1985. "Of Strategies, Deliberate and Emergent." *Strategic Management Journal* 6, 257-272.

Mitchell, Terence R. 1982. "Motivation: New Directions for Theory, Research, and Practice." *Academy of Management Review* 7, 80-88.

Mohr, Lawrence B. 1982. *Explaining Organizational Behavior.* San Francisco: Jossey-Bass.

Morgan, Gareth. 1980. "Paradigms, Metaphors, and Puzzle Solving in Organization Theory." *Administrative Science Quarterly* 25, 605-622.

———. 1981. "The Schismatic Metaphor and its Implications for Organizational Analysis." *Organizational Studies* 2, 23-44.

———, ed. 1983. *Beyond Method: Strategies for Social Research.* Beverly Hills: Sage Publications.

———. 1986. *Images of Organization.* Beverly Hills: Sage Publications.

———, and Linda Smircich. 1980. "The Case for Qualitative Research." *Academy of Management Review* 5, 491-500.

Mossholder, Kevin W., and Arthur G. Bedeian. 1983. "Cross-Level Inference and Organizational Research: Perspectives on Interpretation and Application." *Academy of Management Review* 8, 547-558.

Nagel, Thomas. 1971. "Brain Bisection and the Unity of Consciousness." *Synthese* 22, 396-413.

O'Reilly, Charles A., and David Caldwell. 1979. "Informational Influence as a Determinant of Perceived Task Characteristics and Job Satisfaction." *Journal of Applied Psychology* 64, 157-165.

Payne, D., and D. S. Pugh. 1976. "Organizational Structure and Climate." In *Handbook of Industrial and Organizational Psychology,* edited by M. D. Dunnette, 1125-1173. Chicago: Rand McNally.

Peter, J. Paul. 1979. "Reliability: A Review of Psychometric Basics and Recent Marketing Practices." *Journal of Marketing Research* 16, 6-17.

———. 1981. "Construct Validity: A Review of Basic Issues and Marketing Practices." *Journal of Marketing Research* 18, 133-145.

Peters, Thomas J., and Robert H. Waterman, Jr. 1982. *In Search of Excellence: Lessons from America's Best-Run Companies.* New York: Harper & Row.

Pfeffer, Jeffrey. 1982. *Organizations and Organization Theory.* Boston: Pitman.

———, and Gerald R. Salancik. 1978. *The External Control of Organizations: A Resource Dependence Perspective.* New York: Harper & Row.

Pondy, Louis R., Peter J. Frost, Gareth Morgan, and Thomas C. Dandridge, eds. 1983. *Organizational Symbolism.* Greenwich, Conn.: JAI Press.

Popper, Karl R. 1959. *The Logic of Scientific Discovery.* London: Hutchinson.

Putnam, Hilary. 1962. "What Theories Are Not." In *Logic, Methodology, and the Philosophy of Science: Proceedings of the 1960 International Congress,* edited by Ernest Nagel, Patrick Suppes, and Alfred Tarski, 240-251. Stanford: Stanford University Press.

Quine, Willard Van Orman. 1960. *Word and Object.* Cambridge, Mass.: MIT Press.

———. 1961. "Two Dogmas of Empiricism." In *From a Logical Point of View,* 20-46. New York: Harper & Row, 1961.

———, and Joseph S. Ullian. 1970. *The Web of Belief.* New York: Random House.

Quinn, James Brian. 1980. "Managing Strategic Change." *Sloan Management Review* 21, 3-20.

Ramsey, Frank P. 1950. *Foundations of Mathematics.* New York: Humanities Press.

Roberts, Karlene H., Charles L. Hulin, and Denise M. Rousseau. 1978. *Developing an Interdisciplinary Science of Organizations.* San Francisco: Jossey-Bass.

Rokeach, Milton. 1973. *The Nature of Human Values.* New York: The Free Press.

Rorty, Richard. 1979. *Philosophy and the Mirror of Nature.* Princeton: Princeton University Press.

Rosenblueth, Arturo, and Norbert Wiener. 1968. "Purposeful and Non-Purposeful Behavior." In *Modern Systems Research for the Behavioral Scientist,* edited by Walter Buckley, 232-237. Chicago: Aldine.

———, and Julian Bigelow. 1968. "Behavior, Purpose, and Teleology." In *Modern Systems Research for the Behavioral Scientist,* edited by Walter Buckley, 221-225. Chicago: Aldine.

Ryle, Gilbert. 1947. *The Concept of Mind.* London: Hutchinson.

Sathe, Vijay. 1985. *Culture and Related Corporate Realities.* Homewood, Ill.: Richard D. Irwin.

Schein, Edgar H. 1985. *Organizational Culture and Leadership.* San Francisco: Jossey-Bass.

Schelling, Thomas C. 1984. *Choice and Consequence: Perspectives of an Errant Economist.* Cambridge, Mass.: Harvard University Press.

Schick, Frederic. 1984. *Having Reasons: An Essay on Rationality and Sociality.* Princeton: Princeton University Press.

Schneider, Benjamin, and Douglas T. Hall. 1972. "Toward Specifying the Concept of Work Climate: A Study of Roman Catholic Diocesan Priests." *Journal of Applied Psychology* 56, 447-455.

Schwab, Donald P. 1980. "Construct Validity in Organizational Behavior." In

Research in Organizational Behavior, vol. 2, edited by Barry M. Staw and Larry L. Cummings, 2-43. Greenwich, Conn.: JAI Press.

Sellars, Wilfrid S. 1963. *Science, Perception, and Reality.* London: Routledge and Kegan Paul.

Sen, Amartya K. 1973. *On Economic Inequality.* Oxford: Oxford University Press.

————. 1974. "Choice, Orderings and Morality." In *Practical Reason*, edited by Stefan Koerner, 54-67. Oxford: Basil Blackwell.

————. 1976. "Liberty, Unanimity, and Rights." *Economica* 43, 217-245.

Shapere, Dudley. 1982. "The Concept of Observation in Science and Philosophy." *Philosophy of Science* 49, 231-267.

Silverman, David. 1968. "Formal Organizations or Industrial Sociology: Towards a Social Action Analysis of Organizations." *Sociology* 2, 221-238.

————. 1971. *The Theory of Organizations: A Sociological Framework.* New York: Basic Books.

Simon, Herbert A. 1954. "A Behavioral Theory of Rational Choice." *Quarterly Journal of Economics* 69, 99-118.

————. 1957. *Models of Man.* New York: John Wiley & Sons.

————. 1965. *Administrative Behavior: A Study of Decision-Making Processes in Administrative Organization.* 2d ed. New York: The Free Press.

Skinner, B. F. 1938. *Behavior of Organisms.* New York: Appleton-Century-Crofts.

Smircich, Linda. 1983. "Concepts of Culture and Organizational Analysis." *Administrative Science Quarterly* 28, 339-358.

Staw, Barry M. 1974. "Attitudinal and Behavioral Consequences of Changing a Major Organizational Reward: A Natural Field Experiment." *Journal of Personality and Social Psychology* 29, 742-751.

————. 1976. "Knee-Deep in the Big Muddy: A Study of Escalating Commitment to a Chosen Course of Action." *Organizational Behavior and Human Performance* 16, 27-44.

————. 1980. "Rationality and Justification in Organizational Life." *In Research in Organizational Behavior*, vol. 2, edited by Barry M. Staw and Larry L. Cummings, 45-80. Greenwich, Conn.: JAI Press.

Steers, R. M., and Richard T. Mowday. 1981. "Employee Turnover and Postdecision Accommodation Processes." In *Research in Organizational Behavior*, vol. 3, edited by Larry L. Cummings and Barry M. Staw, 235-281. Greenwich, Conn.: JAI Press.

Stigler, George, and Gary Becker. 1977. "De gustibus non est disputandum." *American Economic Review* 67, 76-90.

Strotz, R. H. 1955. "Myopia and Inconsistency in Dynamic Utility Maximization." *Review of Economic Studies* 23, 165-180.

Taylor, Richard. 1968a. "Comments on a Mechanistic Conception of Purposefulness." In *Modern Systems Research for the Behavioral Scientist,* edited by Walter Buckley, 226-231. Chicago: Aldine.

―――. 1968b. "Purposeful and Non-Purposeful Behavior: A Rejoinder." In *Modern Systems Research for the Behavioral Scientist*, edited by Walter Buckley, 238-242.. Chicago: Aldine.

Thompson, James D. 1967. *Organizations in Action.* New York: McGraw Hill.

Van Fraassen, Bas C. 1981. *The Scientific Image.* New York: Oxford University Press.

Venkatraman, N., and John H. Grant. 1986. "Construct Measurement in Organizational Strategy Research: A Critique and Proposal." *Academy of Management Review* 11, 71-87.

Vroom, Victor H. 1964. *Work and Motivation.* New York: John Wiley & Sons.

Watson, Gary. 1981. "Free Agency." In *Free Will*, edited by Gary Watson, 96-110. New York: Oxford University Press.

Weick, Karl E. 1976. "Educational Organizations as Loosely Coupled Systems." *Administrative Science Quarterly* 21, 1-19.

―――. 1979. *The Social Psychology of Organizing.* 2d ed. New York: Random House.

―――. 1987. "Perspective on Action in Organizations." In *Handbook of Organizational Behavior*, edited by Jay Lorsch, 10-28. Englewood Cliffs: Prentice-Hall.

Weiner, B. 1972. *Theories of Motivation: From Mechanism to Cognition.* Chicago: Rand McNally.

Winter, Sidney G. 1964. "Economic 'Natural Selection' and the Theory of the Firm." *Yale Economic Essays* 4, 225-272.

―――. 1971. "Satisficing, Selection and the Innovative Remnant." *Quarterly Journal of Economics* 85, 237-261.

―――. 1975. "Optimization and Evolution." In *Adaptive Economic Models*, edited by R. H. Day and T. Groves, 73- 118. New York: Academic Press.

Wittgenstein, Ludwig. 1953. *Philosophical Investigations.* New York: Macmillan Company.

Woodfield, Andrew. 1976. *Teleology.* New York: Cambridge University Press.

Zimbardo, Philip and Greg White. 1971. "The Stanford Prison Experiment: A Simulation of the Study of the Psychology of Imprisonment Conducted August 1971 at Stanford University." Unpublished.

Zucker, Lynne G. 1977. "The Role of Institutionalization in Cultural Persistence." *American Sociological Review* 42, 726-743.

―――. 1983. "Organizations as Institutions." In *Perspectives in Organizational Sociology: Theory and Research*, vol. 2, edited by Samuel B. Bacharach, 1-47. Greenwich, Conn.: JAI Press.

INDEX

ABOUT THE AUTHOR

Edwin Hartman teaches business policy and strategy, organizational behavior, and business ethics at Rutgers University. Previously he taught at the University of Pennsylvania, where he was also assistant dean and vice dean of the College of Arts and Sciences. He has been a consultant both independently and with Hay Associates. He received undergraduate degrees in philosophy from Haverford College and in classics from Oxford University, a Ph.D. in ancient philosophy from Princeton University, and an M.B.A. from the Wharton School. He is the author of *Substance, Body, and Soul: Aristotelian Investigations* and coauthor, with Daniel R. Gilbert, Jr., R. Edward Freeman, and John J. Mauriel, of *A Logic for Strategy*.

ISBN 0-88730-251-3

90000